418.407
PHI
(TEEN)

Philpot, Don K.

Reading actively in middle grade social studies

SEP 2 8 2020

PRAISE FOR *READING ACTIVELY IN MIDDLE GRADE SOCIAL STUDIES: TEACHERS AND STUDENTS IN ACTION*

"Middle level educators realize the need to connect reading strategies and thinking across disciplines. This text not only provides theory and strategies with specific examples based on social studies teachers' work with content standards, there is also a deep connection to planning and assessing student learning.

"Every social studies teacher needs both literacy and strategies for presenting social studies content. Philpot shares exemplary samples, rationales, and tools for planning engaging lessons. This text bridges social studies planning with a thorough connection to reading practices that enhance deeper thinking.

"I loved how this book integrates practical reading theory and strategies with social studies lessons. In addition, the focus on intentional, rich lesson planning provides students with multiple opportunities to engage in social studies content blends what we know about the learning needs of young adolescents. Philpot gives social studies teachers multiple tools to engage young adolescents."—**Nancy Ruppert, professor, University of North Carolina Ashville, and past president, Association of Middle Level Education Board of Trustees**

"Don K. Philpot's book, *Reading Actively in Middle Grade Social Studies: Teachers and Students in Action,* explains before, during, and after processes used in reading social studies texts. Social studies teachers stand to learn a lot about vocabulary, linguistic elements, text structure, and other aspects of texts that will help them help their students read for understanding. If you are a social studies teacher with students who struggle to read the textbooks in your classes, this book is for you."—**Cynthia Shanahan, professor emerita in Curriculum and Instruction, University of Illinois at Chicago; former professor of Literacy, Language and Culture; executive director of the Council on Teacher Education; and associate dean of Academic Affairs, University of Illinois at Chicago**

Reading Actively in Middle Grade Social Studies

Reading Actively in Middle Grade Social Studies

Teachers and Students in Action

Don K. Philpot

ROWMAN & LITTLEFIELD
Lanham • Boulder • New York • London

Published by Rowman & Littlefield
An imprint of The Rowman & Littlefield Publishing Group, Inc.
4501 Forbes Boulevard, Suite 200, Lanham, Maryland 20706
www.rowman.com

6 Tinworth Street, London SE11 5AL, United Kingdom

Copyright © 2019 by Don K. Philpot
Reproduced by permission from Tim McNeese, *The Rise and Fall of American Slavery: Freedom Denied, Freedom Gained* (Berkeley Heights, NJ: Enslow, 2004), pages 18–22.
Reproduced by permission from Pearson Education Inc., *myWorld Geography* (Boston: Pearson Education Inc., 2011), pages 511, 523, 530, 532, 533, 534–35, 535, 543, 544, 549.
Reproduced by permission from Ettagale Blauer and Jason Lauré, *South Africa* (New York: Children's Press, 2013), pages 53–56.
Reproduced by permission from Pearson Education Inc., *Prentice Hall Civics: Government and Economics in Action* (Boston: Pearson Prentice Hall, 2009), pages 431, 498.

All rights reserved. No part of this book may be reproduced in any form or by any electronic or mechanical means, including information storage and retrieval systems, without written permission from the publisher, except by a reviewer who may quote passages in a review.

British Library Cataloguing in Publication Information Available

Library of Congress Cataloging-in-Publication Data

Names: Philpot, Don K., author.
Title: Reading actively in middle grade social studies : teachers and students in action / Don K. Philpot.
Description: Lanham : Rowman & Littlefield, [2019] | Includes bibliographical references and index. | Summary: "This book focuses on assigned reading events in middle grade social studies courses and the 14 actions proficient readers take before, during, and after reading to comprehend assigned course texts including textbook chapters, book chapters, passages, and articles"—Provided by author.
Identifiers: LCCN 2019012955 (print) | LCCN 2019022368 (ebook) | ISBN 9781475843989 (cloth) | ISBN 9781475843996 (pbk.)
Subjects: LCSH: Reading (Middle school) | Reading comprehension—Study and teaching (Middle school) | Social studies—Study and teaching (Middle school)
Classification: LCC LB1632 .P46 2019 (print) | LCC LB1632 (ebook) | DDC 418/.40712—dc23
LC record available at https://lccn.loc.gov/2019012955
LC ebook record available at https://lccn.loc.gov/2019022368

Contents

Acknowledgments ix

Introduction: Reading This Book xi

1 Reading in the Middle Grades 1

2 The Reading Cycle 9

3 Before Reading Actions 31

4 During Reading Actions I 51

5 During Reading Actions II 79

6 During Reading Actions III 113

7 After Reading Actions 137

8 Mediational Practices 157

References 183

Index 189

About the Author 193

Acknowledgments

My understandings about young people's reading development, school reading events, mediated reading instruction, and proficient reading in and beyond the middle grades and content area courses have been largely shaped and reshaped by researchers and teachers in the fields of education, reading pedagogy, stylistics, systemic functional linguistics, and text linguistics. To individuals in these fields, whose writings, conversations, suggestions, and modeling continue to challenge and inspire me, I am deeply indebted.

Even more so, I am deeply indebted to the young people I have been privileged to teach and learn from over the past 40 years, children and adolescents alike, who loved or hated to read, excelled or struggled in school. These young people sat and conversed with me for hours, often one on one, and opened their minds to me as I endeavored to help them to be better readers.

My understandings about informational texts and the demands they place on middle grade students in social studies and other content area courses have been greatly refined by discussions I have had over the past seven years with my undergraduate and graduate students at Shippensburg University. My model of the reading cycle and specific understandings about one or more before, during, or after reading actions emerged from these discussions. Sincere thanks to all of you.

I am grateful to those of you who took the time to read my book prior to publication and endorse its content. Your endorsement means a great deal to me.

Finally, I am grateful to John Fitzgerald, general accounts manager at Pearson (South Central Pennsylvania), who provided program materials that helped me to better understand the reading needs of middle grade students in social studies courses, and to Sarah Jubar, my editor at Rowman & Littlefield, who supported me in this writing venture from beginning to end. Without the generous support of these two individuals, my book would not have materialized.

Introduction
Reading This Book

This book focuses on students' development as proficient readers in middle grade social studies courses. All the information presented in this book—all social studies topics, texts, chapter vignettes, descriptions and illustrations of specific proficient reading actions and mediational practices, and all questions posed—pertain to middle grade teaching and learning and middle grade teachers and students.

For the purposes of this book, to make the information presented in forthcoming chapters as clear, relevant, coherent, developmentally appropriate, and useful as possible for middle grade social studies teachers, we will limit the "middle grades" to grades 6–8 and selected textbooks and supplementary texts to those that are commonly used in middle grade classrooms.

Throughout this book the full range of textbooks published by Pearson Education for grades 6–8 social studies courses is used for illustrative purposes. These textbooks, which include *myWorld History* (Karpiel et al. 2012), *myWorld Geography* (Chu et al. 2011), *myWorld American History* (Davidson, Stoff, and Bertolet 2016, 2019), and *Prentice Hall Civics* (Davis, Fernlund, and Woll 2009), are all focal points of core programs published by Pearson, whose texts appear in print and digital formats.

In this book we will also limit the scope of a middle grade reading event in important ways. A reading event, defined simply, is a *sustained period of time spent with an assigned text in a coordinated first encounter trying to understand it*. For the purposes of this book, we will focus on reading events in grades 6–8 social studies courses completed at home or at school, which focus on the main text in an assigned textbook chapter or supplementary text and require sustained silent reading for 15 minutes or more.

Throughout this book we will focus on reading events themselves, while recognizing that reading events in grades 6–8 social studies courses are part of larger learning events that engage students in summative and critical discussion, rereading, and writing that help students to achieve specific learning outcomes. At the completion of a reading event, students often answer questions about important ideas in an assigned text, discuss these ideas with their classmates and teacher, reread and annotate the text to better understand it, and engage in writing to inform, explain, compare or contrast, or persuade.

However, focusing on reading events themselves, the actions proficient readers take to complete these events successfully, and mediational practices that can optimize students' reading experiences and learning in no way suggests that the larger learning context is less important. At no point in this book is a recommendation or appeal made for a return to earlier times when learning events in grades 6–8 social studies courses were almost exclusively concerned with reading textbook chapters and answering questions.

Multimodal experiences that engage middle grade students in speaking and writing for various purposes, in various hands-on classroom investigations, field experiences, problem-solving tasks, and project work all enhance student learning, as do reading events. In fact, students' understandings and developing insights about the social sciences can be greatly enhanced by proficient reading and well-managed reading events.

This book has been written expressly for the purpose of helping middle grade social studies teachers like you understand what proficient reading entails and how classroom reading events can be managed to optimize student learning.

The book is organized in three parts: chapters 1 and 2 focus on the name of middle grade reading events and a model of reading I call the reading cycle; chapters 3–7 focus on essential actions proficient readers engage in before, during, and after reading to understand a text; and the final chapter, chapter 8, focuses on mediational practices, practices that teachers can use to mediate a reading event in one or more phases.

Chapter 1 identifies the four main purposes for reading in middle grades and examines the similarities and differences between reading events in middle school, high school, and college. The chapter also identifies four essential reading skills, which are not specifically delineated in popular instructional frameworks.

Chapter 2 introduces and explains the reading cycle, a model of proficient reading that anchors and informs the reading phase actions and mediational practices discussed in chapters 3–8. This chapter introduces the three phases of school reading events and the distinctive sets of actions that proficient readers take to achieve their reading goal.

Chapters 3–7 focus in turn on the actions proficient readers take in the before, during, and after phases of a reading event. Altogether there are 14 proficient reading actions. Each of these actions is described and illustrated using either a chapter from one of the middle grade social studies textbooks previously cited, published by Pearson Education, or a supplementary text.

Four before reading phase actions are examined in chapter 3: clarifying goal and purpose, generating expectations, activating knowledge, and developing knowledge. Chapters 4–6 in turn examine six during reading phase actions, two per chapter. Chapter 4 examines the actions of visualizing and reading fluently, chapter 5 reading for understanding and inferencing, and chapter 6 formulating and building coherence. Chapter 7 examines four after reading phase actions: summarizing, reconfiguring, assessing, and clarifying.

Chapter 8 describes a set of mediational practices that aims to help students in middle grade social studies courses to read assigned texts proficiently. Information about these practices aligns with information about the reading cycle and specific reading actions described in chapters 2–7. The practices explored in this chapter, including image previewing, terminology cubing, and selective reading guides, prompt middle grade students to take appropriate and coordinated action in one or more phases of a reading event to understand the main ideas in an assigned text and to learn specific vocabulary.

This book is primarily intended for grades 6–8 social studies teachers but will be useful for other educators as well. Teachers in intermediate grades who are responsible for delivering social studies curricula, high school teachers who deliver general and specialized courses in the social sciences, reading specialists, literacy coaches, English as a second language teachers, special education teachers, learning assistance teachers, teacher educators, preservice teachers, teachers in graduate programs, district curriculum directors, and school administrators will all benefit by reading this book and considering the ideas presented.

Readers of this book will confirm and question their existing beliefs about proficient reading and gain insights about proficient reading actions and their optimal use by middle grade students. Readers' transformative thinking about middle grade students' reading experiences and social studies teachers' key role as mediators in these experiences is assisted throughout the book by fictional accounts of teachers and students working together to optimize student learning.

This book can serve as the focal point for professional development initiatives engaged in by individual teaching faculty, teaching teams, or members of a professional learning community. It is informed by and aligned with the standards adopted by all stakeholding professional organizations: the Association for Middle Level Education (AMLE), the National Council for the Social Studies (NCSS), and the International Literacy Association (ILA).

1

Reading in the Middle Grades

Mr. Buckley's seventh grade students are learning about ancient Greece in social studies. Sections 3 and 4 in chapter 10 of their textbook focus on democracy in Athens and oligarchy in Sparta. In the first two sections of the chapter, students learned about ancient Greek society and the rise of city-states. Mr. Buckley has prepared a handout, a written preview for sections 3 and 4, which he reads to his students, who follow along.

He identifies the topic students will read about in their textbook—contrasting forms of government in ancient Greek city-states—and states its relevance for students. Then he reads a paragraph he wrote about contrasting forms of government in two contemporary societies—one democratic, the United States, and the other oligarchic, Saudi Arabia. Three questions follow this paragraph:

1. *Who has power in these societies?*
2. *Which society would you prefer to grow up in?*
3. *What are the priorities of government leaders in these societies?*

He reads these questions to his students, gives them several minutes to respond to one or more of the questions with a partner, then calls on four partnerships to share their responses with the class.

Two of the partnerships responded to question 2. Alaina, Becky, Max, and Reid all prefer to grow up in a democratic society. Alaina would have more opportunities in a democracy, being a girl. She wants to be an architect and can do this in a democracy. Becky wants to have lots of kids like her mom and aunt, and plans to work full-time at some point, maybe even run her grandpa's delicatessen when he retires. Max goes with his dad on business trips overseas and can do this in a democracy. Reid loves to snowboard and play lacrosse and doesn't think these sports would be allowed in an oligarchic society.

Next in his written preview Mr. Buckley has delineated the main ideas in sections 3 and 4, which he now reads to his students:

SECTION 3 MAIN IDEAS

1. An innovative military formation and a series of reforms resulted in the first democratic city-state.
2. Three political bodies made up the democratic government in ancient Athens: the assembly, the council, and the courts.
3. Political decisions in ancient Athens were made directly (not representatively) by citizens.

SECTION 4 MAIN IDEAS

1. Ancient Sparta was essentially governed by two kings.
2. Ancient Sparta was a military society by choice.
3. Spartan boys were raised and extensively trained to be soldiers.
4. Opposing values created tensions between ancient Sparta and Athens.

Finally, before directing students to begin reading, Mr. Buckley reads the following directions for reading sections 3 and 4:

1. Locate Athens and Sparta on the map (p. 319).
2. Preview the images and "Closer Look" feature (pp. 312–22).
3. The introductory paragraphs in section 3 briefly recount the military actions of an Athenian leader called Isagoras, who attempted to prevent a democratic leader from turning Athens into a democracy. These paragraphs are interesting but not highly relevant.
4. Be alert for information related to the main ideas.
5. Read continuously at an optimal rate.

INTRODUCTION

Mr. Buckley, like most middle grade social studies teachers, wants his students to learn relevant content from textbooks and other texts. Students' learning of social studies content is enhanced by relevant and mediated reading experiences. Students in Mr. Buckley's seventh grade social studies class learn about ancient societies like Athens and Sparta, in part, by reading about these ancient city-states in the course textbook. Reading experiences that enhance students' learning are mediated: so before his students read about ancient Greece in their course textbook, Mr. Buckley provides them with a written preview.

This book focuses on the cyclical nature of reading, the actions proficient readers take to understand social studies textbooks and other informational texts, and mediational practices that aim to enhance middle grade students' learning of social studies content through reading. Three associated questions will be addressed in this book:

1. What actions do proficient readers take to understand assigned course texts?
2. How do these actions relate to each other?
3. What mediational practices best support middle grade students' development as proficient readers and enhance their learning of course content through reading?

READING IN MIDDLE GRADES

Students in sixth, seventh, and eighth grade social studies courses read textbooks and other texts for four main purposes. First, they read to learn course content. They read to expand their knowledge about topics and the vocabulary associated with these topics. Second, they read to develop their general proficiency as readers. They read to develop their ability to generate expectations about texts, to identify unknown words, to identify paragraph topics, to make inferences, and to build coherent understandings about texts. They read to understand the aims of texts, textual points of view, particular usage of language, and the ways ideas are organized and developed.

Third, students read to develop proficiency as readers of field-specific texts, texts specifically intended for practitioners in the social sciences. Social studies texts differ from texts in other fields in measurable ways. Fourth, students read to value reading as an essential tool for learning about the world and human experiences.

In middle grade social studies courses, students read a range of texts that expand their understandings about civics and government, economics, geography, and history. Within these fields students read to learn about a range of topics including branches of government, taxation, and mass media; consumption, production, trade, and corporations; geographical features, and physical systems; and historical sources, state history, United States history, and world history.

Students in middle grade social studies courses often read chapters in required course textbooks. For decades, Pearson Education has published textbooks for middle grade social studies courses (e.g., *Prentice Hall Civics, myWorld Geography, myWorld History*). In addition to course textbooks, students often learn social studies content from books, magazines, and websites, all of which may be written for specific audiences or for general interest. Moreover, middle grade students routinely learn about history by reading primary source documents such as personal letters, journals, official records, and written speeches.

READING BEYOND MIDDLE GRADES

Through the middle grades and beyond, in high school and college, students will continue to develop proficiency as readers in social science courses. College reading events in the social sciences are similar to middle and high school reading events in many ways. In this book a reading event is defined as a sustained period of time spent with an assigned text in a coordinated first encounter trying to understand it. Reading events in college, high school, and middle school are similar in terms of the skills and dispositions required of readers, textual demands, and task specifications. These similarities are shown in table 1.1.

Reading events in all three levels of schooling require students to read print and digital texts with increasing proficiency, to manage the scope of new ideas presented in these texts, and to read silently, patiently, and persistently.

Table 1.1. Reading Events Compared

Characteristics	Source	College	High School	Middle School
focus on print and digital texts	text	●	●	●
require increasing reading proficiency	reader	●	●	●
introduce many new ideas and terms	text	●	●	●
require silent reading	reader	●	●	●
require patience and persistence	reader	●	●	●
are primarily completed at home	task	●	●	○
are primarily independent (solitary) reading events	task	●	●	○
involve sustained reading with few interruptions	reader	●	●	○
require students to identify main ideas on their own	reader	●	○	○
require students to set their own purpose for reading	reader	●	●	○

Developmental differences between middle school and the other two levels of school reading events are shown in the second half of the table. Middle grade social studies teachers may not expect their students to read all assigned texts at home or independently; assigned texts may be read in whole or part in class, with a partner or groupmates.

Middle grade reading events are often interrupted, or mediated, to optimize student learning; in both middle and high school grades students' efforts to identify main ideas during and after reading are often mediated by teachers. In middle grades, uniquely, students are provided with a reading purpose. As students begin college, having developed proficiency as readers through successful reading events in middle and high school social studies courses, they are better prepared to meet the demands of college reading events.

Beyond the middle grades, in high school and college, reading events in social science courses will, as in middle grades, focus on textbooks, specialized books, and websites. Pearson Education produces textbooks for both levels of schooling. Their collection of textbooks for high school include: *World History*, *Magruder's American Government*, *Prentice Hall Psychology*, and *Economics*. Their college collection consists of such titles as *Understanding Society*, *Cultural Anthropology*, *The Philosopher's Way*, *Psychology*, and *History of the United States*.

In introductory and more specialized undergraduate college courses, students will be required to read assigned texts independently: to understand their purpose for reading particular selections, to read attentively and with interest, to activate relevant topic knowledge, to understand the main ideas in any given text and the ways they relate to each other, to make inferences, and to read assigned texts in a timely manner, all without support from their professor.

Proficient reading at all three levels of schooling involves a distinctive set of skills that differs from Bloom's (1956) taxonomy of educational objectives and other taxonomies related to cognition and reading. Most teachers are familiar with Bloom's taxonomy from their teacher preparation programs. This influential and enduring taxonomy includes six levels of educational objectives that reflect increasing cognitive complexity:

1. *Knowledge*, recalling or recognizing ideas previously presented
2. *Comprehension*, using ideas that have been learned more substantively than simply recalling or recognizing them
3. *Application*, using ideas substantively in new situations and contexts
4. *Analysis*, breaking ideas down into component parts
5. *Synthesis*, combining ideas to form new understandings
6. *Evaluation*, making judgments about ideas presented or learned

Few PK–12 teachers are familiar with Barrett's (1972) taxonomy of reading comprehension, although it has been influential in the field of reading education. Barrett's taxonomy spans cognitive and affective domains and includes four levels of comprehension:

- *literal*, recalling or recognizing ideas that are explicitly stated in a text
- *inferential*, using directly and indirectly stated ideas to speculate about a text
- *evaluation*, making judgments about a text
- *appreciation*, being aware of the craftmanship of a text

While Bloom's (1956) and Barrett's (1972) taxonomies are useful frameworks for instructional planning and assignment development, they are not particularly useful for planning, understanding, and mediating school reading events.

Proficient reading in and beyond middle grade social studies courses involves a set of skills not specifically delineated by Bloom's (1956), Barrett's (1972), or other taxonomies. To read proficiently, middle grade students use these skills in coordination before, during, and after reading. This book identifies, describes, and illustrates the full set of skills used by proficient readers to complete school reading events. For now we will focus on four skills, which for the sake of convenience and comparative purposes we will call essential reading skills. Proficient readers use the first skill—knowledge activation—before reading; the next two skills—word identification and idea identification—during reading; and the fourth—reconfiguring the text—after reading. These four skills are described briefly in table 1.2.

Table 1.2. Four Essential Reading Skills

Level	Description
knowledge activation	bringing to mind personal schematic understandings about a topic
word identification	recognizing or decoding nonacademic and academic vocabulary
idea identification	identifying important ideas in a text presented directly or indirectly
reconfiguring the text	reworking an earlier mental representation of a text to better reflect the important ideas presented

LOOKING BACK AND AHEAD

Reading events in middle grade social studies courses are both similar to and different from high school and college reading events in social science courses. A reading event was defined earlier in this chapter as a sustained period of time spent with an assigned text in a coordinated first encounter trying to understand it.

Teachers like Mr. Buckley, a middle grade history teacher, aim to prepare their students to read textbooks and other course materials proficiently, to learn course content from mediated and independent reading experiences, and to value reading as an essential tool to learn about the world. To enhance his students' understanding about the contrasting forms of government in ancient Greece, Mr. Buckley used a mediational reading practice known as the written preview.

To read proficiently, middle grade students use sets of skills or mental actions in coordinated ways before, during, and after reading. The next chapter presents a cyclical model of reading called the reading cycle and examines each set of mental actions that proficient readers use to achieve their reading goal for each reading event.

2

The Reading Cycle

Miss Kyle, an eighth grade social studies teacher, will spend the next nine weeks of the term exploring the physical and human geography of Asia with her students and draw extensively on the resources offered by Pearson's myWorld Geography *program (Chu et al. 2011), whose textbook includes individual units on Southwest Asia (unit 6), Central and South Asia (unit 7), and East and Southeast Asia (unit 8).*

In the interest of time, Miss Kyle will focus on six chapters in the textbook, as shown in table 2.1. Each chapter is divided into three sections and includes a "myStory" feature. These sections offer geographical, historical, and contemporary perspectives on life in the region, and the introductory "stories" offer personal vignettes of young people living in these regions.

Within 30 minutes of reviewing her program materials, Miss Kyle decides to begin her comprehensive unit on Asia with all three regional overviews and all nine stories. As shown in table 2.2, she will focus on the regional overviews in week 1 and the stories in week 2.

The regional overviews span 15 textbook pages and consist of maps, photographs, and charts. Miss Kyle will use these resources during week 1 to orient her students to each region. She will also use the guiding ques-

Table 2.1. Unit Overview

Unit	Region	Chapter	Number & Topic
6	Southwest Asia	16	Arabia and Iraq
		17	Israel and Its Neighbors
7	Central and South Asia	19	Central Asia and the Caucasus
		20	South Asia
8	East and Southeast Asia	21	China and Its Neighbors
		22	Japan and the Koreas

Table 2.2. Partial Unit Overview: Weeks 1–2

Week	Focus	Units	Chapter & Sections	Page Range
1	Regional overviews	6–8	16–17; 19–20; 21–22	580–85; 674–79; 736–41
2	My stories	6–8	16–17; 19–20; 21–22	587–89; 615–17; 645–47; 681–83; 705–07; 743–45; 771–73; 799–801

tions included in the teacher's guide and the "In-Flight Movie" resources. In week 2 Miss Kyle will use all nine stories and her own resources. These stories span two to three textbook pages and consist of paragraphed text and surrounding photographs.

Miss Kyle has read each story with great interest and will mediate students' reading experiences of these stories to optimize their learning about each young person showcased and to pique her students' interest about the countries and people they will soon explore. During week 2 she will guide students' reading of two stories, one about Askar (chapter 19) and one about Xiao (chapter 21). She wants her students to do the following:

- *to understand their purpose (i.e., objectives) for reading these stories and aim to achieve their unchanging reading goal, which is to understand the main ideas presented in a text and be able to use these ideas at a later date*
- *to be prepared for their forthcoming encounters with important words and be able to identify these and other new words using their word-building knowledge*
- *to read continuously, identify paragraph topics, distinguish between main ideas and supporting details, register important ideas, and get a sense of each story as a whole*
- *assess the effectiveness of their reading actions, think about the text in new ways, and clarify their understandings about important words and ideas*

On Monday Miss Kyle will guide students' reading of Askar's story. For the next three days students will read and report on one of the seven remaining stories in jigsaw groups. On Friday Miss Kyle will provide a brief summary of the stories students have read and then use Xiao's story in chapter 21 to transition to a two-to-three-week exploration of China and its neighbors (chapter 21) and Japan and the Koreas (chapter 22).

First thing in week 2, on Monday, Miss Kyle will review the first set of unit handouts and guide students' reading of the first story. The first handout will be a simple collage of the showcased young people, Askar and Nancy, whose individual story cards are featured at the start of each chapter. The second handout will focus on vocabulary specific to each story that students will aim to acquire by the end of the unit.

On this second handout Miss Kyle included four words for Askar's story *(*Kyrgyzstan, Kyrgyz, Manas, Bishkek*)* and six words for Nancy's story *(*Palampur, Samriddhi, Changar, chutney, plantation, microcredit*)*. Miss Kyle recorded these words on sticky notes while reading the stories and will reproduce the two full sets of words as a table.

Miss Kyle will help students to decode selected words in each column of the handout using their phonics and word-building knowledge (e.g., their knowledge of non-English sounds, syllabication, Greek and Latin roots), then return to the list of words for Askar's story, their main focus for the day, and discuss the meaning of these words.

Students will see on page 680 that Kyrgyzstan is the name of a Central Asian country and that Bishkek is a major city in this country. Miss Kyle will tell students that, when referring to the people of Kyrgyzstan, you simply remove the suffix -stan, and say, the Kyrgyz people, and that for Kyrgyz people, Manas, pronounced /mŏ' nə/, is a cultural hero.

Most of Monday's class will be spent on Askar's story. Students' overarching reading purpose or objective for all nine stories in the unit will be the same: to discover what life is like for young people like themselves who live in different parts of Asia. Askar's story focuses on six topics; all are paragraph topics that Miss Kyle identified from her careful rereading of the story. Students' specific reading objective for Askar's story will focus on these topics: students will aim to learn about Askar's life—his morning routine, his interests and chores, his living arrangements, information about his town, a pressing regional problem, and his aspirations.

Students will read the story continuously without interruption and independently. When they are finished, Miss Kyle will guide their completion of a two-column note-making table, which focuses on Askar's life in one column and their own lives in the other. A partial view of this note-making table is shown in figure 2.1.

The next day, on Tuesday, students will be assigned to groups based on their selection of another story and will read about, make notes on, and share their insights about this new individual in small groups. Students will complete a note-making table independently for the new story, develop expertise about their selected individual, teach their classmates about this individual, and learn about other individuals selected by their classmates.

Students may select stories from all but chapter 21, Xiao's story, and will complete their note-making tables using the paragraph topics provided by

ASKAR'S LIFE	YOUR LIFE
MORNING ROUTINE	MORNING ROUTINE
INTERESTS & CHORES	INTERESTS & CHORES
LIVING ARRANGEMENTS	LIVING ARRANGEMENTS
TOWN INFORMATION	TOWN INFORMATION
PRESSING REGIONAL PROBLEM	PRESSING REGIONAL PROBLEM
ASPIRATIONS	ASPIRATIONS

Figure 2.1. Partial View of Note-Making Table

Miss Kyle. Paragraph topics differ from story to story and in many cases are not easily identified. The following week, on Monday, Miss Kyle and her students will begin their exploration of China and its neighbors.

INTRODUCTION

Students in Miss Kyle's eighth grade social studies course will better understand the topic of Asia and other course topics as a result of mediated reading experiences provided by their teacher. These experiences are informed by new understandings about the cyclical nature of reading, reading processes and outcomes, proficient reading actions, and the specific demands of content area texts.

This chapter focuses on the reading cycle and the actions proficient readers engage in to achieve their ultimate reading goal. We will continue to make the case that successful school reading events are the result of students' coordinated use of proficient reading actions in the before, during, and after phases.

THE READING CYCLE

This book defines a reading event as a sustained period of time spent with an assigned text in a coordinated first encounter trying to understand it. Eighth grade students in the opening vignette will complete an important reading event at the start of their unit on Asia. This event will focus on the "my-Story" feature in students' geography textbook. It has specific starting and end points, engages students in sustained silent reading for 10–15 minutes or more, focuses on paragraphed text and words, and is linked to other activities within a larger learning event or learning framework.

Reading events are cyclical in nature. A *cycle* is a round or series (of processes or actions) that repeats (*OED Online* 2018). As shown in figure 2.2, a reading event consists of three phases of reading actions: a before, during, and after phase.

From a process perspective, shown in figure 2.3a, readers orient themselves to a new text in the before reading phase, sustain their attention on the text and read it mindfully for understanding in the during reading phase, and consolidate their understandings about the text in the after reading phase. From a product perspective, shown in figure 2.3b, the distinctive outcome of each respective phase is readiness, comprehension, and retention.

Within each phase of a reading event, proficient readers use a coordinated set of actions to achieve their ultimate and unchanging reading goal. Each phase in the reading cycle, as shown in figure 2.4, has a distinctive set of ac-

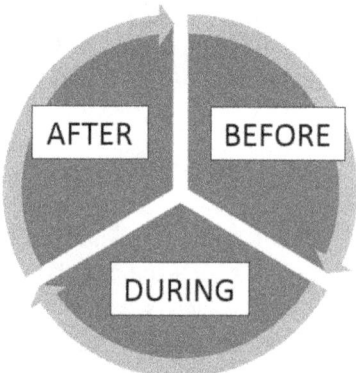

Figure 2.2. Reading Phases

a. Reading Processes   b. Reading Outcomes

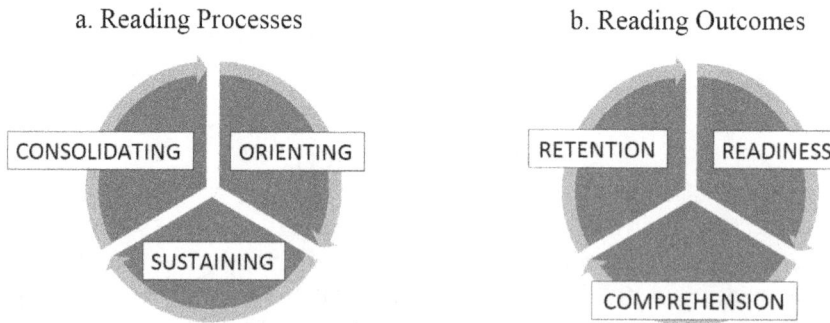

Figure 2.3. Reading Processes and Outcomes

THE READING CYCLE
PHASES ✋ PROCESS | PRODUCT ✋ MENTAL ACTION

PHASE	PROCESS | PRODUCT	MENTAL ACTION	
BEFORE	**ORIENTING** **Readiness**	clarifying goal & purpose generating expectations	activating knowledge developing knowledge
DURING	**SUSTAINING** **Comprehension**	visualizing reading fluently reading for understanding	inferencing formulating building coherence
AFTER	**CONSOLIDATING** **Retention**	summarizing reconfiguring	assessing clarifying

Figure 2.4. The Reading Cycle

tions: orienting actions, sustaining actions, and consolidating actions. In the before reading phase proficient readers clarify their reading goal and specific intentions for reading a text, generate expectations about the words and ideas they will encounter, activate relevant topic knowledge, and develop a preliminary understanding of a topic that is new to them.

In the during reading phase proficient readers visualize important ideas, read fluently, read for understanding, make inferences, register ideas, and build a coherent understanding of an assigned text as a whole. In the after reading phase proficient readers summarize the important ideas they encountered in the text, reconfigure their earlier understandings about a text as a coherent whole, assess the effectiveness of the reading event, and clarify their understanding about specific words and ideas.

Proficient readers use these sets of orienting, sustaining, and consolidating actions to prepare themselves for an optimal reading experience (readiness), to understand the words and ideas they encounter (comprehension), and to retain these understandings for use in larger learning contexts (retention). These sets of actions are essentially *mental* actions, actions completed in our heads—our mental-life actions—although they are often supplemented by physical or verbal actions, *doing* or *speaking events* such as writing or talking to a classmate.

The terms *mental action, doing*, and *speaking* reveal an important influence on the author's understandings about reading, in general, and proficient reading, reading informational texts, and reading instruction in middle grades and beyond, in particular. These terms are used by linguists to analyze the ways our lived experiences are construed by spoken and written language.

Halliday and Matthiessen (2014), both leaders in the specialized field of systemic functional linguistics, identify six types of verbs or processes that people use to communicate their experiences to others. Three of the six are most relevant here: material (doing-focused), mental (thinking-focused), and verbal (saying-focused) processes (e.g., drink, ride; remember, think; tell, explain). The author's understanding about the nature of texts, how they are written and read, has been greatly enhanced by the insights of linguists and others whose research findings are derived from systemic functional analyses.

The author's understanding about proficient reading actions and the cyclical nature of reading events has also been shaped by an important research monograph and two figures that appear in professional development books on reading published for teachers. The research monograph *Verbal Protocols of Reading: The Nature of Constructively Responsive Reading* (Pressley and Afflerbach 1995) provides insights about the actions of proficient readers, actions that are both automatic and conscious.

Figure 5.2 in *Teaching for Comprehending and Fluency: Thinking, Talking, and Writing about Reading, K–8* (Fountas and Pinnell 2006, 53) shows the dynamic relationship between reading processes and outcomes. Figure 6.1 in *Content Area Reading and Learning* (Lapp 1989, 60) illustrates the learning cycle: how people acquire and modify their understandings about the world through learning experiences. Information creates an understanding, which modifies prior knowledge, which generates purpose, which directs attention, which selects information, and on the cycle goes.

PROFICIENT READING ACTIONS

The forthcoming chapters provide detailed information about each proficient reading action included in the author's model of reading and illustrations of each action using a variety of texts. This chapter provides descriptions of each action and illustrates the action for clarity using chapters selected by Miss Kyle in Pearson's *myWorld Geography* textbook (Chu et al. 2011, hereafter referred to as the course textbook or geography textbook). The limits imposed on reading events at the end of the last chapter hold for this and subsequent chapters and bear repeating.

You will recall that for the purposes of this book we are limiting a reading event to an assigned reading event completed at home or at school that focuses on a textbook chapter in whole or in part, and its main text or a comparable supplementary text that requires sustained silent reading typically for 15 minutes or more. It will be helpful to remember, while reading these brief descriptions, that the 14 proficient reading actions described are foremost mental actions.

Before Reading Phase Actions

Proficient reading in the before reading phase consists of four actions:

1. Clarifying your goal and objectives for reading a text
2. Generating expectations about the words and ideas you will encounter in a text
3. Activating relevant topic knowledge
4. Developing background knowledge about a topic that is new to you

Clarifying the Reading Goal and Objectives

At the start of a new reading event middle grade students ready themselves to read an assigned text by clarifying their reading goal and objectives. Their unchanging reading goal is to understand the main ideas presented in an assigned text and be able to use these ideas at a later date.

Their reading objectives will be determined partly by their personal interests and needs and partly by the larger learning context and their teacher. Students will read the text purposefully and attentively, aim to acquire content, develop particular interests in the topic, achieve the learning outcomes, connect the ideas they encounter in the text in a coherent way, and take appropriate mental actions throughout the reading event.

Generating Expectations

Middle grade students optimize a reading experience by spending 5–10 minutes in the before reading phase orienting themselves to an assigned text, leafing or clicking through it from beginning to end and generating expectations about the ideas they will read about and the ways these ideas are organized and illustrated.

By previewing a text, students gain preliminary insights about the organization and comparative importance of the ideas presented. They note the sectioning of the text, the number of sections and their comparative lengths; read the section headings; note the location and number of important words and dates—names and terms; register ideas and consider their relevance; and spend several minutes or more examining interesting images.

Generated expectations about a text, gained by previewing, will help students to complete a reading event successfully. They will help students to plan the reading event and allocate a reasonable amount of time to complete it. They will motivate students to read the text, read it strategically, relate to it, and view the associated images with interest. They will also help students to connect the ideas they encounter in and across paragraphs.

Activating Relevant Topic Knowledge

The action of activating involves bringing to mind one's current knowledge about a topic, bringing this knowledge forward in one's mind to be affirmed or modified by new learning experiences and information. The range and depth of knowledge middle grade students are able to activate about a topic will vary, as will the relevance of the knowledge they activate about a particular topic. But the specific knowledge students activate will relate closely to ideas they will encounter in the text.

Students are best prepared to comprehend and retain topic-related ideas during and after reading when they activate highly relevant topic knowledge before reading. For the topic of the physical and human geography of China, students are better positioned to affirm and modify their understandings about this topic—to expand, refine, or correct their understandings during and after reading—by activating specific geographical knowledge about China—the physical features and climate of China, land use in China, and the current environmental challenges faced by China and its neighbors as the region continues to develop.

Developing Background Knowledge

At times middle grade students will know little or nothing about a topic they will read about in their course textbook. This was the case for Miss Kyle's students at the start of week 2, who had never heard of the Central Asian country of Kyrgyzstan and knew nothing about it. To develop her students' knowledge about the country and its people, which would help them to understand "Askar's Story" in their course textbook, Miss Kyle guided their viewing of the map of Central Asia on page 680 and the 13 photographs that accompany the featured story.

For this particular reading event and chapter, Miss Kyle's students viewed a map and photographs to develop entry-level knowledge about the chapter topic. For other reading events students might view a short video, view images or read about a topic online, listen to excerpts from an audiobook or podcast, or listen to their teacher or a classmate, family member, or guest share their knowledge about the topic.

During Reading Phase Actions

Proficient reading in the during reading phase consists of six actions:

1. Visualizing
2. Reading fluently
3. Reading for understanding
4. Making inferences about important ideas encountered in a text
5. Formulating a text
6. Building a coherent understanding of a text

Visualizing

During reading, visualized content takes the form of one or several flashing images in the mind triggered by a word or group of words encountered in an assigned text. For example, the first time students read the featured story "Xiao's Lake" in chapter 21 of their course textbook, images of an algae bloom and bloated dead fish might flash in their minds, as they did for their teacher.

Miss Kyle spent several summers at her sister-in-law's cabin on a freshwater lake in Manitoba, about seven hours north of Minneapolis. Until the government took action to clean up the lake, algae blooms were common. Algae would actually wash ashore at her feet while she sat on the beach with her nieces and nephews. Then not long ago she saw a disturbing image in a documentary of an enormous algae bloom in the north part of the lake as observed from space. Many of the bloated dead fish that used to float to shore in past summers had died because of those blooms.

The photographic image of an algae bloom and cinematic image of bloated dead fish could be triggered roughly midway through Xiao's story when information is presented about the lake near the family orchard. These two triggered images and the words that triggered them are shown in table 2.3. The action of visualizing during reading is largely automatic and focuses on things and people's doings.

Table 2.3. Visualized Content in Xiao's Story

Triggering Words	Triggered Image	Experience	Type of Image
algae bloom	an algae bloom	observed thing	cinematic
		viewed satellite image	photographic
suffocated fish floated to the surface, belly up	a bloated dead fish	observed thing	cinematic

Reading Fluently

Middle grade students read assigned texts fluently when they read in a forward motion, sustain an optimal speed, use their phonics and word-building knowledge to identify unknown words, and read accurately.

Students who maintain a continuous forward motion in the during reading phase read in a flowing rightward direction, left to right (over and down), line by line, sentence by sentence, paragraph by paragraph, and by doing so reach the end of a text quicker than students who disrupt the flow of their reading and constantly backtrack. By maintaining a forward motion, students are able to achieve and sustain optimal speeds that will vary from text to text but are no less than twice the speed at which we speak in our everyday conversations.

Leveled texts for a particular grade or grade band (e.g., grade 8, or grades 6–8) will contain many words that students, for whom the text is intended, will automatically recognize. These texts will also contain words that students will not recognize, mainly specialized words that are new to them. The word *depression*, which appears in the chapters about Southwest Asia in the geography textbook, has a specialized meaning. In the field of geography, the word *depression* refers to a place, a stretch of land that dips, whose center is lower than its margins.

To maintain a continuous forward motion during reading, students must identify each new specialized word they encounter swiftly and skillfully. They do this by using their knowledge of word sounds and word parts—their phonics, word-segmenting, and word-building knowledge.

Phonic elements in English words include single vowels and consonants and combinations of vowels and consonants. In the during reading phase of a reading event, students use their knowledge of phonic elements, their phonics knowledge, to identify unknown words.

While reading about the southwest region of Asia in their course textbook, Miss Kyle's students will encounter the specialized word *dynasty*. The identification of this word, shown in table 2.4, requires a unique set of phonic element knowledge.

Table 2.4. Examples of Phonics Knowledge Used to Identify New Words

Knowledge	Unknown Word
	dynasty
schwa	dynasty /ə/
long vowel	dynasty /ī/, /ē/
consonant blend	dynasty /st/

To identify the word *dynasty*, students will draw on their knowledge of specific vowel sounds and consonant blends. They will need to know that the letter *a*, in the second unaccented syllable of the word, has an indecisive sound (formally called a schwa), that the letter *y* in the first and third syllables makes two distinctive long vowel sounds /ī/ and /ē/, and that the letters *s* and *t*, appearing together, make a blended sound.

To identify unknown words during reading, students also use their knowledge of English base words, Greek/Latin roots, prefixes, and suffixes. Two words that Miss Kyle's students will encounter in their course textbook as they read and learn about Asia are shown in table 2.5. The English base word *urban* is easily identified in the first word. To this base word is added the derivational suffix *-ize* (to make) and the inflectional suffix *-d,* which denotes a past action.

The second word, *desalination*, contains the Latin root *sal* (salt) and four derivational affixes—one prefix (*de-*, denoting removal) and three suffixes

Table 2.5. Examples of Word-Building Knowledge Used to Identify New Words

Knowledge	Unknown Word	
	urbanized	desalination
base word	urban	
Greek/Latin root		sal
inflectional suffix	-d	
derivational prefix		de-
derivational suffix	-ize	-ine
		-ate
		-ion

(*-ine*, made of, pertaining to; *-ate*, involved in a process; and *-ion*, an action or condition). The three derivational suffixes change the root from a noun to an adjective to a verb and back to a noun.

To read a text in a forward motion at an optimal speed, students need to identify the unknown words they encounter swiftly and accurately, using their knowledge of word sounds and word parts. Fluent reading depends in part on accurate word identification. It also depends on students' ability to read sentences accurately as they were intended to be read in terms of their grammatical structuring and punctuation.

For the featured story "Asuka: A Girl on the Go," Miss Kyle's students will repeatedly draw on their knowledge of English phrasing and both simple and complex sentence punctuation to read the story fluently. Students will read groups of words as units rather than as individual words.

For example, when reading the following first paragraph of Asuka's story, students will read the boldfaced and underlined words as units. They will read the boldfaced words as noun groups, consisting of a thing and the words that describe it (identical apartment blocks; the drab, box-shaped buildings; the third-year high school student; the family's pet turtle); and they will read the underlined words as a phrasal verb (stands out) and groups of prepositional phrases as a unit (onto the top of their walls).

> In the bamboo- and concrete-covered hills of Yokohama, a cluster of **identical apartment blocks** <u>stands out</u>. **The drab, box-shaped buildings** have numbers stenciled <u>onto the top of their walls</u> to identify them. On the third floor of one of the apartment buildings, in a small apartment no bigger than an average American living room, lives Asuka. **The third-year high school student** shares the apartment with her father, her grandmother, her 15-year-old brother, **the family's pet turtle**, and Max, a pet rabbit. (Chu et al. 2011, 171)

To read this and other assigned texts fluently, Miss Kyle's students will also use their knowledge of punctuation marks—periods, commas, hyphens, apostrophes, quotation marks, dashes, parentheses, semi-colons, and colons.

Reading for Understanding

In the during reading phase of a reading event, middle grade students who read for understanding will likely achieve their reading goal of understanding the main ideas presented in a text and being able to use these ideas at a later date. To read for understanding involves extracting important meanings from a text, paragraph by paragraph. Students who read for understanding during reading identify paragraph topics and the ideas closely related to these topics, track the development of ideas within individual paragraphs, and distinguish between main ideas and supporting ideas.

The quantity and quality of meaning extracted from a text during reading depends partly on students' paragraph-by-paragraph identification of important ideas and partly on their knowledge of word meanings, concepts, and the way texts are structured. In their unit on Asia, Miss Kyle's students will read about contemporary life in Central Asia and the Caucasus in chapter 19, section 3 in the course textbook and will use their knowledge of word meanings, concepts, writing structures, and textual transitioning to expand their understandings about the political organization of countries in this part of Asia (the focus of sections 3B and 3C).

In "Challenges for New Nations" (section 3B), students will encounter the transitional words *still* and *meanwhile* and the comparison structure. In "Building New Governments" (section 3C), students will encounter the concepts of election fraud and repressive (governments) and the specialized words *task*, *collapsed*, and *economy*.

The quantity and quality of meaning students extract from these sections will depend in part on their knowledge of transitional words (their knowledge of conjunctions, and the ways conjunctions are used to link ideas across paragraphs), informational writing structures (distinctive ways that ideas are presented in informational writing), concepts (linked words and ideas that form larger units of meaning), and individual word meanings (the distinctive ways words are defined and used in informational texts). Informational writing structures are explored at length in chapter 5 of this book.

Inferencing

Informational texts such as the *myWorld Geography* textbook (Chu et al. 2011) aim to present ideas explicitly. Chapter 16, section 1B in this specific textbook has been purposefully designed to convey information directly to middle grade students about gas and oil fields on the Arabian Peninsula, a striking physical feature in this geographic region.

Section 1B, "Oil and Gas Riches," consists of four paragraphs. It also includes two images: one image, a cutaway drawing, that shows an oil and gas field in a fold trap; and a second image, a map, that shows the location of oil fields on the Arabian Peninsula, the location of tectonic boundaries in proximity to these fields, and the direction of plate movements in the region. Information about the rich reserves of oil and gas on the Arabian Peninsula is conveyed directly to readers through these images and the short four-paragraph text. From the text, aided by the images, students will learn explicitly about the evolution and location of fold traps (what materials and processes caused these traps to form, and where these traps formed).

Yet however explicit, direct, and logical informational writing aims to be in these and other textbooks produced for middle grade social studies courses, certain meanings can only be extracted by the action of inferencing. This book defines inferencing as the action of extracting meaning from understated ideas, and limits these understated ideas to paragraph topics and the main ideas presented in paragraphs. Paragraph topics may or may not be clearly articulated in a text, and when they are not, students will need to infer them. Students will also need to infer each paragraph's main idea or ideas that, along with the paragraph topic, structure the paragraph's meaning.

Textbook writers and publishers aim to produce considerate texts but do not explicitly identify main ideas for middle grade students, paragraph by paragraph. Students will need to identify main ideas for themselves and do so economically. To maximize the meanings they extract during reading, students will need to engage in two types of inferencing: paragraph topic and main idea inferencing.

As explicitly—directly and logically—as the ideas in section 1B, "Oil and Gas Riches," appear to be conveyed to readers in chapter 16, Miss Kyle's students will need to infer the paragraph topics and main ideas shown in table 2.6.

Table 2.6. Ideas That Need to Be Inferred

Paragraph	Paragraph Topic Key Words	Main Idea Key Words
1	folding	seabed
		death of living things
		forces
		folds
2	location	nearness to plate
		nearness to water

Formulating

To formulate a text during reading is to give shape to the text being read. The during reading action of formulating is a three-prong action that involves the mental registration and storage of important ideas encountered in an assigned text, the ordering of these ideas, and the formation of new understandings about one or more of these ideas. For all course readings, proficient readers like Ryan in Miss Kyle's class will automatically engage in this three-prong action without being prompted by their teacher.

In week 5 of their nine-week study of Asia, Miss Kyle assigns chapter 20, section 1 in the course textbook for independent reading and allocates 20 minutes of class time to complete this task.

The region of South Asia is the focus of chapter 20, a region that includes the countries of India, Pakistan, Sri Lanka, Bangladesh, and three others. Section 1 spans eight pages of text and focuses on South Asia's landforms, climate, land use, population growth, settlement patterns, and cultural exchanges through trade and settlement. Ryan and his classmates, given the go-ahead, begin to read. They have already completed the before reading phase with Miss Kyle and will complete the during and after reading phases now on their own, within the given time frame.

Ryan reads this section on South Asia with great interest and takes the appropriate actions to achieve his reading goal. He reads the text fluently, reads for understanding, extracts meanings from understated ideas, and visualizes things like Mount Everest, the Ganges River, sweltering weather, and torrential rainfall. At the halfway point in his reading, at the end of section 1C, he has mentally registered and cached important ideas about the region's physical features, climates, and primary uses of land, ordered these ideas sequentially as he encountered them in the text, and gained a new understanding about the Himalaya Mountains.

He has registered the ideas of India's collision with Asia, famous mountains, two important rivers, different climates, monsoons, and the prevalence of farming, all in sequence. In section 1A he learned that the Himalaya Mountains at the northeastern edge of the region, which include Mount Everest, the tallest mountain in the world, came into being 90 million years ago with the collision of two land masses: one that drifted over from Africa, a subcontinent (the Indian subcontinent), and the other, a fully fledged continent, Asia.

Ryan will learn the next day that the majority of his classmates, like him, formed a new understanding about the Himalayas while reading section 1. His other formulations will be similar to and different from the formulations of other proficient readers in his class.

Building Coherence

During reading, proficient readers begin to develop a whole and coherent understanding of a text. They draw on their expanding repository of ideas identified and registered to build a coherent mental representation of a text incrementally. Such representations will be coherent if the ideas represented are connected in thoughtful ways and form a logical, meaningful whole. Middle grade students who build coherent mental representations of texts during reading create networks of ideas and topics within and across sections that reach back to and substantively expand students' understanding about the chapter topic.

A possible mental representation for chapter 21, section 2A in the *myWorld Geography* textbook (Chu et al. 2011), "The Empires of China and Mongolia," is shown in figure 2.5. Representations such as this take the form of a web at whose center is a section topic, here "Chinese & Mongolian Empires," the focus of the reading event.

The branched ideas in figure 2.5 are drawn from section headings or paragraphs. The branched ideas "Chinese empire" and "Mongolian empire" are derived from section headings. Topic sentences and main paragraph ideas provide the branched ideas of "Beginnings," "Chinese Emperors," "Chinese accomplishments," and "Unification." Finally, the branched ideas of "Conquest" and "Duration" are inferable from sentences in the last paragraph.

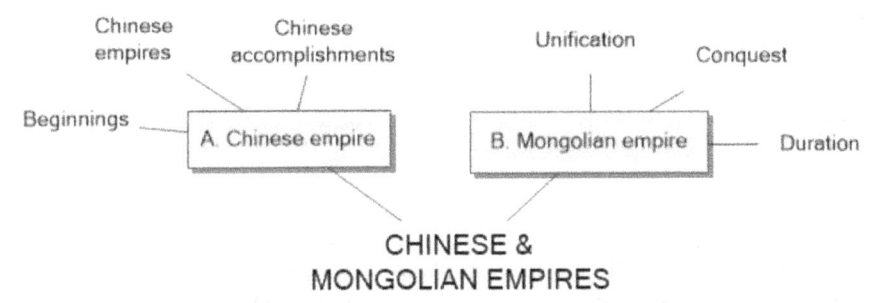

Figure 2.5. Mental Representation of Assigned Text

After Reading Phase Actions

Proficient reading in the after reading phase consists of four actions:

1. Summarizing the main ideas
2. Reconfiguring the text in whole or part
3. Assessing the overall quality of the reading event
4. Clarifying meanings (words, terms, and ideas)

Summarizing

To demonstrate their understanding of an assigned text in the after reading phase of a reading event, middle grade students will produce a mental, verbal, or written summary of the text in which they delineate the text's main ideas accurately, systemically, and succinctly. An after reading summary typically retains the ordering of ideas in the source text and may consist of complete sentences or bulleted phrases.

At the end of week 1 of their study, Miss Kyle's students produced written summaries for chapter 16, section 3, "Arabia and Iraq Today," in their course textbook. These single-paragraph summaries consisted of one statement about the main section, three topic and two to four summative statements about the topics in each subsection, 3A–C. A summary that may have been produced by one of her students follows. The first sentence summarizes topic-related information provided in the introductory paragraph, and subsequent sentences summarize information related to the subsection topics of religion, the economy, and modernization.

> Modern Arabia and Iraq have unique qualities that make them stand out from other countries in the world. Islam is the dominant religion in these two countries. People who have adopted this religion are called Muslims. Muslims share some basic beliefs about the world but participate in different cultural activities and hold varying political views. Oil production and sales are centrally important to the economies in Arabia and Iraq. Both countries have become rich selling oil to nations around the world including the United States. Each country, however, is trying to diversify its economy. Over the past 50 years Arabia and Iraq have become very modern countries. Many Arabs and Iraqis own televisions and computers, but women's rights are still restricted.

Reconfiguring

Proficient readers build a representation of an assigned text during reading, which they then reconfigure after reading to consolidate their understandings about the text and its central topic. Both representations are built primarily from identified and registered section and paragraph topics, are internally coherent, and accurately reflect the important ideas presented in a text. After reading representations, however, differ from during reading representations in significant ways. They are physical, not mental, representations, are more specific and detailed than during reading representations, and include ideas from during reading mental representations that have been rearticulated and reorganized.

Figures 2.6 and 2.7 are the author's own representations for chapter 22, section 2, "History of Japan and the Koreas," in the *myWorld Geography*

Figure 2.6. During Reading Representation

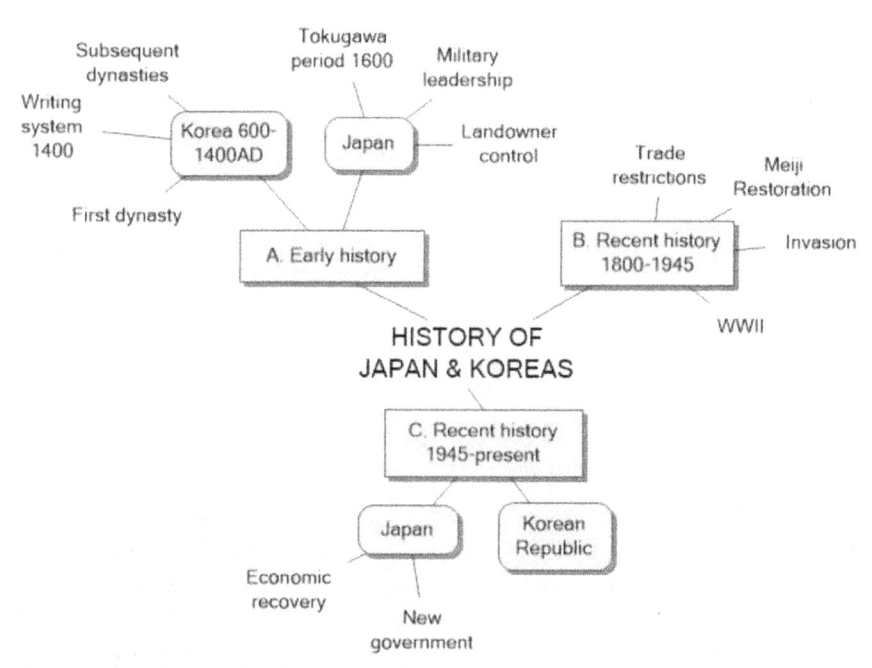

Figure 2.7. After Reading Representation

textbook (Chu et al. 2011). Figure 2.6 simulates the mental representation the author built for this section during reading, and figure 2.7 is the actual physical representation he produced after reading. The differences between these two representations illustrate the distinctive features of a reconfigured text produced in the after reading phase of a reading event, differences in terms of form, detail, and reconstituted meanings. The reconfigured text represented in figure 2.7 includes:

- up to three levels of branching (e.g., writing system 1400, military leadership)
- dates (e.g., 1800–1945)
- clustered ideas (e.g., early history of Japan, early history of the Koreas)
- branched ideas not included in the during reading representation (e.g., Meiji Restoration)
- reconstituted topics (e.g., Recent History ← Conflicts and connections + WWII to present day)
- rearticulated meanings (e.g., first dynasty ← kingdoms; trade restrictions ← relations with Europeans)

Assessing

Middle grade students gain valuable insights about a reading event as a whole through the action of assessing, a two-prong action that involves personal reflection and evaluation. After reading a text like "History of Japan and the Koreas" in the *myWorld Geography* textbook (Chu et al. 2011), proficient readers will take a few minutes to think quietly, calmly, and carefully about each preceding phase of the reading event, assign a value to their overall comprehension of the text, and identify particular words and ideas they did not fully understand during reading.

Clarifying

Middle grade students will be confused about some of the words, terms, and ideas they encountered in an assigned text during reading and will need to resolve these confusions—or clarify their understandings about a text—after reading in order to achieve their reading goal. During reading students may be confused about the meaning of a word or concept, the meaning of a sentence, or the meaning of a whole paragraph or section. Students have at least four options for resolving these confusions. They can reread the portion of text that led to their confusion; cross-reference a word, term, or idea; annotate the text in new ways; and question the text.

To understand the important ideas about Israel and its neighbors presented in chapter 17, section 1 of their geography textbook, Miss Kyle's students will need to engage in the after reading action of clarifying. Section 1 consists of four parts. Sections 1A–C focus on the region's physical characteristics and section 1.4 on its human characteristics. Section 1 as a whole focuses on all four countries in the region: Israel, Lebanon, Jordan, and Syria. This fourfold focus makes tracking and understanding ideas specific to any one country challenging during reading.

In section 1C, for example, whose focus is the region's main sources of water, students will read about the region's aquifers, three important rivers, the abundance of freshwater in Lebanon, water shortages in Syria and Jordan, and water resources that all four countries compete over. After reading section 1C on their own, students will need to clarify their understandings about specific words and concepts (e.g., aquifer, scarce resource, limited resource, desalination plant, disagreements, agreements, water loss) and how the word *thirsty* in the first-level heading "Water for a Thirsty Region" relates to the accompanying image of an Israeli farmer watering his crops.

Most importantly, students will need to clarify their understandings about the location of shared resources in the region, such as aquifers, the Euphrates and Jordan Rivers, and the Sea of Galilee, and each country's access to and use of these contested resources.

LOOKING BACK AND AHEAD

Middle grade social studies teachers like Miss Kyle use their knowledge about reading events and the actions proficient readers engage in to achieve their reading goal to mediate assigned readings in their courses. Reading events, as defined in this book, are cyclical events that consist of before, during, and after phases. This chapter presented a cyclical model of reading called the reading cycle and briefly described each distinctive set of proficient reading actions delineated in this model. Proficient readers use these sets of actions, all essentially mental actions, to optimize their reading experiences and learn course content.

This chapter is foundational for the chapters that follow. The next chapter focuses specifically on the before reading phase of a reading event and provides detailed information about and examples of the four actions that help middle grade students to prepare themselves for optimally productive reading experiences in their social studies courses.

3

Before Reading Actions

"Here are your tasks," says Mrs. Harper, showing her next slide. *A moment ago Mrs. Harper told her sixth grade students that they will complete these tasks with their side partner and report their observations together; to put away their extra textbooks, as only one is needed per partnership to complete the tasks; and for now to keep their books closed. Mrs. Harper highlights each task with her laser pointer.*

"First," says Mrs. Harper, *"when I give the word, flip through chapter 1, and look quickly at the images. Spend about five seconds on each but no longer than that for now. There are lots of images in the chapter, about 30, and some are more useful than others. Focus on the images, not the text. Refrain from reading anything for now, even the captions.*

"Second," says Mrs. Harper, *"return to the images on these four pages: pages 58, 64, 65, and 68. These images are important images in the introduction and three sections in the chapter. Select one of the images to focus on for the remaining tasks.*

"Two tasks remain. Third," says Mrs. Harper, *"look closely at your image and talk about it expansively with your partner. What do you do see in the image? That's one of the questions you want to answer for yourselves. Remember on Monday I talked expansively about the image of the skull in the first section? Do this now with your partner: talk expansively about your image. Now answer this question with your partner: What will this section of the chapter be about? To answer this question, keep your image in mind.*

"In other words," says Mrs. Harper, *"I want you to use the image to generate expectations about the text, to anticipate what the text is about. This fourth task speaks for itself. Share some of your observations and one expectation with the class."*

Mrs. Harper and her sixth grade students are embarking on a study of human origins, the first unit in their myWorld History textbook (Karpiel et al. 2012). The first chapter focuses on early people and consists of three main sections: "Studying the Distant Past," "Hunter-Gatherer Societies," and "Populating the Earth." Among the partnerships that Mrs. Harper calls on today to share are Trevor and Delaney. Everyone turns to the image on page 64 in their textbooks.

"It's a caveman," says Delaney. "He's holding a sharp stick. His feet are covered with dust." "Dusty ashes," says Trevor. "He's crouching by a fire, but the fire is out. The wood is all burned. His arms are covered with ash dust too." "He's not very tall. But he sure looks strong," says Delaney. "He's reaching out with both arms. He's right-handed like me, like Trevor too."

"That's an interesting observation," says Mrs. Harper.

Kayla and Ian focused on this image too. "He has a moustache," says Kayla, "and a very large head, a very thick neck. His eyebrows jut out from his head." "He's very muscular," says Ian. "He's wearing furry shorts. He looks like he's digging in the ashes." "Like he wants to cover himself with ashes," says Kayla. "We couldn't figure out why."

"What do you expect to read about in this section?" asks Mrs. Harper.

"How people like him survived long ago. That's what we thought," says Ian.

"We'll probably read about caveman tools and what they were used for," says Delaney.

Kim and Erin focused on a different image. Everyone now turns to page 68 in their textbooks. "We picked this image because it was mysterious," says Kim. "We really didn't know what we were seeing at first. Then I spotted the baby," says Erin. " 'That isn't a baby,' I said," says Kim. "Then I saw that it was. 'It's looking right at us,' I said."

"It looks like a toddler," says Mrs. Harper.

"We decided it was a girl," says Erin. "A girl with her dad. Both are wearing hats. The dad's hat is pointed. The girl's hat is striped." "That's snow in the background," says Kim. Then Kim speaks again: "They're going somewhere. The girl is bundled up in the saddle, holding on to two posts. Erin called them saddle posts." "The picture starts to get brighter the more you look at it," says Erin.

"What animal is that she's sitting on?" asks Mrs. Harper.

Tyler raises his hand. "A reindeer," he says. "I know lots about reindeer."

"The dad is making sure that the saddle doesn't move and the girl is safe," says Erin. "They're taking their pots and food. That's their food in that gray bag tied to the post. I bet there's water in that metal container."

"What do you expect to read about in this section?" asks Mrs. Harper.

"I expect to read about people on the move," says Erin.

"And their reasons for moving," says Kim.

Tyler raises his hand again. "Animals carried things like blankets and food, like the reindeer in the picture. They made it easier for people to move. I expect to read about that," says Tyler.

"Very good," says Mrs. Harper. "These images really do get us thinking about the text and the important information that we'll read and learn about shortly. Let's look at the headings now and see what they can tell us about the text."

INTRODUCTION: BEFORE READING PHASE ACTIONS

Middle grade students are more likely to read attentively and learn from an assigned text if they briefly explore the text first with their teacher and classmates to get a sense of what the text is about and how it is organized. Generating expectations about a text, which Mrs. Harper helped her sixth grade students do for the chapter about early people, is one of four mental actions proficient readers engage in before reading to achieve their reading goal. These four actions include:

1. Clarifying one's reading goal and purpose
2. Generating expectations about a text
3. Activating topic knowledge
4. Developing topic knowledge

In this chapter each of these four before reading actions is explained in detail and illustrated using the chapter on early people in the *myWorld History* textbook (Karpiel et al. 2012) and several supplementary texts including a chapter from the specialized book *Every Bone Tells a Story* (Rubalcaba and Robertshaw 2010). Already you are rightly asking yourself key questions about the four actions that you will seek to answer while reading on. Your questions likely include the following:

- How will Mrs. Harper's students clarify their reading goal and purpose for each chapter or chapter section they will read?
- What expectations will Mrs. Harper's students generate about individual chapter sections and each chapter as a whole?
- What knowledge about the topic of early people is best for Mrs. Harper's students to activate before reading?
- What basic knowledge about early people might some of Mrs. Harper's students need to acquire before they attempt to read any assigned texts?

CLARIFYING ONE'S GOAL AND PURPOSE

Statements and Questions

Proficient readers clarify their reading goal and purpose before reading an assigned text. To clarify means to make clear, to set forth clearly (*OED Online* 2018). Proficient readers clarify their reading goal and purpose for reading an assigned text by reminding themselves about their ultimate reading goal and by understanding and specifying their objectives for reading that text. One's purpose for reading consists of multiple reading objectives.

This section addresses the following questions:

- What is the ultimate goal for any school reading event?
- What do middle grade students aim to do with an assigned text? What are their personal and assigned reading objectives?
- How do students best clarify their goal and objectives for reading?

Clarifying Your Reading Goal

As stated in the previous chapter, the ultimate goal of all school reading events is to understand the main ideas in an assigned text and be able to use these ideas at a later date. Proficient readers, mindful of the during and after phases of the reading event, aim to identify and understand the main ideas about the topic explored in the text, and to use these ideas to enhance their understanding about the topic subsequent to the reading event.

Before reading an assigned text, students will simply clarify their reading goal: "I'm aiming to understand the main ideas in this text and be able to use them at a later date." All students will benefit from having this statement recorded on the cover of their notebooks or in another accessible location. Some students will refer to this written statement in whole or part to remind themselves of their reading goal. Some will remind themselves mentally or verbally. Others may prefer a question-answer approach: "What is my goal for reading this text? To understand its main ideas and be able to use them at a later date."

Students who clarify their reading goal before reading will be rewarded for doing so during and after reading. They will read an assigned text intentionally, focus on identifying and understanding the main ideas presented and developed, read attentively to acquire specific knowledge about the given topic, and experience greater success refining and expanding their understandings about the topic through post-reading event discussion and analysis.

Illustration

Mrs. Harper has directed her students to read chapter 1, section 1 for homework, the section called "Studying the Distant Past." Five or so minutes before packing them up and sending them on to their next class, she directs her students to open their textbooks to page 58, where section 1 begins, and to clarify their reading goal with their side partner.

Trevor and Delaney have been side partners for several weeks and know the routine. Today Trevor will clarify his reading goal and Delaney will affirm it. Trevor knows his reading goal by heart and no longer needs to refer to the written statement on the cover of his notebook. He turns his notebook over and says confidently, "I'm aiming to understand the main ideas in this section and be able to use them at a later date." Delaney affirms Trevor's statement as accurate and complete, comparing it to the written statement on the cover of his own notebook. Both partners turn to their teacher and give her a thumbs-up.

Clarifying One's Reading Purpose

Proficient readers do more than simply clarify their reading goal before reading an assigned text. They also clarify their reading purpose—their multiple reading objectives. There are two sets of reading objectives: a teacher-assigned set and a self-assigned set.

Teacher-assigned reading objectives focus on specific topic knowledge, general content knowledge, the coordination of ideas within an assigned text, connecting ideas across learning contexts, and personal inquiry. Before reading an assigned text, proficient readers clarify five teacher-assigned reading objectives:

1. To expand one's knowledge about the topic
2. To acquire general content knowledge on one's own
3. To understand the ideas presented in a text in a coherent way
4. To connect ideas presented in a text to ideas presented in class
5. To develop a personal interest in some aspect of the topic

Proficient readers also clarify self-assigned reading objectives that focus on topic relevance, attentiveness to an assigned text, and forthcoming actions during and after reading that will help them to achieve their ultimate reading goal. There are three self-assigned reading objectives:

1. To make the ideas in the text personally relevant for oneself
2. To read attentively
3. To take appropriate reading actions before, during, and after reading

Illustration

A minute has passed since Mrs. Harper directed her students, in side partnerships, to clarify their reading goal for the section about studying the distant past in their world history textbooks. All of her students have now responded with a thumbs-up, indicating that they have clarified their reading goal with their partner. Now Mrs. Harper helps her students to clarify their reading objectives and calls on Erin to explain one of her self-assigned reading objectives.

"I'm aiming to make the ideas in this section personally relevant for myself," says Erin.

"Yes, personal relevance makes reading much more interesting for you," says Mrs. Harper. Next she calls on Ian.

"I'm going to read the section attentively and not get distracted," says Ian.

"Where will you seat yourself at home to read this section?" asks Mrs. Harper.

"At my desk," says Ian.

"What about you, Erin?" asks Mrs. Harper. "Where will you seat yourself to read this section attentively?"

"The downstairs couch," says Erin.

Mrs. Harper nods her head and poses her next question to Delaney. "What's the last self-assigned reading objective?"

Delaney refers to the cover of his notebook, then tells Mrs. Harper that he is going to remind himself to take appropriate actions before, during, and after reading, to really understand the main ideas in the section.

"Name one during reading action you'll take," says Mrs. Harper.

"I'll read for understanding," says Delaney.

"Name one after reading action you'll take," says Mrs. Harper.

Delaney refers to his notebook cover, then says, "I'll clarify my understanding about new words."

Mrs. Harper now shifts to teacher-assigned reading objectives, points to the poster on the wall with the key words *topic knowledge*, *content knowledge*, *coherence*, *learning contexts*, and *interest*, and calls on Kylie to clarify one of these objectives, beginning with the phrase "I'm aiming to . . ."

"I'm aiming to expand my knowledge about studying the past," says Kylie.

"Good," says Mrs. Harper. "Scientists study the past using special methods and tools. You want to expand your knowledge about those methods and tools. Nick, what are you aiming to do?"

"I'm aiming to develop an interest in the early human called 'Lucy.' I've never heard of her before," says Nick.

Mrs. Harper now addresses the students, who minutes ago affirmed their reading goal with their partner, and directs these students to clarify the remaining teacher-assigned reading objectives with their partner, to use simple statements as they have done in the past. Once her students have clarified the remaining objectives related to content knowledge, coherence, and learning contexts, and given her a thumbs-up, she sends them on to their music class.

Reading and Learning Goals and Objectives

The two-prong action of clarifying one's goal and purpose for reading an assigned text within the context of a social studies unit such as Mrs. Harper's sixth grade world history unit on early people is a supportive action that helps students to achieve the unit's broader set of learning outcomes that reflect national and state social studies standards. To achieve one's reading goal and objectives at the end of a reading event will help students to achieve their learning goals and objectives. But these two sets of goals and objectives are distinctive.

While completing their unit on early people, for example, Mrs. Harper will prompt her students to clarify their reading goal and purpose for each reading event and help her students to achieve specific learning targets related to the unit topic, the theme of time, continuity, and change, and several state world history standards. Throughout the unit Mrs. Harper will engage her students in questioning, acquiring knowledge, processing ideas, and demonstrating their understanding about the unit topic and theme productively.

GENERATING EXPECTATIONS

Statements and Questions

Proficient readers generate expectations about an assigned text before reading it. An expectation refers to the action of anticipating or foreseeing something, and to generate means to bring into existence (*OED Online* 2018). In other words, before reading an assigned text, proficient readers bring the text into existence in terms of its organization and content.

This section addresses the following questions:

- How do middle grade students generate expectations about an assigned text from a chapter overview, section titles and headings, section length, and sequencing?
- How do students generate expectations about the words they will encounter in an assigned text?
- How can students use images to generate expectations about an assigned text?

The Structure of Assigned Texts

Students will likely be required to read a wide range of texts in middle grade social studies courses, including textbook chapters, book chapters, program handouts and supplementary digital texts, news and government reports, magazine articles, and a host of primary source documents such as speeches, government bills, and letters. The structure of these texts will vary from simple to complex. Personal letters will be structurally simpler than web-based texts with multiple sections, sidebars, and hyperlinks.

On a continuum of structural complexity, book and textbook chapters, such as those selected by Mrs. Harper for her unit on early people, lie at the midway point. These two texts are used below to explicate the before reading action of generating expectations about assigned unit texts.

Generating Expectations about Text Organization

Pearson's *myWorld History* textbook (Karpiel et al. 2012) is organized by units. Twelve units appear in the textbook, and like the first unit, "Origins," each includes a unit overview and several chapters. A core concepts handbook appears at the front of the book, and a world atlas, glossary, and index appear at the back. Each chapter, like the first chapter, "Early People," includes a "myStory" feature, numbered sections, and assessments.

Regrettably, the textbook does not include a chapter outline with each chapter, which Mrs. Harper's students would have used to learn about the organization of their first chapter on the topic of early people. A chapter outline provides quick information about chapter sectioning: how many sections are in the chapter, how long each section is, and which section is longest. In the absence of such an outline, Mrs. Harper has taught her students to use the contents page as a chapter outline.

Once students have brought the chapter as a whole into existence, they will do likewise with section 1, the focus of their assigned reading. Students will want to know the section topic, how the section begins and ends, how it is sectioned, and what special features are present.

Illustration

A week ago Mrs. Harper and her students explored the organization of the sixth grade history textbook, the larger textual context of their first assigned reading. They turned to the table of contents and shared their observations about the topics examined and the organization of chapters. They noted the location and organization of the core concepts handbook on pages vi–vii;

skimmed the list of story titles and primary sources on pages xxii–xxiv; then skimmed through the atlas and glossary at the back of the book.

Today, before assigning the first section of chapter 1 for reading homework, Mrs. Harper wants her students to prepare themselves for reading by noting specific organizational details about the chapter as a whole. She directs them to turn to the table of contents.

Individual students answer her first set of questions more quickly and easily than her second set. **First set of questions:** What is the chapter topic? Early people. How does the chapter begin? With an exposé on Mary Leakey. How many sections are in the chapter? Three. What are the first, second, and third section topics? Studying the distant past, hunter-gatherer societies, and populating the earth. **Second set of questions:** Roughly how long is each section? Six, four, and eight pages. What is the average length of each section? Six pages. Which is the longest section? Section 3.

"Excellent," says Mrs. Harper. "Now turn to section 1 on page 58, 'Studying the Distant Past,' and answer this next set of questions." **Third set of questions:** What is the chapter topic? Studying the distant past. How does section 1 begin? With an introduction. How many level one sections are there? Two. Are there any level two sections? Yes. How many? Two and two. How does section 1 end? With a section assessment. Any conclusion? No. Any special features? A closer look feature. "A closer look feature that focuses on an archaeological dig," says Mrs. Harper. "I see that phrase in the first paragraph.

"Nicely done," says Mrs. Harper. "Now let's turn our attention to the section headings themselves and think about them for a moment."

Generating Expectations from Section Titles and Headings

Section titles and headings are easily identified throughout the *myWorld History* textbook (Karpiel et al. 2012). They are similarly styled in upper- and lowercase, use the same font style, and are aligned with the left margin. Level one headings appear in orange, level two headings in blue, and section titles in an outline font with a blue border and orange fill. Section titles and headings appear in large, medium, and small font sizes, respectively.

Proficient readers generate expectations about the ideas they will encounter during reading using section titles and headings. They locate and read the section title and level one and two headings, then focus on the key words in each, connect these key words to each other, and finally generate a sentence that captures the gist of the section.

For example, one possible sentence that captures the gist of section 1 in the chapter on early people is this: Scientists hunt for the fossilized remains of early people in Africa to study and learn about the distant past. This sentence uses key words from the section title and both levels of headings: "study," "hunt," "fossils," "remains," and "Africa."

Illustration

Ian, Kayla, and all their classmates have been charged with the task of generating expectations about section 3 in the chapter on early people, "Populating the Earth." Mrs. Harper has given them five minutes to make a list of key words for the section, then to generate two complete sentences that capture the gist of the section. Because the section consists of four level one sections, Mrs. Harper directs her students to generate two sentences and refers to the sections as 3A, 3B, 3C, and 3D.

Kayla takes responsibility for the section title and sections 3A and 3B, and Ian for sections 3C and 3D. Their combined list consists of the following key word ideas:

- Section title: populating, earth
- Section 3A: human migration, theories, new evidence
- Section 3B: adapting, environments, changing climate, warmth, forming communities
- Section 3C: culture, art, cave paintings
- Section 3D: religion, beliefs, practices, burial

Mrs. Harper has just spoken with several partners about their lists, breaks in, and directs her students to limit their focus to no more than eight words, to circle these words and leave the other words for now. "We'll come around to all the words in the end," she says.

Ian and Kayla manage to include seven key words in the two sentences they generate, which they share with the class when called on: Early people migrated to live in new places and adapted to new environments by helping each other. Art and religion helped these early communities to survive.

Generating Expectations about Words

Proficient readers generate expectations about the words they will encounter during reading. They generate expectations about the types of words they will encounter in a text, the distribution and grouping of more challenging words in a text, and specific topic-related words they will seek to understand and add to their personal vocabularies.

The words that middle grade students encounter in assigned social studies textbooks and supplementary texts may be classified as common, general academic, or field-specific. Common words such as *animal, families, move,* and *feel* enable people to communicate about the world and share their everyday experiences easily with others.

General academic words such as *mammoths, clan, migrate,* and *populate* and field-specific words such as *Homo sapiens* enable people to communicate more specifically about the world and its workings and speculate about or evaluate ideas within or across fields. More complex texts typically include more general academic and field-specific words than simpler texts, which tends to make them more challenging to read and understand.

In the *myWorld History* textbook (Karpiel et al. 2012), general academic and field-specific words are formatted for easy identification. General academic "key terms" are shown in boldface and yellow highlighting. Other important general academic words are underlined. In section 1, "Studying the Distant Past," the key terms *anthropology* and *fossil* are boldfaced and highlighted, and the general academic word *evidence* is underlined. Field-specific words such as *Homo sapiens* and *Paleolithic* in section 2 are shown in italics.

Key terms in the textbook are listed at the start of each section. These lists contain three to seven "terms," some of which are proper nouns (people, places), foreign words (e.g., mestizo), naturalized words (e.g., mosque), and occasionally, some common words (e.g., alphabet). Six key terms are listed in section 1, "Studying the Distant Past," the terms *anthropology, archaeology, prehistory, fossil, geologist,* and *artifact*.

Unfortunately, key term lists do not help students to generate expectations about the range and number of unknown general academic and topic-related words they will encounter in an assigned text and the relative location of these words to each other. In fact these lists may actually mislead students into believing that the only words they should aim to acquire for any reading event are a small set of key terms.

Before reading the text, students will optimally prepare themselves for the assigned reading event by answering the following questions:

1. (a) What words or terms appear in bold? (b) Where are they located? (c) What words or terms appear in italics? (d) What words are underlined and defined for me on the page? (e) Do I understand these underlined words?
2. (a) What known topic-related words do I see? (b) What known proper nouns do I see? (c) Where are these proper nouns located? (d) What general academic words or terms do I see that do not appear in bold?

3. (a) What unknown words or terms do I see? (b) Will these words or terms slow me down during reading? If so, (c) what will I do to keep moving forward?

Illustration

Twice this week, Mrs. Harper helps her students to generate expectations about the words they will encounter in this week's assigned texts, a chapter section in their course textbook and part of a chapter from the information book *Every Bone Tells a Story* (Rubalcaba and Robertshaw 2010). On Monday she directs her students to open their textbooks to the start of section 1 on page 58 and locate the key terms at the top of the page. She reads the terms twice out loud, once on her own, and once with her students reading along with her.

"These are some of the words you'll encounter in this section," says Mrs. Harper. "You'll read about two fields of study, anthropology and geology (prehistory), and two specialists in these fields, archaeologists and geologists. These scientists use specialized terms such as *fossil* and *artifact* to learn and communicate with others about prehistoric periods and people. You'll spot all of these key terms easily during reading," says Mrs. Harper. "They appear in bold and yellow highlighting." Then pointing at each key word on page 58, she adds, "Here are four of them straight off, one, two, three, four—four in the first four paragraphs."

Mrs. Harper then directs her students to locate other important words in section 1, first underlined and italicized words, then proper nouns. "There are only two underlined words and one italicized word in this section," says Mrs. Harper. "Make a mental note of these words, then in your notebook record 10 proper nouns you spot in this section. Do this quickly. Generating expectations about words in a text shouldn't take long."

Erin and her classmates get straight to work. Erin leafs through the section and quickly locates the underlined words *evidence* and *conclude*. Then she locates the italicized term *Homo habilis*, which appears twice in the text, in the same paragraph as the word *evidence*. Erin now turns her attention to proper nouns and manages to record six before she and her classmates are timed out. Mrs. Harper calls on her to share the first five proper nouns on her list.

"Earth, Mary Leakey, Louis Leakey, East Africa, Donald Johanson," says Erin.

"Good," says Mrs. Harper. "Two places, three people (all scientists). The names of people and places are often hard to pronounce, as you know from experience. You want to pronounce these names correctly, which helps you to remember them, important names like Leakey and Johanson, and the names of important landforms. How many of you spotted Olduvai Gorge? A gorge is like a canyon. Two really important names appear on page 63 and close together, the names of important early people. One name begins with L and the other A. Kim, I saw these names on your list. Tell us what they are."

"Lucy and Ardi," says Kim.

Mrs. Harper nods her head, then moves to the side board and reveals a list of 10 words that are highly relevant for the section on studying the distant past. Mrs. Harper reads them out loud and calls them special topic-related words. The list includes the words *remains, footprints, skeleton, dating, DNA, campsite, excavating, discovery, fragments,* and *tests.* "Jot these words in your notebook, locate them with your partner, and note their locations. I'll give you two minutes to do this."

Later that week, in the second half of her class on Friday, Mrs. Harper prepares her students to read their next assigned text over the weekend, the last three sections in a chapter on Otzi the Iceman, the name given to the mummified remains of a late Neolithic hunter found in the Otztal Alps in 1991. None of her students have heard of the Iceman, so Mrs. Harper plays a short video that provides basic information about him: his discovery, appearance, and age.

Mrs. Harper assigns the last three sections in the chapter for homework and now helps her students to generate expectations about the words they will encounter in each section. "In the first section, 'Artifacts,' " says Mrs. Harper, "you can expect to encounter words related to the Iceman's belongings, his clothing and gear. See if that's true. Look at paragraph two. Yes, there's the word *clothing*, and his gear consists of feathered arrows, bones, flint tools, and arrowheads."

Mrs. Harper then points out that the second section provides a detailed description of the Iceman's belongings, which scientists like Markus Egg (whom students will read about in the first section), whom students will read about in the first section, have pieced together through their scientific investigations. "Here is a complete list of Otzi's belongings," says Mrs. Harper, referring to pages 151–54. "Record these words in your notebooks, starting with the first one, *bum bag*, and ending with *marble*. Isn't that interesting! One of Otzi's belongings was a marble."

At the side board, Mrs. Harper reveals a list of words that relate to Otzi's death, the focus of the third and final section in the chapter. Both single words and phrases appear in her list, including *sliver of bone, bone fragment, flint arrowhead, lodged, entrance wound, pierced, cuts,* and *immobilized.* Students copy the list in their notebooks then, as directed, quickly turn back to the first section, "Artifacts," to end the class.

"I've spent the last part of today's class helping you to generate expectations about the words you'll encounter in this new unit text," says Mrs.

Harper in summary. "These words largely relate to the Iceman's belongings and death. You'll also encounter words related to the condition and restoration of artifacts and medical procedures."

She records this information on the board and directs her students to copy it. "You'll read about these medical procedures last. You'll also read about the scientist who conducted these procedures to unlock the mystery of Otzi's death. On Monday, you'll share your thoughts with me about this chapter."

Generating Expectations from Images

Pearson's *myWorld History* textbook (Karpiel et al. 2012), like most social studies textbooks produced for the middle grades, is filled with images that aim to help students to learn curricular content. An image refers to any picture or graphic reproduced in a digital or print format (*OED Online* 2018). The types of images that commonly appear in course textbooks and specialized books include photographs, maps, line drawings, charts, and various types of graphs.

The chapter on early people includes three types of images: photographs, maps, and line drawings. Section 1 specifically includes numerous photographs, a map of Africa, and two line drawings. Some of the photographs feature early human skulls, newly excavated artifacts, and archaeological tools. Both line drawings appear in composite images. One line drawing appears with three photographs at the bottom of page 59, photographs that feature a cave painting, radioactive dating technology, and a well-used rock pick and chisel.

Before reading an assigned text that includes individual or composite images like those in the chapter on early people, students will optimally prepare themselves for the reading event by examining one or two images that appear in the text and responding to the following questions:

1. What type of image am I looking at?
2. (a) What do I see in the image? (b) What people do I see? (c) What do they look like? (d) What are they doing? (e) What things do I see? (f) What do they look like? (g) How are they used?
3. What will I likely read about in the text that relates to this image?

Illustration

Before reading section 3, the last section in the chapter on early people, Mrs. Harper's students will work in pairs to generate expectations about the ideas they will encounter in the section using one of three images. "You'll recall in a previous class," says Mrs. Harper, "that we used the first image in the section 'Animal Transportation' to generate expectations about the chapter as a whole. Today we'll narrow our focus to section 3 and three images, all composite images: 'Migration Routes,' 'Big Game Hunting,' and 'Burial Sites.' Let's see what expectations we can generate about the content of this section using these three composite images."

Kim and her partner Erin are randomly assigned the first image, "Migration Routes." They locate the image in their textbooks then turn to their special set of questions for viewing images at the front of their notebooks. Erin reads the first question aloud, and she and her partner quickly answer in turn: "We're looking at a map."— "A map of the world."

The second question asks about people and things. "There are no people," says Kim, "just lines, lots of them, long ones, red ones." "The key says they're possible migration routes of early people," says Erin. "So that's why Mrs. Harper called this image 'Migration Routes,' " says Kim. "The lines are routes. The arrows show the direction the early people went," says Erin.

"What are these dates for?" asks Erin, pointing at Europe and Australia. "They're all dates in the past: BC," says Kim. "This one in Africa is the oldest, 200,000–150,000 BC. The first people lived right here," says Kim, pointing to central Africa. "I get it," says Erin. "The first people migrated away from here, from central Africa, around 200,000 years ago, going north and south along these routes."

Kim traces the routes out of Africa with her finger. She notices that early people first reached Europe about 45,000 years ago and India about 15,000 years before that. Now Erin takes a turn tracing the routes with her finger, following the arrows left and right. When she reaches Australia, all at once she is confused. "What's going on here?" she asks Kim.

"Time for a swim," says Kim jokingly. Several arrows point to the ocean.

"Here's something else I don't get," says Erin. "People reached South America before they reached Florida. They reached Florida 13,000 years ago and the tip of South America 11,000 years ago. Or am I getting it backward?"

At this point, Mrs. Harper interrupts and directs each partnership to record their expectations about the content of section 3 in a one-to-two-sentence statement, which they will then share with their classmates. "Each partnership will begin their statement with the same phrase," says Mrs. Harper. "In this section I will read about . . ."

ACTIVATING KNOWLEDGE

Statements and Questions

All informational texts focus on a particular idea, a topic. Proficient readers activate their existing knowledge about the topic explored in an assigned text, which they subsequently draw on, expand, or reconstitute during reading. To activate one's knowledge about a topic means to make that knowledge active (*OED Online* 2018), to bring it into consciousness, to bring it forward in one's mind. People acquire knowledge about a range of topics through their lived experiences at home and at school by doing things, by seeing and hearing things, and by reading.

This section addresses the following questions:

- What knowledge is best activated about assigned reading topics?
- How do middle grade students best articulate their activated topic knowledge?

Activating Relevant Topic Knowledge

In addition to clarifying their goal and purpose for reading an assigned text and generating expectations about the ideas they will encounter during reading, proficient readers also prepare themselves for a reading event by activating knowledge about the text's central idea, its topic. Activating knowledge is a deliberate action, both conscious and purposeful. One's knowledge about a topic is activated by two simple questions: What topic am I going to read about in this text? And what specifically do I know about this topic?

For section 1, "Studying the Distant Past," in their course textbook, Renata, one of Mrs. Harper's students, reported this in response to the two questions: "I'm going to read about the ways scientists study early people and piece together their lives. I know some things about the early people called Neanderthals. There are pictures of them coming up. They lived in caves and looked different from us. They were shorter, stocky. Scientists have learned about Neanderthals and other early people by studying their skulls and bones. They know where these early people lived, what animals they hunted, what tools they used, and how they died."

Renata's activated knowledge about the scientific study of early people is significantly informed by the expectations she recently generated about the text with her partner Gina. It also reflects information about specific early people, the Neanderthals, which was shared by her classmates Delaney and Trevor a week ago when they generated expectations about the chapter as a whole, using the image of the Neanderthal man by a fire in section 2. Activated topic knowledge will be more substantive, specific, relevant, and useful if students have already generated expectations about the text and noted its organization, headings, words, and images.

With guidance, Renata and her classmates were able to activate even more specific knowledge about the section topic than reported above, knowledge specifically related to the topics explored in sections 1A–C. Mrs. Harper went on to ask her students what they knew specifically about the methods scientists use to date human fossils, the types of artifacts that scientists have recovered from ancient campsites, and important details that scientists have learned about prehistoric life from their studies of Ardi and Lucy, two famous early people.

Illustration

"Today," says Mrs. Harper, projecting her first slide, "I want you to work with your side partner to activate your knowledge about the four topics listed on this slide." Several days have passed since Mrs. Harper assigned section 1 for homework, and for homework tonight she will assign section 2, "Hunter-Gatherer Societies." "You and your partner," continues Mrs. Harper, "will activate your knowledge about early people who met their needs partly by hunting and partly by gathering." Four topics appear on her slide: hunting and gathering, tools, uses of fire, and the ways these early people organized themselves into communities.

"Now turn over your handout," says Mrs. Harper. "This is a knowledge activation guide for section 2. The guide contains four sets of questions. Each set focuses on one topic shown on the slide." Mrs. Harper reads the first set of questions aloud: What do you know about the ways early people hunted and gathered? What did these early people hunt? What do you know about their hunting techniques? What did these early people gather? When and where did they gather these things? What do you specifically know about early hunter-gatherers?

"This first set of questions will get you started," says Mrs. Harper, "and the guide as a whole will really help you and your partner to activate specific and expansive knowledge about early hunter-gatherers."

Trevor, whose partner is still Delaney, knows a lot about hunting and the hunting techniques people used in prehistoric times. Hunters killed game with spears, game like deer, elk, and bison. They made the spears themselves out of wood and sharp rocks. They heated the wood over coals to strengthen it and chipped at the rocks until they were pointed and sharp. You needed help to kill a big animal like a bison. You couldn't do it on your own. People hunted in groups. Sometimes they traveled many miles, following an animal before they actually killed it. Then they had to haul the meat home a long distance.

Delaney knows lots about tools. His grandpa is a carpenter and owns a shop where he makes custom furniture. But his grandpa's tools are not like the tools early people used. Most prehistoric tools were made from rocks.

"Steel wasn't around back then," says Delaney. "All of my grandpa's tools are made out of steel." Rocks were very important to early people. Delaney knows this for a fact. Prehistoric hammers and axes had heads made of rock. Prehistoric people made spearheads and arrowheads out of rocks. "They must have been pretty smart to do that," says Delaney.

DEVELOPING KNOWLEDGE

Statements and Questions

Proficient readers may have no existing knowledge about the topic explored in an assigned text and will need to develop basic knowledge about the topic before reading the text. To develop means to acquire (*OED Online* 2018). A basic level of topic knowledge is best acquired by speaking with others, reading summative information about the topic, or viewing a short video. Proficient readers who are able to activate basic knowledge about a topic before reading have no need to develop knowledge at this stage.

This section addresses the following questions:

- How do middle grade students determine their current level of topic knowledge?
- What informational resources should students draw on to develop basic knowledge about an assigned reading topic?
- How much time should students devote to developing basic knowledge about an assigned reading topic?

Developing Topic Knowledge

Middle grade social studies teachers like Mrs. Harper use program textbooks purposefully to help their students to acquire knowledge about historical, political, geographic, and economic topics. Students who have no knowledge about a topic they will soon be reading about will likely struggle to acquire substantive knowledge about the topic during reading. Students will be more successful reading an assigned text and will be more likely to achieve their reading goal by approaching texts knowledgeably, even somewhat knowledgeably. Students therefore benefit by developing a basic level of understanding about a topic before reading about it.

Students who are unable to activate any relevant knowledge about the topic of an assigned text, a textbook chapter or supplementary text, can spend several minutes talking about the topic with a peer, teacher, parent, or other adult; reading summative information about the topic online; or viewing a video clip or photographs.

Illustration

Before reading the section on early hunter-gatherer societies in their course textbook, Mrs. Harper's students activated their knowledge about hunting and gathering, prehistoric tools, uses of fire, and the ways early hunter-gatherer communities were organized. Near the end of the section, in 2B, students will also read about Neanderthals. In the event that her students cannot activate any specific knowledge about these early people, Mrs. Harper will show a four-minute video that provides basic information about them.

Twice previously, Mrs. Harper has helped her students to develop basic knowledge about assigned chapter topics. Earlier today she helped her students to develop basic knowledge about hunter-gatherers by engaging them in knowledge activation with partners. Students who could not activate specific knowledge on their own about, say, prehistoric tools or uses of fire learned about these topics from their partnership interactions. Mrs. Harper also helped her students to develop basic knowledge about Otzi the Iceman a week ago by showing them a short video.

Determining that most of her students have insufficient knowledge about Neanderthals, Mrs. Harper plays her video. Students then read the following handout summary she prepared:

> **Basic Information about Neanderthals**
>
> Neanderthals are our closest human relatives. They lived in Europe and Asia from 400,000 to 40,000 years ago and were eventually absorbed in modern human societies. Neanderthals were the first humans to survive a glacial ecosystem. Their bodies and brains were well adapted for a cold climate. Neanderthals had a relatively sophisticated culture. They built shelters, made clothing, created advanced tools, and buried their dead. Their tools, art, and DNA tell us that Neanderthals were very resilient. Their innovations, creativity, and social behavior were very much like *Homo sapiens* today.

LOOKING BACK AND AHEAD

Before reading an assigned text, proficient readers take four actions. They clarify their goal and purpose for reading the text, generate expectations about the text, activate specific knowledge about the text's topics, and develop basic knowledge about topics that are new to them. These four before reading actions will typically take students 5–10 minutes to complete on their own and longer if working with a partner or if mediated by their teacher. The next three chapters focus on the second phase of school reading events, the during reading phase. The during reading actions of visualizing and reading fluently are the focus of chapter 4.

GROUNDING: BEFORE READING PHASE ACTIONS

This chapter is grounded in goal theory (Schunk 2016) and schema theory (Anderson 2013). It draws on discussions of images (Kress and Van Leeuwen 2006), goals and expectations (Schunk 2016), goal-directed learning (Alexander and Fox 2013; Fox and Alexander 2017), and purpose setting (Ruddell and Unrau 2013).

4

During Reading Actions I

Mr. Rivera has taught the seventh grade civics course for 19 years at his school. His course textbook, Prentice Hall Civics: Government and Economics in Action *(Davis, Fernlund, and Woll 2009), published by Pearson, is forthcoming in a new edition but for now continues to offer his students excellent information about such topics as the Constitution and Bill of Rights, the government's role in the economy, foreign policy, and criminal justice.*

For the past two years Mr. Rivera has worked closely with his school's literacy coach, Mrs. Donovan, to provide reading-related support for students in his civics course. He and four other social studies teachers at his school met with Mrs. Donovan for the first time two years ago to talk about the challenges students face reading social studies materials. At the end of that very enlightening conversation, Mr. Rivera accepted Mrs. Donovan's invitation to work with her to develop ways of supporting students' reading in social studies courses.

For the next several weeks, while studying crime and criminal proceedings with his seventh graders as part of a larger unit on criminal and civil justice, Mr. Rivera aims to help his students to read assigned sections in their civics textbook and several book chapters fluently. Specifically, after consulting with Mrs. Donovan about the first textbook chapter, chapter 20: "Criminal and Juvenile Justice," he will help his students to identify complex nouns and abstract subjects, both of which figure prominently in chapter 20. He also aims to help his students to limit the visualizing they do during reading.

"There are lots of complex nouns in our course textbook," he tells his students. "Lots are classified nouns like these: property crimes, violent crimes, victimless crimes, suburban communities, rural communities. *These are some of the classified nouns you'll encounter today in your assigned reading in chapter 20, section 1, sections 1A and 1B."*

*Mr. Rivera records two examples on the board (*property *crimes,* violent *crimes), boxes each example, and explains that classified nouns have two parts: a classifier (*property, violent*) and a classified thing (*crimes*). "We read these words together as a single unit, not as individual words," says Mr. Rivera, tracing the box around each example. "I located five classified nouns in section 1B on page 537. I mentioned two of these already, but the other ones are new. Skim page 537 now, and record all the classified nouns you come across. Do this independently. Go."*

Five minutes later, having recorded, boxed, and reviewed the examples of classified nouns collected by his students from page 537, Mr. Rivera refers to these boxed examples as his first reading tip of the day. "Read all classified nouns as single units of meaning. That's tip 1."

He clicks to his next slide, a two-column table with the headings "Personalized Doings" and "Depersonalized Doings" and four blank rows, which are blank for the moment. "Tip 2," says Mr. Rivera. "Read the abstract subjects you encounter in section 1B as they are. Here's what I mean by abstract subjects. Section 1B focuses on different types of crime. Ordinary citizens like us think mostly about crimes in personalized ways, but social scientists, lawyers, lawmakers, and many other professionals think mostly about crimes in depersonalized ways."

Mr. Rivera directs his students' attention to the left side of the table, clicks his mouse, and reveals four personalized criminal actions beneath the heading "Personalized Doings." "All of these actions focus on people," he says. "People steal things. People shoplift at stores. People paint graffiti on sidewalks and buildings. People break windows. All four actions focus on people. All are personalized actions. But personalized actions are not the focus of section 1B," says Mr. Rivera, revealing four complementary actions on the right side of the table: the depersonalized actions of stealing, shoplifting, painting graffiti, and breaking windows.

"Depersonalized actions like these are the focus of section 1B," says Mr. Rivera. "Social scientists who study crime (we call them criminologists) depersonalize criminal actions like these to understand them scientifically. Depersonalizing an action in English is simple: simply remove the personal subject people *and add the suffix* -ing *to the verb. Simple."*

That part is simple. But as Mr. Rivera recently learned from Mrs. Donovan, sentences that begin with abstract subjects like stealing or shoplifting can be challenging for middle grade students to read and understand. Middle grade students, especially those who struggle to read, do not expect to encounter a verb at the beginning of a sentence, and such encounters, if not anticipated, trip them up, slow them down, and confuse them. Nine sentences in section 1B begin with abstract subjects, and three of these begin with double subjects (e.g., breaking windows and painting graffiti, stealing company secrets, and not paying taxes).

"Expect to encounter a good number of depersonalized actions in section 1B," says Mr. Rivera. "Read them as they are, as abstract subjects. Don't get hung up trying to figure out who is stealing what or who is stealing which company secrets. Simply recognize these actions as crimes that anyone could commit. That's my second reading tip of the day."

Before advancing to his next slide, his last slide of the day, Mr. Rivera commends his students for their attentiveness. "My reading tips are important," he tells his students. "When you recognize words like classified nouns and abstract subjects quickly, you get to the end of the text quicker, read more attentively, and better understand the ideas you've read about. There's one last thing you can do get through a text quicker," he says, advancing to his last slide, a list of words that his students will encounter in section 1B. "Tip 3, limit the visualizing you do when you encounter these particular words in section 1B."

Mr. Rivera reminds his students that their civics textbook is an informative text, not a creative text like a novel. "Visualizing often, reading creative texts, is appropriate and helpful," says Mr. Rivera. "But too much visualizing while reading informative texts like section 1B in your textbook can slow you down, distract and confuse you. You'll encounter these words in section 1B," says Mr. Rivera, referring to the listed words on his slide, the words shoplifting, breaking windows, stealing a car, cheating, killing, murder, robbery, *and* gambling. *"These words can derail you during reading, triggering picture after picture in your head."*

Mr. Rivera calls on several students to share the pictures triggered in their heads by the words shoplifting *and* murder. Carla shares a flashback image of two young women in handcuffs being led back into the store where they shoplifted socks. Robbie shares a cinematic image of a drive-by shooting and a teenage boy lying bloody and lifeless in the grass, killed by the drive-by shooter.

"All of these words will trigger pictures in your head during reading, slow you down, distract you, even confuse you," says Mr. Rivera. "You can't let them do that. Limit the visualizing you do during reading. Read a bit faster to stop these words from triggering pictures in your head. If a picture is triggered, prompt yourself to read on. That's tip 3."

INTRODUCTION: DURING READING PHASE ACTIONS

Middle grade students like Mr. Rivera's will better understand assigned texts in social studies courses by reading fluently and visualizing strategically during reading. The during reading phase of any reading event is more complex than the before and after reading phases. In the during reading phase proficient readers engage in six coordinated actions to achieve their ultimate reading goal of understanding the main ideas in a text and being able to use these ideas at a later date. These six actions include:

1. Visualizing
2. Reading fluently
3. Reading for understanding
4. Making inferences about important ideas presented in an assigned text
5. Formulating a text
6. Building a coherent understanding of an assigned text as a whole

This chapter focuses on the first two during reading phase mental actions: visualizing and reading fluently. Each of these actions is explained in detail and illustrated using chapters 20 and 21 in the *Prentice Hall Civics: Government and Economics in Action* textbook (Davis, Fernlund, and Woll 2009) and chapters from the specialized books *Youth in Prison* (Smith and McIntosh 2007), *Juvenile Justice* (Haugen 2013), *America's Prisons* (Lasky 2016), and *Juvenile Crime* (Gerdes 2012).

VISUALIZING

Statements and Target Questions

All readers—proficient and non-proficient alike—visualize during reading. To visualize means to picture things in your mind; to form a mental picture of something once seen but no longer physically present (*OED Online* 2018). Mental pictures are triggered by particular words that readers encounter in a text, words like *shoplifting* or *murder*. The frequency of visualizing, the duration of each visualizing event, and the specific content and form of any image triggered in a reader's mind all differ from reader to reader. Proficient readers, however, purposefully limit the frequency of their visualizing when reading informational texts.

This section addresses the following questions:

- How do visualized images and visuals differ?
- What types of images are triggered in middle grade students' minds during reading, and what do these images focus on?
- When is visualizing helpful? When is it not helpful?
- How can students modulate the frequency of their visualizing?

Visuals versus Visualized Images

Middle grade social studies textbooks like Mr. Rivera's seventh grade civics textbook contain an impressive number of informative, relevant, and highly engaging images related to the topics explored.

Chapter 20 in the *Prentice Hall Civics* textbook (Davis, Fernlund, and Woll 2009, hereafter referred to as the civics textbook), which focuses on criminal and juvenile justice, contains 26 images in all, including photographs of a crime scene, a young person playing a violent video game, an actual police badge used by officers in Florida, a pair of handcuffs, a lawyer speaking to a jury, and a community crime watch sign. Textbook publishers include such images, or visuals, to help students to process and understand chapter content.

Visuals, or published images, such as photographs, maps, drawings, and other types of figures featured in social studies textbooks, are more useful to students before and after reading than during reading (see chapters 3 and 7 of this work). Visualized images, on the other hand, affect students directly during reading and can negatively impact their efforts to understand a text.

A visualized image, or mental picture, is a mental rendering of something seen, stored in memory, then retrieved (i.e., recalled). Visualized images may be static or dynamic and focus on people or things. The visualized images shared by Mr. Rivera's students in the opening vignette, triggered by the words *shoplifting* and *murder*, are recalled visual experiences that are largely dynamic and focus on real-world events, people in action.

Visualized Things, People, and People in Action

Static images of nonliving things are commonly triggered during reading. The static images of the Pentagon (a satellite view), an MP3 player with earbuds, a storefront, a broken storefront window, graffiti on the side of a building, an arrest warrant, a credit card, and a handgun may all flash one at a time in the minds of Mr. Rivera's students as they read to learn about adult and juvenile crime in chapter 20 of their civics textbook and chapter 3 in *Youth in Prison* (Smith and McIntosh 2007).

Images of people, also triggered during reading, may flash in the minds of Mr. Rivera's students as they read chapters 20 and 3. Static or dynamic images of a judge, a jury, a jogger being mugged in a park, a man being locked up in a jail cell, a teenage girl dropping her schoolbooks on the living room table, and a teenage boy jokingly pointing a gun at his girlfriend, any of these images, or others, may be triggered in the minds of Mr. Rivera's students during reading.

Image-Triggering Nouns and Verbs

Visualized images are triggered by one or more words that students encounter in assigned texts. The word *murder*, a simple noun, is sufficiently evocative on its own to trigger the dynamic image of a drive-by shooting, as in the opening vignette. Images of real-world events, people, and things may be triggered by simple single-word nouns like *murder* or more complex multi-word nouns like *a rebellious child* (a described noun) or *an electronics store* (a classified noun), whose meanings are conveyed both by a noun and an associated descriptive or classifying word. Images may also be triggered by proper nouns such as *the Pentagon*.

While reading chapters 20 and 3, Mr. Rivera's students will encounter simple and complex nouns that may trigger static or dynamic images in their minds of people or things. They will encounter simple nouns such as *arson* and *prosecutor*, proper nouns such as *the World Trade Center* and *Mexican Americans*, described nouns such as *new technology*, and classified nouns such as *violent crimes*, *a poor neighborhood*, and *minimum-wage jobs*.

Visualized images can also be triggered by the reported doings or actions of people in assigned texts. Dynamic images of people in action are readily triggered by action words, verbs, and the people, places, or things associated with them.

The actions of two teenagers, Kate and Mitch, are individually reported on in chapters 20 and 3 in personalized accounts of a burglary and an accidental shooting. Dynamic images of these two people in action—of Kate entering her house by the front door, slamming the door behind her, and dropping her schoolbooks on the family room table; and of Mitch pointing a gun at his girlfriend, pulling the trigger, killing her, and fleeing the scene—all these visualized actions may be triggered during reading.

Visualizing Strategically

Visualized images triggered during reading may help or hinder students' efforts to understand an assigned text. Visualized images triggered by people's reported actions in personalized accounts like Kate's and Mitch's will undoubtedly enhance students' understandings of abstract concepts such as burglary and homicide. Indeed personalized accounts, and the actions of real or fictional people reported in these accounts, aim to vivify the reading experience, concretize ideas, connect other people's experiences to our own, and help students to better understand the range and complexity of problems people face in their lives.

The visualized images of people and things triggered by nouns and verbs in narrative texts like personalized accounts can have an ameliorative effect on students' attentiveness during reading and their incremental understandings about the narrative taking shape. Comparable images triggered by nouns and verbs in informational texts, and frequently by nouns, will adversely affect students' efforts to read attentively and understand the ideas encountered. Mr. Rivera rightly identifies chapters 20 and 3 as informational texts and advises his students to read these chapters accordingly, limiting the frequency of their visualizing.

Mr. Rivera also rightly advises his students to refrain from visualizing depersonalized actions like stealing, shoplifting, and other abstract subjects that appear in chapters 20 and 3. An English teacher would likely identify these words grammatically as gerunds—verbs, ending in *-ing*, that function as nouns—and illustrate how gerunds function variously as subjects, subject complements, direct objects, and objects of prepositions.

Mr. Rivera rightly keeps things simple: identifies actions such as stealing and shoplifting as depersonalized actions, explains that social scientists depersonalize actions to understand them scientifically, and advises his students to read such actions accordingly, without visualizing them.

Illustration

Álvaro's seventh grade civics teacher, Mr. Rivera, directs him and his classmates to read the first part of a chapter on juvenile incarceration posted on their class web page. The chapter begins with the biographical accounts of four young people convicted of juvenile assault or murder and sentenced to juvenile detention centers, or youth prison. Mr. Rivera directs his students to read all four accounts quickly, and twice—once for gist, and once with the next day's discussion questions in mind:

1. What's going on for these young people at home?
2. Whom does each young person assault or murder, and why?

In this assigned chapter from the book *Youth in Prison* (Smith and McIntosh 2007), Álvaro will read about four culturally and racially diverse young people, boys and girls ages 13–16, all convicted of serious crimes in juvenile court and incarcerated for the remainder of their childhoods. Each biographical account is roughly one page or less long, and all four accounts should take Álvaro no longer than 10 minutes to read twice.

At home in his room Álvaro clicks on the assigned chapter and begins to read the four accounts quickly for gist. As he reads the first account, of 13-year-old Mitch, images flash in his mind, first of himself playing a video game, then of a gun pointed at a person's head and fired, and then of himself racing frantically from the house. Álvaro stops, reads the sentence again about the gun going off and the girlfriend dying, then reads to the end of the account quickly.

"Read the four accounts quickly," said his teacher. "Don't get sidetracked by images flashing in your head." Álvaro recorded these words in his notebook, which now lies open on his desk. His teacher specially warned him and his classmates that parts of Mitch's account would likely trigger images in their heads but not to let the images sidetrack them. Also in his notebook Álvaro recorded the questions he and his classmates will discuss next day.

Álvaro reads the next account quickly for gist but is sidetracked reading the third by images triggered in his mind of a street gang and his little brother Ciro.

Álvaro starts to read about Daniel, a teenage boy who lives with his uncle. Daniel starts to drink and use drugs, skips school, eventually gets suspended, and joins a local street gang. As a gang member Daniel looks to start trouble in his neighborhood and participates in a drive-by shooting that leaves several rival gang members dead. In the second paragraph of the account, while reading about Daniel's beliefs as a gang member, Álvaro gets sidetracked by a sequence of images that flash in his mind of his eight-year-old brother.

Álvaro reads that members of Daniel's gang believe that eight-year-old children are old enough to be gang members. Reading this triggers an image in Álvaro's mind of his eight-year-old brother Ciro heading off to school with a friend, the way he looked this morning and always looks on a school day. Then other images flash in his mind of Ciro, now in a gang, hanging out with a nasty group of guys, getting high, getting ready to do a job—.

Álvaro suddenly realizes, having reached the end of the paragraph, that these flashing images of his little brother have sidetracked him. Nothing in the last part of the paragraph has registered to him, and he guesses that the name O. G. Black Lazarus, which appears at the end of the paragraph, is the nickname given to Daniel by members of his gang.

Álvaro promptly takes action to get himself back on track, returns to the middle of the paragraph where the images of his brother were triggered, tells himself to stay focused, to focus on Daniel, and reads this third account more quickly to stop himself from visualizing. He learns that he was wrong about the nickname, that it does not belong to Daniel at all, reads the last paragraph quickly, then quickly proceeds to the fourth account, of two good friends, Stacey and Amanda, whose lives take very different turns.

READING FLUENTLY

Statement and Target Questions

Proficient readers read assigned texts fluently. To do something fluently means to do it easily (*OED Online* 2018); to read *texts* fluently means to read them easily—smoothly, effortlessly, and accurately. Smooth, effortless, and accurate reading is achieved by students in and beyond the middle grades who read assigned texts at optimal speeds in a continuous forward motion and use their knowledge of sentence structure and words to read these texts smoothly and identify both known and unknown words quickly and accurately.

This section addresses the following questions:

- What sentence- and word-building knowledge do middle grade students use to read assigned texts fluently?
- What complex nouns and verbs will students encounter in assigned texts?
- What complex subjects will students encounter in assigned texts?
- What types of sentences and complex punctuation marks will students encounter in assigned texts? How do complex sentences challenge readers?
- What phonics, word-building, and word-segmenting knowledge will students use as resources to read assigned texts fluently?
- How are students disadvantaged by relying solely on their phonics knowledge to identify unknown words during reading?
- How do students optimize their speed during reading?

Reading Groups of Words Fluently

Proficient readers recognize the difference between simple and complex groups of words: simple and complex nouns and simple and complex verbs. A simple noun conveys basic information about a thing, and a simple verb basic information about an event. Complex nouns and verbs convey additional information about a thing or an event. Proficient middle grade readers recognize complex nouns and verbs as complex word groups and read each accordingly as a group of words and not as individual words.

Reading Complex Noun Groups Fluently

Middle grade students will encounter four types of complex nouns in their social studies textbooks and other assigned texts: classified nouns, described nouns, compound nouns, and proper nouns. Classified nouns consist of a classifier (a classifying word) and a classified thing. Described nouns consist of a descriptor (a describing word) and a described thing. Compound nouns consist of two or more nouns whose meaning as a whole derives from each noun. Proper nouns are formal names used to identify individual people or things.

Mr. Rivera's seventh grade students will encounter all four types of complex nouns as they read about crime and the criminal justice system in their course textbook and other assigned texts. In the opening vignette Mr. Rivera identifies some classified nouns that his students will encounter in the first assigned text, chapter 20, section 1 in the civics textbook. In each noun group identified, the classified thing is a crime or community (e.g., a violent or victimless crime; a suburban or rural community).

Mr. Rivera's students will encounter a range of classified things in chapter 20, as shown in table 4.1. They will encounter such classified things as (violent, victimless) crimes, (economic) changes, (social) problems, (federal, state) prisons, (maximum, minimum) sentences, and (initial, adjudicatory, dispositional) hearings. One or multiple types of classified things may be mentioned briefly in the assigned chapter or discussed at length. Rural communities, economic changes, social problems, and minimum sentences are merely mentioned at points in the text while multiple types of crimes and hearings are discussed at length in sections 1 and 3.

A classified thing may be a role. In chapter 20, section 2, Mr. Rivera's students will read about one or more types of (court) employees, (court) officials, (probation) officers, and (defense, private, prosecuting) attorneys.

As many described nouns appear in chapter 20 as classified nouns, but all are merely mentioned in the text and not discussed. Some examples of described nouns that Mr. Rivera's students will encounter in the chapter include

Table 4.1. Classified Noun Examples

Classified Noun	Classifier	Classified Thing
violent crimes	violent	a type of crime
nonviolent crimes	nonviolent	
victimless crimes	victimless	
property crimes	property	
white-collar	white-collar	
suburban communities	suburban	a type of community
rural communities	rural	
economic changes	economic	a type of change
social problems	social	a type of problem
federal prisons	federal	a type of prison
state prisons	state	
a maximum sentence	maximum	a type of sentence
a minimum sentence	minimum	
juvenile court	juvenile	a type of court
adult court	adult	
the initial hearing	initial	a type of hearing
the adjudicatory hearing	adjudicatory	
the dispositional hearing	dispositional	
pretrial motions	pretrial	a type of motion

(new) technology, (common) values, (unique) challenges, (good) behavior, (difficult) tasks, and (quick) decisions. The descriptors in this sample provide additional information about the currency, popularity, distinctiveness, agreeableness, demandingness, and speed of the described thing.

Mr. Rivera's students will also encounter many compound and proper nouns in chapter 20. They will encounter such compound nouns as the death penalty, capital punishment, prison populations, a parole board, and neighborhood watch programs; and such proper nouns as the Constitution, the Supreme Court, the Federal Bureau of Investigation, the World Trade Center, and a Miranda warning.

An impressive number of proper nouns appears in two book chapters that Mr. Rivera will require his students to read when, midway through their unit on criminal and civil justice, their focus will shift to juvenile justice and race. In "Why Are Juveniles Incarcerated" (Smith and McIntosh 2007) and "The Juvenile Justice System Should Address Racial Inequalities" (Armour and Hammond 2012), Mr. Rivera's students will encounter proper nouns that identify individual people, groups of people, places, organizations, offices, initiatives, websites, and various published materials (see table 4.2).

Table 4.2. Proper Nouns in Two Unit Readings

Categories	Proper Nouns
Individuals	Mitch, Tomás, Daniel, Stacey, Amanda
Authors	M. A. Bortner, Linda M. Williams, Kathleen Edgar
Ethnic groups	African Americans, Hispanics, Mexican Americans, Asians, Pacific Islanders, Native Americans
Places	States: Arizona; Countries: United States, Canada
Organizations	National Council on Crime and Delinquency Center for Children's Law and Policy National Center for Juvenile Justice John D. and Catherine T. MacArthur Foundation Elizabeth Fry Society
Offices Administrations	Office of Juvenile Justice and Delinquency Prevention Substance Abuse and Mental Health Services Administration
Initiatives	Building Blocks for Youth Models for Change
Books	*Youth in Prison* *Youth Violence, Crime, and Gangs*
Censuses	Census of Juveniles in Residential Placement
Websites	Public Safety and Emergency Preparedness Canada Department of Justice Canada

Proper nouns, always capitalized, are easily recognized during reading both as proper nouns—formal names used to identify specific people or things—and as complex nouns. All of the examples shown in table 4.2 will be readily recognized by middle grade students both as formal names and complex nouns.

Recognizing the other three categories of complex nouns during reading can be more challenging for middle grade students. Students will readily recognize classified, described, and compound nouns as complex nouns but may not be able to tell if a particular noun encountered during reading is a classified, described, or compound noun.

Take, for example, the following complex nouns that Mr. Rivera's seventh graders will encounter in chapter 20 while reading about crime in the United States: poor neighborhoods (described noun), a bank employee (classified noun), new technology (described noun), proper therapy (described noun), and job skills (compound noun). Students will likely identify the second noun, a bank employee, correctly and may want to identify all the others as classified nouns too, reasoning that neighborhoods are being classified as poor or rich, technology as new or old, therapy as proper or improper, and skills as specific job or life skills.

Two easy grammatical tests can help students to identify a complex noun as a classified, described, or compound noun. Compound nouns, which contain two or more nouns and refer to more specific things (e.g., job skills, prison populations), are easy to identify. Other complex nouns can be tested using the inflectional ending *-er* or adverbs *very* or *more* to confirm their identity as classified or described nouns. As shown in table 4.3, classifiers like *economic* and *private* are not gradable, whereas descriptors like *poor*, *new*, *proper*, and *difficult* are.

Middle grade students, however, should not concern themselves about the identity of particular complex nouns encountered during reading but rather aim to read assigned texts fluently in a continuous forward motion at an optimal speed. Fluent reading is achieved in part by students' quick recognition of complex nouns during reading, not by their ability to ascribe a particular identity to a complex noun like classified, described, or compound.

Table 4.3. Tested Complex Noun Groups

Noun Group	Test	Descriptor	Classifier
economic changes	more economic changes		economic
private attorney	more private attorney		private
poor neighborhoods	very poor neighborhoods	poor	—
new technology	newer technology	new	—
proper therapy	more proper therapy	proper	—
difficult tasks	very difficult tasks	difficult	—

Reading Verb Groups Fluently

Fluent reading is also achieved in part by students' quick recognition of complex verbs during reading. Middle grade students will encounter both complex and simple verbs in their social studies textbooks and other assigned texts. Simple verbs are single-word verb groups that convey basic information about an event (e.g., argue, learns, granted). Complex verbs are multi-word verb groups that convey additional information about the occurrence or necessity of an event (e.g., will make, have been suggested, should be given, add up, is trying to prove).

In their civics textbook chapters 20 and 21 and supplementary chapter 3 from the book *Youth in Prison* (Smith and McIntosh 2007), Mr. Rivera's students will encounter a range of simple verbs, like those in table 4.4. In all three assigned texts, these simple verbs appear in present and past tense, singular, and plural forms (e.g., flees, fled; is; have).

Mr. Rivera's students will readily recognize the simple verbs in table 4.4. They will also readily recognize such two- and three-word complex verbs as *will make, was taken, had been passed, may be, would be, may take, might sue, must prove, should think, could order,* and *can be trusted,* all of which appear in chapters 20, 21, and 3. Some complex verbs that students will encounter in these chapters will convey information about events that will happen in the future (e.g., will make) or events that may possibly happen (e.g., might sue, could order).

Table 4.4. Simple Verb Examples

Present Tense		
Chapter 20	*Chapter 21*	*Chapter 3*
is	involves	reports
flees	promises	explore
occurs	learns	experience
accepts	rules	share
decides	include	
protects	settle	
pleads	arise	
have	provide	

Past Tense		
Chapter 20	*Chapter 21*	*Chapter 3*
caused	awarded	fought
crashed		pointed
killed		fled
granted		adjudicated

Students will read about a number of possible events in chapter 21, the chapter on civil justice. In the first part of the chapter, they will read about several property suits that might be litigated in a civil court trial, one involving a car owner and one a homeowner. Students will read about these two possible suits in consecutive sentences: "A car owner might sue a repair shop if the car comes back with a new dent. A homeowner might sue a neighbor whose tree fell over and damaged the homeowner's roof" (Davis, Fernlund, and Woll 2009, 564).

In the same part of the chapter, students will read about possible settlements that may be obtained in suits involving property damages or trespassing. Information about these settlements is conveyed in a short paragraph by complex verbs that include the auxiliary verb *may*:

> Property cases may be settled through compensation or through equity. Payment of money, for instance, may make up for damage to a person's roof. However, courts usually settle trespassing cases through equity. A court may issue an injunction ordering a defendant to stay off the plaintiff's land in the future. (Ibid., 564)

In chapter 21, sections 1 and 3, Mr. Rivera's students will read about the possible outcome of a civil suit involving a factory and town, possible courses of action for tenants and landlords in housing (rental) disputes, and the necessary actions plaintiffs must take in property cases to secure a favorable outcome. Students will read about the possibility that a court could issue an injunction against a factory to stop it from emitting harmful fumes, that tenants can pay for repairs themselves and deduct the cost of these repairs from their monthly rent, and that a plaintiff must prove that the damage to his property was caused by the defendant.

In the last section of chapter 21, "To Sue or Not to Sue," readers are informed that civil trials are typically long and costly. In the last paragraph of the chapter, Mr. Rivera's students will encounter two complex verbs that convey information about necessary actions that people like themselves should (advisedly) take prior to filing a complaint in civil court. Both complex verbs include the auxiliary verb *should*: people, first, should think carefully about resolving a personal conflict in court, and second, people should explore their options thoroughly.

Other two- and three-word complex verbs that Mr. Rivera's students will encounter in assigned textbook chapters and may not readily recognize as verb groups are passive verbs such as *was damaged* and *have been violated*. Passive verbs are used by informational writers to shift the focus of an event from one participant to another, from the active (effectuating) participant to the passive (effected) one. In chapter 21, for example, two

Table 4.5. Passive Verb Examples

Present Tense	Past Tense	Possible/Necessary Events
is mugged	was suspended	may be reduced
is kidnapped	was damaged	may be dropped
are committed	has been gathered	can be treated
are released	have been made	can be held
are sponsored	have been violated	should be given
are allowed	had been parked	must be questioned

passive things, a damaged bike and violated tenancy rights, are made the focus, rather than the repair shop that damaged the bike and the landlord who violated a tenancy agreement.

Complex passive verbs convey information about past, present, possible, or necessary events. All the passive verbs in table 4.5 and others appear in chapters 20 and 21.

In these two chapters, Mr. Rivera's students will read about such present- and past-tense events as a jogger being mugged, a child being kidnapped from the front yard of his house, personal property like bikes being damaged, and vehicles being parked in dangerous locations. Students will also read about such possible and necessary events as prison time being reduced, defendants being held in jail without bail, and many potential jurors being questioned before a final group of jurors is selected.

The most challenging complex verbs that middle grade students will encounter during reading contain four or more words, include a phrasal verb, or consist entirely of a phrasal verb. In chapter 21, Mr. Rivera's students will encounter the following complex verb groups that contain four or more words:

1. has to be settled
2. has not lived up to
3. may also be gathered
4. may even be sentenced
5. does not always have to reach
6. are no longer even provided

The verb groups listed above all convey information about an active or passive present-tense or recurring event that has added complexity. Verb groups 1 and 5 both convey information about necessary events and contain the complex auxiliary verb *has/have to* rather than the more easily recognized auxiliary verb *must*. Verb groups 2 and 6 convey information about negated events, something not achieved (lived up to) or provided, and verb group 5 contains information about a recurring event (i.e., reaching a verdict in a civil trial) that may or may not be achieved (unanimously). Verb groups 3–6 all contain adverbs (also, even, always, longer).

Verb group 2 contains the added complexity of a phrasal verb. A phrasal verb is a group of words that consists of a verb + preposition(s)/adverb. Phrasal verbs challenge readers because their meanings cannot be derived by constituent words. For example, verb group 2 consists of a verb (live) and two prepositions (up, to). To live up to something means to fulfill an expectation (*McGraw-Hill's Dictionary of American Idioms and Phrasal Verbs*, Spears 2006). This meaning cannot be derived from the individual meanings of each word—*live*, *up*, and *to*.

In chapters 20 and 21, Mr. Rivera's students will encounter more phrasal verb groups that contain prepositions than adverbs. Examples are shown in table 4.6. Some of these phrasal verbs convey information about present, past, or possible events (e.g., are looking for, were put together, can shop around), while others stand alone and convey no information about an event (e.g., go against, depend on, make up for). Phrasal verbs also appear in the supplementary chapter 3, as shown in table 4.6.

Table 4.6. Phrasal Verb Examples

Chapters 20 and 21		Chapter 3	
v. + prep.	v. + adv.	v. + prep.	v. + adv.
make up	go against	came from	go without
add up	pay back	went off	run away
give up	put together	picked up	
divide up	shop around	end up	
clear up			
set out			
depend on			
look for			
make up for			
made up of			

Reading Sentences Fluently

Fluent reading is achieved partly by students' quick recognition of complex noun and verb groups like those examined above and partly by their quick recognition of complex subjects, different types of sentences, independent and dependent clauses, and the different ways sentences are punctuated.

Reading Complex Subjects Fluently

In their course textbook, Mr. Rivera's students will encounter many more sentences that begin with simple subjects than complex subjects. While reading about juvenile courts in chapter 20, for example, they will only encounter sentences that begin with simple subjects like *juvenile courts, their goal, most states, a youth, a juvenile, children, these acts*. Elsewhere in chapter 20, students will encounter sentences that begin with complex subjects like these:

1. One of the most important motions
2. This growing population of young defendants and prisoners
3. The terrorist bombing of a federal government office building in Oklahoma City in 1995
4. A large percentage of adults convicted of crimes

These complex subjects focus on one (motion), a particular population, a bombing, or a percentage, and each is made complex by a qualifying phrase/clause or several qualifying phrases. Subjects 1–2 contain a prepositional phrase that conveys additional information about the thing discussed: the one (motion) or a particular population. Subject 3 contains three prepositional phrases, one beginning with *of* and two beginning with *in*. Subject 4 contains a prepositional phrase (of adults) and a qualifying clause (convicted of crimes).

Reading Compound, Complex, and Compound-Complex Sentences Fluently

All four types of sentences—simple, compound, complex, and compound-complex—appear in assigned texts that Mr. Rivera's students will read in their unit on criminal and civil justice. A simple sentence contains one verb group, a compound sentence two verb groups, a complex sentences two or more verb groups, and a compound-complex sentence three or more verb groups. A simple sentence consists of one independent clause, a compound sentence two independent clauses, a complex sentence one independent clause and one or more dependent clauses, and a compound-complex sentence two independent clauses and one or more dependent clauses.

Students' progress through an assigned text—their ability to read an assigned text in a continuous forward motion, maintain an optimal speed, and understand the ideas encountered—will depend in part on their ability to read all four types of sentences appropriately. Proficient readers read simple sentences continuously without pausing and the other three types of sentences with measured continuity and appropriate pausing. And they do this automatically.

The following sentences appear in textbook chapters 20 and 21 and supplementary chapters 3 and 7. Mr. Rivera's students will read these sentences fluently by reading the first continuously without pausing and the others as marked, pausing for a fraction of a second at each double vertical line, which marks the end of each constituent clause, an independent or dependent clause. Students' understanding of whole sentences like the following will be determined largely by their understanding of individual clauses:

1. Minority youth are disproportionately represented throughout juvenile justice systems in nearly every state in the nation. (simple sentence)
2. In high school, Stacey started to get in trouble, || and the court put her into group homes. (compound sentence)
3. In order to make sure that people's rights are protected, || there are many steps that must be taken to decide whether a person is guilty of a crime. (complex sentence)
4. If the police see Jack commit the crime || or if someone reports that Jack has committed the crime, || then the police have probable cause to arrest him. (complex sentence)
5. Although each youth in detention is an individual, || most are between fifteen and seventeen years old, || and in the United States, most juveniles in detention centers are from a minority. (compound-complex sentence)

Complex sentences like 3 and 4 can be challenging for seventh graders to read fluently. Individual clauses in both sentences contain multiple verb groups that can overwhelm students and disrupt the continuity of their reading. Sentence 3 consists of a dependent and independent clause and sentence 4 two dependent and one independent clause. Each clause in these sentences contains multiple verb groups: the independent clause in sentence 3 contains four verb groups (are, must be taken, to decide, is), and both dependent clauses in sentence 4 contain two verb groups each (see, commit; reports, has committed).

Reading Punctuation Fluently

Clause boundaries are conveniently marked—to aid fluent reading—by punctuation marks like commas. Proficient readers routinely use commas to read complex sentences like 3 and 4 continuously with appropriate pausing. They will use the comma in sentence 3 to read the initial dependent clause continuously; and in sentence 4 they will mentally insert a comma between the first two clauses, and use the comma after the second clause to read the final clause continuously.

Clause boundaries can also be marked by semicolons, colons, and em dashes. Whereas commas are commonly used to mark boundaries between independent and dependent clauses, semicolons, colons, and em dashes are used to mark boundaries between independent clauses. Em dashes are also used to offset or emphasize particular information about a thing, information conveyed by a preceding clause.

Commas, as in sentences 3 and 4 above, semicolons, and em dashes all appear in chapters 20, 21, 3, and 7. Sentences 1 to 3 below use a semicolon or single em dashes to mark the boundary of a clause or offset additional information about a thing.

1. His mother had a boyfriend who abused drugs and alcohol; this man also physically abused Tomás's mother and his sisters and brothers.
2. They were still good friends—but Amanda couldn't imagine what Stacey's life was like.
3. In 2002, a jury awarded her over $28 billion in damages—the largest verdict ever in an individual product-liability case.

Identifying Unknown Words

Fluent reading is also achieved by readers' ability to identify unknown words quickly during reading. Proficient readers use their phonics knowledge, word-building knowledge, and word-segmenting knowledge quickly and competently as resources to identify unknown words encountered in assigned texts. That is, they use their knowledge of the ways English sounds are written (phonics knowledge), their knowledge of base words, Greek/Latin roots, prefixes, suffixes, and inflectional endings (word-building knowledge), and their ability to segment words (word-segmenting knowledge) all as resources to identify unknown words.

Mr. Rivera's students will encounter unknown words in all the chapters they are assigned to read in their unit on criminal and civil justice. In chapters 21 and 7, they will encounter such words as *probate, plaintiff, injunction, campaign, arbitrator, marijuana, deteriorate, diagnosed, stigmatize, rationalize, compromise, psychological,* and *larceny*. By identifying these and other new words quickly using their phonics, word-building, and word-segmenting knowledge, students will be able to read their assigned texts fluently with minimal disruption.

Phonics Knowledge as a Word Identification Resource

As noted earlier in chapter 2, phonic elements include single and combined vowels, and single and combined consonants. Single vowel sounds in English may be marked as short using a breve (e.g., ă) or marked as long using a macron (ā). There are five short and long vowel sounds in English (ă, ĕ, ĭ, ŏ, ŭ; ā, ē, ī, ō, ū) and 17 single consonant sounds (b, c, d, f, g, h, j, k, l, m, n, p, r, s, t, v, z), two of which may be hard or soft (c, g). The letters *w* and *y* are both consonants and vowels.

The consonants *s-*, *-r*, and *-l* regularly appear in English words in combination with other consonants. The consonant *s-* appears in the first letter position as in <u>s</u>capegoat, <u>s</u>kewed, <u>s</u>mattering, <u>s</u>nippet, <u>s</u>pecious, <u>s</u>table, <u>s</u>windle. The consonants *-r* and *-l* appear in the second or third letter position as in the examples shown in table 4.7. In all of these combinations, the two or three consonants produce a blended sound.

Table 4.7. Consonant Blend Examples

-r	-l	-r/-l
<u>br</u>utal	<u>bl</u>ackmail	<u>scr</u>een
<u>cr</u>edible	<u>cl</u>aim	<u>spr</u>int
<u>dr</u>opout	<u>fl</u>inch	<u>str</u>ategy
<u>gr</u>aphic	<u>gl</u>obal	<u>spl</u>it
<u>pr</u>obation	<u>pl</u>ead	
<u>tr</u>ansfer		

Pairs of consonants also produce single consonant sounds in English. These combinations of letters are called consonant digraphs (*di* meaning two and *graph* meaning letter). Two groups of digraphs are shown in table 4.8. In the first group, the sound produced by the combination of letters does not reflect the phonetic value of either letter. In the second group, one letter is silent.

Table 4.8. Consonant Digraph Examples

Digraph	Example
ch	<u>ch</u>allenged
ph	eu<u>ph</u>emisms
sh	puni<u>sh</u>ment
th/th	al<u>th</u>ough, reau<u>th</u>orization

Diagraph	Silent Letter	Example
ch, gh, wh, sch	h	te<u>ch</u>nicalities, <u>gh</u>etto, <u>wh</u>ichever, <u>sch</u>eme
wr	w	<u>wr</u>ongdoing
sc	c	adole<u>sc</u>ence
kn, ck	k	<u>kn</u>owledge, ba<u>ck</u>ground

Pairs of vowels also appear in English words. These combinations of letters may produce a single short or long vowel sound or a gliding sound from one vowel to another. Pairs of vowels that produce single short or long vowel sounds are called vowel digraphs. As shown in table 4.9, the vowel digraphs

Table 4.9. Vowel Digraph Examples

Diagraph	Sound	Example
au/aw	/ŏ/	re<u>au</u>thorization, withdr<u>aw</u>n
ea	/ĕ/	w<u>ea</u>pon
oo	/oo/	misunderst<u>oo</u>d
ai/ay	/ā/	pl<u>ai</u>ntiff, betr<u>ay</u>al
ea, ei, ee	/ē/	r<u>ea</u>sonable, s<u>ei</u>zure, disagr<u>ee</u>ment
oa, ow	/ō/	encr<u>oa</u>chment, narr<u>ow</u>
oo, ue	/ū/	sh<u>oo</u>tings, subd<u>ue</u>

au/aw, *ea*, and *oo* produce short vowel sounds, while the vowel digraphs *ai/ay*, *ea/ei/ee*, *oa/ow*, and *oo/ue* produce single long vowel sounds.

Pairs of vowels that produce a gliding or dipping sound from one vowel to another are called diphthongs (*di* meaning two and *phthong* meaning having two sounds). As shown in table 4.10, all diphthongs consist of the vowel *o* in one of four possible vowel combinations: *oi/oy/ou/ow*.

Table 4.10. Diphthong Examples

Diphthong	Sound	Example
oi/oy	/oi/	app<u>oi</u>ntment, empl<u>oy</u>ment
ou/ow	/ou/	insurm<u>ou</u>ntable, c<u>ow</u>ardly

Diphthongs, vowel digraphs, and single vowels can appear in combination with the consonant *-r*. In some vowel + *r* combinations, the original vowel sound is preserved, as in the words <u>dete</u>riorate, <u>ir</u>rational, en<u>for</u>cement, <u>air</u>tight, and pion<u>eer</u>ing. In most cases, however, the presence of an *-r* changes the original vowel sound slightly or dramatically, as in the words <u>ar</u>bitrator, vuln<u>er</u>able, j<u>ur</u>isdictional, mem<u>oir</u>, <u>ear</u>nings, and j<u>our</u>ney.

Finally, diphthongs, vowel digraphs, and the single vowel *i* can appear in combination with the consonant pairing *-gh*. The *-gh* is silent in some of these combinations and produces the sound /f/ in others. Mr. Rivera's students will encounter all of the combinations shown in table 4.11 in assigned unit texts.

Table 4.11. Vowel Combination Examples

Vowels	Sound	Example
ou	/ŭ/	r<u>ough</u>
ei/ai	/ā/	n<u>eigh</u>borhood, str<u>aigh</u>tforward
i/ei	/ī/	overs<u>igh</u>t, h<u>eigh</u>tened
ou	/ō/	alth<u>ough</u>
ou	/ū/	thr<u>ough</u>out
au/ou	/au/	c<u>augh</u>t, th<u>ough</u>t

Word-Building Knowledge as a Word Identification Resource

During reading, Mr. Rivera's students will use their word-building knowledge—their knowledge of morphemic elements—as well as their phonics knowledge—their knowledge of phonic elements, as discussed above—to identify unknown words quickly and proficiently. A morpheme is the smallest unit of language that conveys a specific meaning. Morphemic elements include base words, Greek/Latin roots, prefixes, suffixes, and inflectional endings. Each of these elements is defined and illustrated in table 4.12. Proficient readers use their knowledge of these elements during reading to identify unknown words and read assigned texts fluently.

Table 4.12. Morphemic Elements

Element	Definition and Examples
Base words	free-standing English words examples: crime, treat, prosecute, prison
Greek/Latin roots	ancient Greek/Latin (G/L) elements used to derive new words in English examples: tele (far, G), therm (heat, G), aud (hear, L), spec (look, L)
Prefixes	elements added to the front of base words or Greek/Latin roots that yield derivative words examples: post- (after), sub- (below), trans- (across), anti- (against)
Suffixes	elements added to the back of base words or Greek/Latin roots that yield derivative words examples: -al (like, characterized by), -ful (full of, like), -ity (quality or condition), -less (without)
Inflectional endings	elements added to the back of a base word that change its case, number, tense; or specify a comparison (as comparative or superlative) examples: judge's (possessive case), crimes (number), entered (tense), harshest (comparison: superlative)

Two- to five-letter prefixes and one- to four-letter suffixes appear commonly in middle grade social studies texts. These prefixes, shown below, range in meaning from not (em-/en-) and from (ex-) to wrongly (mis-) and across (trans-), and the suffixes range in meaning from like (-y/-ly) and characterized by (-al/-ic) to make (-ize) and action or process (-ance/-ence/-ent/-ment). Most print dictionaries, many free-access online dictionaries, and other free resources available online provide the meanings of all and more of the affixes shown below and others:

common prefixes: bi-, de-, em-, en-, ex-, im-, in-, re-, un-; dis-, mis-, non-, pre-; anti-, fore-, poly-, post-; inter-, intra-, trans-
common suffixes: -y; -al, -an, -fy, -ic, -ly; -ful, -ist, -ous, -ion, -ant, -ent, -ity, -ate, -ian, -ism, -ize, -ite; -able, -ance, -ence, -less, -ment, -ness

Inflectional endings mainly help readers to classify unknown words as things (nouns), actions/events (verbs), or qualities (adjective/adverb). Inflectional endings in English include the morphemes -*'s*; -*ing*, -*ed*, -*en*; -*er*, -*est*; and -*s*. The ending -*'s* marks possession and is only added to nouns (things, people's names). The endings -*ing*, -*ed*, and -*en* mark tense and are only added to verbs. The endings -*er* and -*est* are added to adjectives/adverbs and mark degrees of comparison. The ending -*s* is added to nouns to mark number and verbs to mark tense/person.

Mr. Rivera's students may use their knowledge of inflectional endings and base words to identify unknown words during reading, words like *convinced* (*convince* + -*ed*, past tense verb), *guarantees* (*guarantee* + -*s*, plural noun), or *narrower* (*narrow* + *er*, an adjective used to compare two things), none of which they may have seen before in print.

But to read their assigned texts fluently, all his students will necessarily use their knowledge of base words, prefixes, and suffixes to identify unknown words like those shown in table 4.13. All these words appear in assigned unit texts and fit one of three patterns: prefix + base word, base word + suffix(es)/inflectional ending, or prefix + base word + suffix(es).

Table 4.13. Identified Word Examples

Unknown Word	Base Word	Prefix/Suffix/Ending
anti<u>social</u>	social	anti-
<u>technical</u>ities	technical	-ity, -s
<u>crim</u>inality	crime	-al, -ity
de<u>sens</u>itize	sense	de-, -ize
dis<u>organiz</u>ation	organize	dis-, -tion
dis<u>proportion</u>ately	proportion	dis-, -ate, -ly

Mr. Rivera's students will also use their knowledge of Greek/Latin roots as they aim to read their assigned unit texts fluently. Words with Latin roots appear regularly in these texts. In chapters 20 and 21, students will encounter the words *verdict, construction, convict, convince, mandatory, injunction,* and *rehabilitated*. These words contain the Latin roots *dict* (say), *struct* (build), *vict/vinc* (conquer), *mand* (order), *junct* (join), and *hab* (hold).

In assigned chapters 5 and 6 from *America's Prisons* (Lasky 2016), students will also encounter words that contain Greek roots, like *archaeologists* (*arch*, ancient), *psychiatric* (*psych*, mind), *geographically* (*geo*, earth), and *philosophy* (*phil*, love).

Students will use their knowledge of Greek/Latin roots as a word identification resource in all their middle grade social studies courses. In their civics, geography, and history courses, middle grade students will encounter words that contain such roots as *corp* (corporate, body), *cred* (credibility, believe), *duc/duct* (deduce, reduction; lead), *fract* (fractious, break), *ject* (interject, throw), *leg* (legislate, law), *port* (transport, carry), *rupt* (disrupt, break), *spec* (suspect, look), *tract* (detract, drag), and *vers/vert* (versatile, revert; turn).

Word-Segmenting Knowledge as a Word Identification Resource

During reading, proficient readers identify unknown words by segmenting them. To segment a word means to take it apart, to separate its constituent elements. Word segmentation can focus on phonic elements, morphemic elements, or syllables. A syllable is a unit of sound that consists of a lone vowel sound or a vowel + consonant(s) sound.

Four segmented words appear below. These words contain four to five syllables, syllables that contain a range of phonic elements: long and short vowels, r-controlled vowels, combinations of vowel and consonant sounds, hard and soft consonants, and consonant blends. Some of these syllables function as a suffix/inflectional ending (-tion, -al, -ment, -s), and one is a Latin root (*dic*, speak).

ar-bi-tra-tors
em-bez-zle-ment
jur-is-dic-tion-al
in-car-cer-a-tion

Many unknown words encountered in middle grade social studies textbooks and other assigned texts are best identified by segmentation that focuses on morphemic elements. Words like *disagreements, disproportionately,* and *criminality* are best identified in this way. Some unknown words, however, are best identified by segmentation that focuses on syllables. Words like *notorious, relinquish,* and *regimented*, which do not contain base words, and words like *adjudication, incarceration, jurisdiction,* and *embezzlement*, whose base words may not be apparent to students, are best identified, at least in part, by syllables.

While some unknown words may be identified by segmentation that focuses on phonic elements, students' exclusive use of phonic segmentation to identify unknown words in middle grade civics, geography, or history texts is not advisable. Phonic segmentation (i.e., the practice of sounding words out left to right) may be useful for smaller words like *civil* or *penal* but is rarely economical for longer words like *deterioration* and *adjudication*.

Sustaining an Optimal Speed

To read a text fluently means to read it continuously at an optimal speed. A reading speed can be determined by the number of minutes taken to read a text in whole or part. In middle grade social studies courses like Mr. Rivera's seventh grade civics course, an optimal reading speed is best measured by the length of time taken to read an assigned text in whole.

To read an assigned whole text fluently at an optimal speed, middle grade students should read that text silently about twice as fast as they would read it aloud. For example, some of Mr. Rivera's seventh graders may take 20 minutes to read chapter 3 aloud, a chapter about juvenile incarceration from the book *Youth in Prison* (Smith and McIntosh 2007). An optimal silent reading speed for this particular chapter would be about 10 minutes.

To read all their assigned unit texts fluently at sustained optimal speeds, Mr. Rivera's students will move from sentence to sentence, paragraph to paragraph, and section to section in a continuous forward motion. They will expect to encounter complex sentences, complex sentence elements (complex subjects, nouns, verbs), and complex punctuation marks (colons, semicolons, em dashes), and respond appropriately. They will use their ability to segment words and their phonics and word-building knowledge as word identification resources.

Proficient readers aim to read assigned texts fluently at sustained optimal speeds. They reach an optimal speed quickly in the during reading phase, monitor their progress, and adjust their reading speed if needed. Proficient readers understand the benefits of fluent reading and costs of disfluent reading and aim to read texts optimally with few interruptions.

Illustration

The following illustration focuses on the fluent reading action of word identification and chiefly middle grade students' use of phonics, word-building, and word-segmentation knowledge to identify unknown words in assigned unit texts. Examples of fluent reading actions involving complex groups of words and sentences have been amply provided above.

Álvaro and his partner Lindsay are busily collecting unknown words from their next assigned unit chapter, Viewpoint 6: "Juveniles Should Be Tried as Adults When They Have Committed Violent Crimes" from the book *Juvenile Justice* (Haugen 2013). Next day, in a group of four, Álvaro and Lindsay will discuss the question: Should juveniles be tried in adult court for violent crimes?

Álvaro and Lindsay's assigned chapter argues yes, and their discussion partners' chapter, Viewpoint 7: "Juveniles Should Not Be Tried or Sentenced as Adults" (McCormick 2013), argues no. Álvaro and Lindsay are skimming through their assigned chapter individually and recording unfamiliar words in their notebooks.

Álvaro and Lindsay collect about 20 words each, then in the time remaining identify as many words as they can using their phonics, word-building, and word-segmenting knowledge. They manage to identify half of the words in their list before their teacher Mr. Rivera times them out. Three headings appear on the board: "Phonic Resources," "Phonic & Morphemic Resources," and "Morphemic Resources." "Viewpoint 6 words first," says Mr. Rivera, looking at Álvaro, whom he calls on first. "Give me two words, Álvaro, and tell me how you identified them."

"My first word is *malicious*," reports Álvaro, "which Lindsay and I identified using our knowledge of Greek/Latin roots and suffixes: *mal* means bad and *-ous* having the quality of. My second word is *unequivocally*. This one has two Greek/Latin roots: *equi* (equal) and *vocal* (voice). The prefix *un-* means not, and the suffix *-ly* means in such-and-such a way, which we learned this week."

"Great," says Mr. Rivera and adds both words below the heading "Morphemic Resources." Ten minutes later, once Álvaro's classmates have reported words from their lists, four to seven words appear below each heading (see table 4.14), and all these words appear in Álvaro's personal list.

Table 4.14. Alvaro's Sorted Word List

Phonic Resources	Phonic & Morphemic Resources	Morphemic Resources
petty	cringed	malicious
slaughter	perpetrated	unequivocally
phenomenon	chronic	cartwheels
truancy	petition	semiautomatic
	adjudication	aggravated
	adjacent	jurisdiction
		insurmountable

LOOKING BACK AND AHEAD

Two of six actions that proficient readers engage in during reading were explored at length in this chapter. These two actions, visualizing and reading fluently, help all readers to achieve their ultimate reading goal of understanding the main ideas presented in a text and being able to use them at a later date.

Proficient readers visualize during reading but limit the frequency and duration of their visualizing for assigned informational texts in order to focus on the important ideas presented in these texts and to move through these texts at optimal speeds. Proficient readers use their knowledge of English sounds, phonics, morphemes, word groups, sentence structure, and sentence punctuation all to read texts fluently in a continuous forward motion—smoothly, effortlessly, and accurately.

Proficient readers also use the actions of reading for understanding and inferencing to achieve their ultimate reading goal. These two actions are the focus of chapter 5.

GROUNDING: DURING READING PHASE ACTIONS

This chapter is grounded in visual grammatics (Kress and Van Leeuwen 2006), alphabetics, vocabulary processes, and fluency (NRP 2000; Kuhn and Stahl 2013; Nagy and Scott 2013; Ash and Baumann 2017), formal linguistics (English phonology, morphology, semantics, syntax), and systemic functional linguistics (Halliday and Matthiessen 2014).

5

During Reading Actions II

Spring Semester

Mrs. Touré and her sixth grade students have just completed a monthlong unit on the physical and human geographical features of Africa. Mrs. Touré has taught this unit three times since her state adopted a set of standards for reading social studies texts in grades 6–12. This is the third year that Mrs. Touré has provided explicit reading instruction aimed at helping her students to identify and track the development of ideas in assigned unit texts.

This is also the third year that Mrs. Touré focused mainly on the southern and eastern region of Africa, which includes the countries of Sudan and Ethiopia to the north, South Africa to the south, the island of Madagascar, and the coastline countries of Somalia, Kenya, and Tanzania. This particular region, one of three, is the focus of chapter 14 in the course textbook, the main unit text. Chapter 13, whose focus is the west and central region, is also an assigned unit text, but Mrs. Touré only touched on this region at the start of her unit. Her students will learn about the north region in a seventh grade cross-curricular unit on Egypt.

Having taught her unit on Africa now for a third time since her state's adoption of the new reading standards, Mrs. Touré affirms to herself that she rightly narrowed the focus of her unit to address these new standards and will teach the unit again with this same narrowed focus. But her next group of students will benefit greatly from reading more about individual countries within the southern and eastern region and reading widely. This coming summer she will spend a day or two online, searching for supplementary texts, a few book chapters and articles.

Summer Break

One rainy morning midway through the summer, Mrs. Touré sits down at her kitchen table to review some promising new texts about Africa—books about Kenya, South Africa, and Sudan and several articles each about Namibia, Kenya, and Rwanda, all obtained from her recent search of the public library catalog and a special database for students, provided free of charge by the library. Mrs. Touré conveniently downloaded the articles directly from the database, all full-color PDFs, and collected the books from the library last night.

Within minutes of leafing through the first two texts, both children's books, Mrs. Touré determines that both are excellent supplementary texts for her sixth grade unit on Africa. The historical chapters in each are particularly interesting, relevant, and informative: each of these chapters complements or extends the information presented in the course textbook, chapter 14, section 2, which focuses on the history of the southern and eastern region, its first inhabitants, first civilizations, colonialism, and independence. These two children's books are simply called Kenya *(Burgan 2015) and* South Africa *(Blauer and Lauré 2013).*

The third book about Sudan, They Poured Fire on Us from the Sky *(Deng, Deng, and Ajak 2005), is not a children's book but presents the personal accounts of three Sudanese boys, all under the age of 10, who fled from their country during its civil war in the late 1980s. The first two chapters captivate Mrs. Touré, but she puts the book aside for now, doubting its appropriateness for her sixth grade study. Let her see what she thinks this evening, after reading further along in the book.*

Mrs. Touré spends the next several hours reviewing her articles: clicks through them quickly, eliminates several straight off, then reads the others attentively, mindful of her students' needs and abilities.

The four articles she eventually selects are excellent new texts for her study. They focus on controversial hunting practices in the southern part of Africa, land dispossession and redistribution in Namibia, recent flooding in Kenya, and local efforts to preserve endangered groups of gorillas in Rwanda. Two of the articles appeared in the New African, *a widely circulated magazine published in Africa, and two appeared in recent issues of* National Geographic. *All four articles will definitely interest her students.*

Later that evening, Mrs. Touré decides that portions of the book about Sudan—portions of Part One, "The Village of Juol," which she just finished reading—are highly appropriate for her unit on Africa. In the first part of the book, the authors Benson and Alepho Deng and Benjamin Ajak recall the first part of their lives, to ages five and seven, living happily and prosperously with their families in the village of Juol in southern Sudan. Their people, the Dinka, were subsistence farmers and pastoralists. They lived in huts with thatched grass roofs. Young Dinka boys liked to play games and roamed the countryside freely.

Mrs. Touré will use portions of four chapters in Part One, roughly 20 pages in all, as assigned texts in her unit. From these texts, Mrs. Touré's students will learn about Africa firsthand, from African people themselves. They will read personal firsthand accounts about the authors' people, the authors' mothers and fathers, family relationships, childhood friendships, cultural practices, everyday problems and events, and the region's geography. Her students will be thrilled to read about the authors' firsthand childhood encounters with such animals as ostriches, monkeys, hyenas, and lions.

Several days later, though, Mrs. Touré has second thoughts about using the book in her unit, even parts of the book. She foresees a problem. Some of her students will be interested to read more about the authors' experiences on their own and get copies of the book online or from the library; and that may be problematic for their parents. Mrs. Touré has now read the book in its entirety and knows how troubling it is. The authors Benson, Alepho, and Benjamin write candidly and descriptively about their experiences as orphans and child refugees in a war-torn country; and their experiences are harrowing.

Students will need to talk with their parents about these experiences if reading the book on their own. Mrs. Touré wonders how many parents will agree to do this, if any agree at all, or will they flatly object to her using the book in the first place, even portions of it? Her principal may even object to her using the book in sixth grade, thinking that the book is more appropriately explored with older students. She will speak to him in the fall.

Spring Semester

Mrs. Touré begins her unit on Africa this year as she did a year ago, with one exception. After guiding her students' reading of the introductory section of unit 5 in their course textbook, she skips ahead to chapter 14: "Southern and Eastern Africa," previews the chapter with her students, then introduces the new texts she selected in the summer to enhance her students' understandings about the southern and eastern region, the unit's central focus.

She begins the unit on Monday. By Friday, she has completed a quick overview of the west and central region, chapter 13 in the course textbook, which she plans to return to at the end of the unit, to bring the unit full circle. For next Monday, her students will read the "myStory" feature in chapter 14 about a young South African man named Khulekani and complete a paragraph topics outline she created for this text. The outline, completed by all of her students independently, will provide baseline information about their ability to identify paragraph topics in grade level texts.

In the second half of class on Monday, Mrs. Touré projects a photocopy of the physical geography section 1A in chapter 14 and directs her students to read the section and paragraph topics added to the text in pencil. The original section heading, "Remarkable Land and Water," has been struck out and replaced by the section topic Physical Features: Land & Water, and a paragraph topic is printed neatly flush right above each paragraph. The paragraph topics include Remarkable Physical Features, Valleys & Mountains, Lakes & Rivers, Swamps, and Deserts.

"We'll start with the paragraph topics," says Mrs. Touré. "For each paragraph, we'll ask ourselves the question: What words in this paragraph help me to generate a paragraph topic? I'll go first. Paragraph 1. Question: What words in this paragraph help me to generate the paragraph topic Remarkable Physical Features? Answer: physical features.*" She circles the words directly on the text with her pencil. "And here's the word* remarkable *in the heading," she says and circles it too. "That's all for paragraph 1. Now for paragraph 2. Your turn," she says.*

Her students easily identify the paragraph topic key words for paragraphs 2–5, and when all six key words are circled, Mrs. Touré looks curiously at her students. "I'm surprised," she says, looking at the text. "I didn't expect these key words to appear where they do. I expected them to appear in the first sentence in their paragraphs, but only two of them do, physical features *in paragraph 1 and* lakes *in paragraph 3. The other key words appear in the second, third, fourth, and fifth sentences in their paragraphs."*

Mrs. Touré now projects a paragraph topics outline for this short section of text, section 1A, and reviews it quickly with her students. The outline, shown below, is formatted identically to the ones she collected from her students earlier today for the myStory text.

A. *Physical features: land & water*
   1. *Remarkable physical features*
   2. *Valleys & mountains*
   3. *Lakes & rivers*
   4. *Swamps*
   5. *Deserts*

"Now for the main ideas," says Mrs. Touré, projecting a second photocopy of the text, which is comprehensively marked with paragraph topics, paragraph topic key words, and main idea key words. "I underlined the main idea key words in this copy of the text and marked their location in the margin with a check mark. Here in paragraph 1, four main idea key words are underlined: diverse, impressive, landscapes, *and* wildlife. *In other words, when reading paragraph 1, you want to understand above all else that the physical features*

of southern and eastern Africa are diverse and impressive in terms of landscapes and wildlife."

In paragraph 1, the paragraph topic key words physical features *and the four main idea key words,* diverse, impressive, landscapes, *and* wildlife, *are distinct, but in paragraphs 2–5, the main idea and paragraph topic key words correspond—they are one and the same. Consequently, all of the key words previously circled are now both circled and underlined. Mrs. Touré urges her students not to be confused by this, that when reading these paragraphs, they want to understand above all else that southern and eastern Africa have valleys, mountains, lakes, rivers, swamps, and deserts. "Don't get lost in the details," she says.*

Details about these six main ideas appear on a map in the textbook. All of the lakes, rivers, and deserts named in the text, as well as the Great Rift Valley, Victoria Falls, and several other physical features omitted from the text, including the Serengeti Plain, Ethiopian Highlands, and Okavango Basin, appear on a physical map above the text on page 531. "Read the text now yourselves," says Mrs. Touré. "Read it quickly, check out the map, and tell me this: Why did I caution you before not to get lost in the details? What was I getting at?"

Her students tell her that too many names appear in the text, names that are hard to keep straight. Victoria, Zambezi, Sudd, Namib—which are which, mountains, rivers, lakes? "These names are paragraph details, details also shown on the map, 12 names in all," says Mrs. Touré. "Paragraph details like these can easily distract you. Always focus on the main ideas. Read the details quickly for gist. Don't get sidetracked. That's what I was getting at before."

Mrs. Touré has included this information about paragraph details on today's first handout, a copy of the fully marked section 1A text and its corresponding paragraph topics outline, which she will distribute momentarily. In the few minutes remaining in today's class, she neatly circles back to the section heading and asks her students why she revised it. Why did she keep the words land *and* water *and replace the word* remarkable *with the geographical term* physical features?

They have one minute to talk about these questions with a neighbor before she answers them herself. A minute later, she tells her students that section 1A is essentially about physical features—land features in paragraphs 2 and 5 and water features in paragraphs 3 and 4. Her revised heading "Physical Features: Land & Water" best encapsulates the information presented in the section. The word remarkable *is misleading. The authors should not have used it.*

Mrs. Touré has prepared two handouts for today. She distributes them quickly, almost out of time. The second handout is a partially marked copy of section 1B, "Patterns of Ecosystems," the next section in chapter 14. Mrs. Touré directs her students to read section 1B on this second handout, circle one or two paragraph topic key words in each of the six paragraphs, and create a paragraph topics outline for the section. Her directions appear at the top of the handout.

"Tomorrow," says Mrs. Touré, finishing up, "we'll take a look at the paragraph topic key words you circled in this section, then focus on several informational writing structures used by the authors to convey information about the region's ecosystems. Expert readers use these structures to generate questions about the text, to better understand it. More about that tomorrow. Try to locate these structures yourselves. They are listed here on the handout: the comparison and causal explanation structures."

INTRODUCTION: DURING READING PHASE ACTIONS

Middle grade students are best positioned to read, understand, and learn from assigned texts in social studies courses like Mrs. Touré's sixth grade world geography course if they are able to identify paragraph topics, track the development of ideas in and across paragraphs, identify the patterned ways ideas are presented in texts, and infer meaning from understated ideas. In other words, students' achievement of specific course learning outcomes will be greatly enhanced by students' ability to read for understanding and infer meanings from assigned texts.

These two during reading mental actions—reading for understanding and inferencing—are the focus of this chapter. Each of these actions is explained in detail and illustrated using the texts identified in the opening vignette: chapters 13–14 in Pearson's *myWorld Geography* (Chu et al. 2011) and books and articles about the countries of Kenya, South Africa, Sudan, Namibia, and Rwanda.

The articles featured in this chapter include "Floods Everywhere and Not a Drop to Drink" (Kubakura 2015), "Mercury Rising! Namibia: Land of the Brave?" (Ankomah 2015), "The Gorillas Dian Fossey Saved" (Royte 2017), and "Should We Kill Animals to Save Them?" (Paterniti 2017).

READING FOR UNDERSTANDING

Statements and Target Questions

The ultimate goal of reading is to understand the main ideas presented in a text and be able to use these ideas at a later date. Proficient readers achieve this goal by taking deliberate action before, during, and after reading—by clarifying their reading goal (before reading), reading for understanding (during reading), and clarifying their understandings (after reading).

Reading an assigned informational text for understanding involves the ongoing extraction of essential information about the prominent topic explored in the text. The quality of information extracted by readers from any given text will largely be determined by readers' understandings about the ways ideas are communicated in information texts and readers' ability to track major ideas.

This section addresses the following questions:

- How are informational texts structured?
- What knowledge about key structural elements do proficient readers use to read informational texts for understanding?
- How do meanings flow in informational texts?
- What is the relationship between topic identification, titles, headlines, and headings?
- How do middle grade students apply word and conceptual meanings during reading?
- How do students use their knowledge of informational writing structures and auxiliary paragraph structures to extract and track meanings?
- How does goal-oriented and purposeful reading help students to read for understanding?

The Structure of Informational Texts and Flows of Meaning

Presentational Structures

Informational texts like those selected by Mrs. Touré for her sixth grade study of Africa present information in structured ways. Chapter 4: "Creating Kenya," from the specialized book *Kenya* (Burgan 2015) and the *New African* article "Mercury Rising! Namibia: Land of the Brave?" (Ankomah 2015) use a simple chapter/article-section structure to inform readers about two African countries. Chapters 13–14 in the *myWorld Geography* textbook (Chu et al. 2011, hereafter referred to as the geography textbook) use the more complex chapter-section-subsection structure to inform readers about two African regions.

Proficient readers use their knowledge of the ways texts are structured for particular communicational purposes (i.e., to inform, recount, explain, or persuade) as well as their basic understandings of key structural elements—topics and ideas—to read for understanding.

Key Structural Elements: Topics and Ideas

For informational texts, whose primary communicational purpose is to inform, topics are best understood as subjects and ideas as thoughts. A topic is the subject of a communication. An idea is a thought about the subject of a communication. Social studies textbooks, specialized books, and many magazine articles communicate tiers of information about an overarching topic/subject, as illustrated by the following topic overview for the article "Mercury Rising! Namibia: Land of the Brave?" (Ankomah 2015). This two-tier topic overview includes four section topics. (Paragraph topics are not included in this overview.)

> Article topic: Rising tension over land ownership in Namibia
> Section topics: 1. Land ownership in Namibia. 2. Namibia: past and present. 3. Land negotiations. 4. Rising tensions.

Section topics in this *New African* article about Namibia are logically ordered to advance readers' understandings about the article's overarching topic. The first section identifies the issue of land ownership in Namibia. The second and third sections provide systematic information about the historical impact of colonialism on land ownership and the current status of land negotiations between native Namibians and the government. The fourth section reports on the rising tensions between existing landowners, prospective landowners, and government negotiators.

Section A–C topics in chapter 14, section 1 in the geography textbook are also logically ordered, whereas section topics in chapter 4 in the book about Kenya are chronologically ordered. Sections 1A–B in chapter 14 present logically ordered information about nonliving and living things in southern and eastern Africa, human uses of land, and water resources, respectively.

Chapter 4, on the other hand, presents chronological information about the chapter topic—Kenya's history from prehistoric times to present day. Chapter 4 section topics include the first people, European exploration (1498–1505), European rule (1512–1944), independence and nation building (1950–1969), and recent times (1978–2010).

Proficient readers use their knowledge about topics and the ways they interrelate within the overall structure of informational texts like textbooks, specialized books, and articles to read for understanding. More significantly, though, proficient readers use their knowledge about ideas and the integral relationship between paragraph topics and ideas to read for understanding.

Flows of Meaning

In informational texts, ideas/thoughts about an overarching topic are communicated to readers incrementally paragraph by paragraph, section by section. To understand these texts, readers must be able to track the incremental meanings presented to them. Proficient readers are able to track the two-way flow of meanings in informational texts, from larger to smaller and smaller to larger units of meaning, as represented below:

chapter topic > section topics > paragraph topics > main ideas
main ideas → paragraph topics → section topics → chapter topic

This two-way flow of information from larger to smaller and smaller to larger units of meaning is observable in all 10 chapters of the specialized book *South Africa* (Blauer and Lauré 2013). The flow of information from smaller to larger units of meaning in the section titled "The Union of South Africa" in chapter 4 is shown in outline form below. This section, labeled section G, consists of three paragraphs. Two main ideas (a–b) are communicated about each paragraph topic (1–3), whose incremental meanings inform readers about the section topic (G).

G. South Africa unions: 1910–1930

1. Union formations

   a. formation of the Union of South Africa
   b. formation of the African National Congress

2. Legislative restrictions on native South Africans

   a. enactment of Natives' Land Act
   b. subsequent landownership laws

3. Living conditions for native South Africans

   a. hardships
   b. political resistance

Supporting Ideas

Supporting ideas/thoughts (i.e., supporting details) are purposefully omitted from this outline. In the during reading phase of a reading event—for the first whole reading of an assigned text—proficient readers focus not on supporting ideas but on the flow of information primarily in an upward direction, from smaller to larger units of meaning beginning with main ideas. Middle grade students will undermine their efforts to read for understanding by focusing on minutiae. Supporting details for this section in chapter 4 will be explored later in this chapter.

Topics, Titles, Headlines, and Headings

Topics, titles, headlines, and headings correspond when words that appear in the one also appear in the other. For example, the first three section topics for chapter 4 in the book about South Africa all correspond to the first three section headings. The topic words *early settlers*, *European arrival*, and *European communities* also appear in the section headings "Early Settlers," "Europeans Arrive," and "European Communities."

Chapter topics may or may not correspond to chapter titles in textbooks and specialized books. Chapter titles and topics in chapters 13–14 in the geography textbook correspond, while the majority of chapter titles and topics in the book about South Africa, including chapter 4, do not. Chapter titles in many specialized books published for middle grade students function more as eye-catching headlines than topic identifiers.

Article topics too may or may not correspond to article titles. The topic and title of the Kenyan article about flooding correspond, while the topic and title of the Namibian article do not. The non-correspondence of chapter/article topics and titles is understandable, of course, given that a topic denotes the subject of a communication and a title the name of a published work.

Section topics and headings in three assigned unit texts selected by Mrs. Touré have a high degree of correspondence. Twenty-three of 25 section topics and first level headings correspond in chapters 13–14 in the geography textbook, and 12 of 13 section topics and headings correspond in chapter 4 in the book about South Africa.

In Mrs. Touré's set of articles, however, there is considerable variability in the correspondence of section topics and headings. Only two of five headings that appear in the articles about Kenya and Namibia correspond to section topics, one in each article.

Identifying Chapter and Section Topics: Easy Identifications

Chapter and section topics that correspond to chapter titles and section headings are easily identified by middle grade students. For chapter 14 in the geography textbook, the chapter topic and individual topics for sections 1E and 2A2–4, for example, are easily identified. All correspond exactly to the chapter title and section headings: southern and eastern Africa (chapter topic/title); disease (section 1E topic/heading); Nubia & Aksum, Bantu Migrations, Great Zimbabwe (sections 2A2–4 topics/headings).

But not all section topics and headings correspond exactly in this text. In chapter 14 and other chapters in the geography textbook, some section topics and headings correspond closely but not exactly. In chapter 14, section topics for 1E, 2A1, and 2A5 are derived from minor changes to section headings:

environmental challenges ←"Challenges of the Environment," first people ← "Earth's First People," and Arab influences ← "Arab Influence."

Seven of 11 section topics for chapter 4 in the book about Kenya and one of two section topics in the article about Kenya correspond to section headings and are easily identified. Section topics in each text are derived by minor changes to section headings, by subtracting or reordering words (e.g., British rule ← "The Path to British Rule," independence ← "Towards Independence," nation building ← "Building a Nation," and household displacements ← "47,000 households displaced"). Five section topics in these same texts, however, do not correspond and can only be derived by inferencing.

Identifying Paragraph Topics and Main Ideas in Textbooks and Specialized Books

The identification of paragraph topics and main ideas in the geography textbook and specialized books about Kenya and South Africa can be easy or challenging. Paragraph topics and main ideas in any informational text are both derived from paragraph key words. The precision of these key words and their visibility to readers will determine the degree to which paragraph topics and main ideas are identifiable without inferencing.

Paragraph Topic Identification: Easy Identifications

Five of nine paragraph topics in chapter 14, section 1C, "Riches from the Land," in the geography textbook are easily identified. Sample identifications for three paragraphs on pages 534–35 follow. Paragraph topics appear first, then topic sentences. In each topic sentence, paragraph topic key words are underlined:

mineral amounts ← Not all countries have an abundance, or large <u>amount, of minerals</u>.
farm land use ← People also <u>use</u> the <u>land</u> in this region to <u>farm</u> and raise animals.
land irrigation ← Because so much of the region is dry, many farmers <u>irrigate</u> their <u>land</u>.

Main Idea Identification: Easy Identifications

An outline of chapter 4, section G in the book about South Africa was presented above. None of the paragraph topics in this section about South African unions are identifiable without inferencing, but five of six main ideas communicated in the section are easily identified. Sample identifications follow for the first two paragraphs on pages 52–53 in this section. Main ideas appear first, then main idea source sentences. In each source sentence, main idea key words are underlined:

> formation of the Union of South Africa ← In 1910, Britain brought together four of the colonies in the region—Natal, Free State, Orange, and Transvaal—to <u>form the Union of South Africa</u>.
> formation of the African National Congress ← In 1912, black South Africans <u>created the African National Congress</u> (ANC) to fight for full citizenship.
> enactment of Natives' Land Act ← In 1913, they <u>enacted</u> the <u>Natives' Land Act</u>.

Using Knowledge to Read Continuously for Meaning

To extract essential meanings from assigned texts during reading, proficient readers use more than their knowledge about the ways texts are structured to inform and the way meanings flow in informational texts. To read for understanding, proficient readers also use their knowledge of word meanings, concepts, informational writing structures, and auxiliary paragraph structures; and their efforts are goal-oriented and purposeful.

Using Definitional Knowledge to Read for Understanding

Mrs. Touré transitions to the next topic in the course textbook, the history of southern and eastern Africa, by providing a quick historical overview of one country in the region, Sudan, and introducing her students to the authors of the book *They Poured Fire on Us from the Sky* (Deng, Deng, and Ajak, 2005), Benson, Alepho, and Benjamin. A childhood story about a hyena and lion, recounted in the book by Benjamin, is the next assigned unit text.

Benjamin is a young boy in his story. Back in the early eighties, when he was four years old, he and other young boys were responsible for tending the family goats, grazing them in the fields beyond the village and keeping them safe. Benjamin learned firsthand that unprotected goats got killed by hyenas on the outskirts of the village, and he learned to protect his goats by looking big and dangerous, a ploy he learned from his father.

His father instructed him and the other boys to hold thick branches on their heads and stand them straight up, to make themselves look tall, like men; then to jump up and down on the spot and make lots of noise. So today, while grazing their goats beyond their village, Benjamin and his friends have armed themselves with sticks and spring into action when the next hyena strikes.

But here a lion enters the story.

The extent to which Mrs. Touré's students are able to extract essential meanings from this text will be determined in part by their understanding of essential content words they encounter. To understand the experience conveyed by Benjamin's story, students will use their definitional knowledge of essential content words like *graze, dense, herd, commotion, bolt, frenzy,* and *kid goat*:

> Young boys graze (= put to feed on grass) their family goats beyond the village.
> The bush was dense (= thickly treed) at the edge of the field.
> The boys herded (= drive) their goats back to the village.
> The boys and goats return to the village in a great commotion (= tumultuous activity).
> A goat bolted (= make a sudden escape) at the sound of the rustling bush.
> A little bunch of goats went into a frenzy (= a state of near madness).
> A kid goat (= young goat) squeals among the tall grass.

Using Conceptual Knowledge to Read for Understanding

To extract essential meanings from course textbooks like the geography textbook, middle grade students will draw on their personal stores of conceptual knowledge. While reading chapter 14, section 1B, for example, Mrs. Touré's students will use their conceptual knowledge about ecosystems to extract important information about the distinctive cluster of ecosystems in southern and eastern Africa. In section 1B students will read about and view five ecosystems that distinguish the region:

1. Tropical and subtropical forest
2. Tropical or subtropical grassland or savanna
3. Mediterranean brush
4. Desert and desert brush
5. Mountain grassland and brush

Very little information about these five ecosystems is presented in section 1B. To read the section for understanding—that is, to understand the distinctive pattern of ecosystems in southern and eastern Africa—students must draw on their conceptual knowledge about each ecosystem and apply it during reading. Mrs. Touré's students know from previous grades, for example, that the savanna ecosystem, which resembles the American prairies, consists of many miles of grasslands and trees that are able to survive droughtlike conditions. Their understanding about patterns of ecosystems in southern and eastern Africa will be greatly advanced by this knowledge.

More broadly, Mrs. Touré's students will use their knowledge of core geographical concepts to extract important information from all assigned texts in their unit on Africa. During reading, they will use their knowledge of location, landforms, temperature zones, and ocean currents for chapters 13–14, section 1 in their course textbook; their knowledge of the water cycle, climate change, and urbanization for the article about Kenya; and their knowledge of timelines, historical sources, political systems, and colonization for the historical chapters from the specialized books about Kenya and South Africa. Information about all these concepts is presented in the core concepts handbook at the start of the geography textbook.

Using Text-Building Knowledge to Read for Understanding

Middle grade students are best equipped to extract important information from assigned unit texts when they are knowledgeable about the ways texts are structured or built. Informational texts communicate information to readers in larger and smaller structural units. Three of these units were discussed above: chapters, sections, and paragraphs. Informational texts like those selected by Mrs. Touré for her study of Africa also present information using other structural units whose communicational focus, purpose, and span vary. In this book, these other structural units are referred to taxonomically as informational writing structures.

Eleven informational writing structures are described and illustrated below. As shown in table 5.1, these structures include the bulleted list structure, two types of numbered structures, the causal and consequential explanation structures, and others. More than half of these structures have the same communicational focus. Identified in the table as type 2 structures,

Table 5.1. Informational Writing Structures

Type	Focus of Communication	Informational Writing Structures
1	supporting details	bulleted list, numbered offset list, numbered inset list
2	paragraph topic	question and answer, problem and solution, **comparison**, evaluative, **causal explanation**, consequential explanation
3	section topic	factorial explanation, fact stream

Note. The three type 2 structures shown in boldface may improperly be conflated by middle grade teachers and students. As will become clear in the following discussion, these three structures differ significantly from the compare-contrast essay, point-counterpoint essay, and cause-effect essay, respectively.

these structures communicate information about a paragraph topic in systematic ways. The other structures shown in the table, identified as type 1 or 3 structures, communicate information about smaller or larger units of meaning (e.g., supporting details or section topics).

Type 1 Informational Writing Structures

Type 1 informational writing structures include the bulleted list, numbered offset list, and numbered inset list structures. These writing structures communicate information about the smallest units of meaning—supporting details.

1. Bulleted list structure

The bulleted list structure communicates information about supporting details in a bulleted vertical list. Bulleted lists like the example below are typically introduced by a complete sentence and colon; appear at the end of paragraphs; and present details simply using key words.

A bulleted list appears in chapter 13 of the geography textbook. Section 3D in that chapter identifies some of the ways that West and Central African leaders are working to improve the quality of life for native Africans in the region. The bulleted list appears in the first paragraph in the section "An Eye Toward the Future." This first paragraph focuses on the goal of regional development. Two main ideas are presented in the paragraph, encapsulated by the key words *promoters* and *factors*. Details about the second main idea, a set of factors that will lead to the goal of regional development, are identified using the bulleted list structure.

> The African Union, along with many foreign aid agencies, has identified these key factors in getting rid of poverty and promoting development in Africa:
> - democracy
> - women's rights
> - development of infrastructure
> - development of social services (such as education and health care) (Chu et al. 2011, 523)

2. Numbered offset list structure

The numbered offset list structure communicates information about supporting details in an offset vertical list numbered 1–n. Numbered offset lists are typically introduced by a complete sentence and colon; appear at the end of paragraphs; and present details using key word phrases or complete sentences of varying lengths. These lists typically provide more expansive information about a main idea than bulleted lists.

No such lists appear in the texts selected by Mrs. Touré for her unit on Africa. In other geography units or in other middle grade social studies courses, students may encounter such lists in assigned texts, most likely in assigned articles. Numbered offset lists rarely appear in middle grade social studies textbooks published by Pearson. None of these lists appear in the geography textbook or *myWorld American History* textbook (Davidson, Stoff, and Bertolet 2019).

Four numbered offset lists do appear in the *Civics* textbook (Davis, Fernlund, and Woll 2009), all in the unit on the government and the economy; and two of these are shown below, the first partially, the second fully:

First Numbered Offset List Example

Below are six reasons that the government has become involved in our economy.

1. *Businesses have sometimes earned profits unfairly.* Some businesses have driven competitors out of business or made secret agreements with competitors to fix prices at high levels. Some have also deceived consumers through false or misleading advertising.
2. *Working conditions have sometimes been unsafe and inhumane.* Workers have sometimes been badly treated. Some have been required to work long hours for low pay. Others have had to use dangerous machinery or chemicals without protection (Davis, Fernlund, and Woll 2009, 431; italics in the original).

Second Numbered Offset List Example

To do so, the government sets an economic stabilization policy. It reflects three economic goals:

1. To promote economic growth
2. To maintain stable prices
3. To ensure full employment (Davis, Fernlund, and Woll 2009, 498)

These two lists appear in chapters 16 and 18, respectively. Chapter 16 focuses on the government's role in the economy and chapter 18 on public finance. The first list consists of six numbered items. Each item identifies a specific reason for the government's involvement in the economy and includes additional details about the identified reason. All six items are similarly structured: reason statement + expansion sentences. The second list consists of three numbered items—three goal statement predicates. The list provides details about the government's economic stabilization policy, its goals.

3. Numbered inset list structure

The numbered inset list structure is a second type of numbered list. In contrast to the type 1 numbered offset list, this type 2 numbered inset list communicates information about 2–n supporting details within one or more paragraphs. Each detail or group of detail sentences is commonly headed with an ordinal number word (e.g., first, second), but may also be headed with the words *one* and *another*. Like type 1 structures, numbered inset lists are typically introduced by a complete sentence and colon.

Numbered inset lists appear in all of Mrs. Touré's assigned texts about Africa. One such list appears in the article about Namibia. Shown below, this list spans two paragraphs and consists of two numbered groups of supporting details identified by the ordinal number words *first* and *secondly*. The two paragraphs focus on the centrality (importance and priority) of land issues in Namibian politics (the paragraph topic). The two-part reason (two basic facts) for the political prioritization of land issues (the main idea) is expanded upon in the numbered inset list.

> As a result, today, "land is a central issue in Namibian politics and, in order to grasp this," says the Dutch/UNDP study of 2005, "two basic facts need to be explained: the first is that about 40% of land in Namibia is commercial, surveyed and fenced land and is overwhelmingly in the hands of a white minority [including absentee European landowners who live permanently in Germany, Italy and elsewhere].
>
> "Secondly, 45% of the Namibian population lives on about 7% of the territory's surface, situated mostly in the north of the country. Most land there is not surveyed and fenced, and it is held by individuals with large residential communal rights." (Ankomah 2015, 12; quotation marks in original)

Type 2 Informational Writing Structures

Type 2 informational writing structures include the question and answer, problem and solution, comparison, evaluative, causal explanation, and consequential explanation structures. All of these writing structures communicate information about paragraph topics.

4. Question and answer structure

The question and answer structure presents a paragraph topic in the form of a question, whose answer follows in the same or subsequent paragraph. The question in this structure may be a WH-type question beginning with the word *who*, *what*, *when*, *where*, *why*, or *how*. Or it may be a YES/NO-type question beginning with the word *is*, *do/does*, or *have* in the present, past, or future tense, a speculative word like *can* or *would*, or an appraisal word like *should*. The answer to the posed question may be stated directly or, as in the forthcoming example, indirectly.

Mrs. Touré's students will encounter a question and answer structure in the *National Geographic* article about trophy hunting. The last section of this article consists of seven paragraphs. In five of these paragraphs—paragraphs 1 and 4–7—the writer concludes his firsthand account of the killing of an old bull elephant during a 12-day elephant hunt in southern Africa. This account is interrupted by a question and answer structure spanning paragraphs 2–3.

In paragraph 1, the trophy hunters close in on their target, an old bull elephant; and in paragraph 2, shown below, the writer interposes a question about the impact of killing old bull elephants. This interposed question is answered in paragraph 3 by a biologist with expertise on elephants, whom the writer likely interviewed after the 12-day hunt.

> Would killing an old bull like this one help save all those other elephants in Nyae Nyae?
> Old bulls, says Caitlin O'Connell, a biologist and elephant researcher focused on how the animals communicate, are a font of wisdom, deciding when and where the herd will move in search of water, imposing an order on pachyderm society. "Contrary to myth, elephant bulls are very social creatures," she says. "They move in groups of up to 15, and they maintain a strict hierarchy. The older bulls exert a very important regulatory impact on the herd and an emotional-social influence on the younger bulls." Younger bulls in musth, a heightened state of aggression during which testosterone levels can be 10 times as high as normal, will be more likely to fight each other when an older bull is absent. (Paterniti 2017, 99)

The writer essentially asks the expert in paragraph 2 if killing old bulls positively impacts elephant herds; and the expert answers him indirectly no, killing old bulls has the opposite impact. In his response to the writer's question, the expert provides details about the important role that older bulls play in elephant herds and special knowledge they possess, and implies that without them, the safety of the herd is actually threatened.

5. Problem and solution structure

The problem and solution structure presents or restates a paragraph topic as a problem whose solution and solution details follow in the same or subsequent paragraph. This structure is signaled explicitly or implicitly: it may be signaled explicitly by the words *problem* and *solution* or signaled implicitly by synonyms for the word *problem* (e.g., challenge, difficulty) or synonyms for the words *solution* or *solved* (e.g., resolved, combated). The structure may also be implied by the negation of a topic sentence, as illustrated by the forthcoming example.

Mrs. Touré's students will regularly encounter problem and solution structures in their course textbook. One of these structures appears in chapter 13, section 1E. In this section of the chapter, students will read about the problem of disease in many parts of West and Central Africa.

Section 1E consists of five paragraphs. The problem and solution structure, shown below, spans the last three paragraphs. The structure is signaled explicitly by the word *problem* in the section heading, "The Problem of Disease." It is then signaled implicitly in paragraph 3 by the negation of the paragraph topic in the second sentence: people *cannot* afford to protect themselves from some diseases (problem). A solution to this problem follows in subsequent paragraphs and is explicitly signaled by the word *combat* in paragraph 5.

> Some diseases are both treatable and preventable, Sadly, many people in this region cannot afford to take even the simplest measures to protect themselves.
> Nigerian doctor Emmanuel Miri visits rural villages to educate communities on disease prevention and treatment.
> Local education programs like Miri's are helping to combat many diseases.
> (Chu et al. 2011, 511)

6. Comparison structure

The comparison structure presents details about the similarities and differences between two topics. The structure spans one or two paragraphs and aims to help readers to clarify their understandings about two topics that might easily be confused or conflated. Topics are explicitly identified, and their similarities presented first. The structure may be signaled explicitly by the words *similarities* and *differences* or signaled implicitly by synonyms for or derivations of the words *similarity* (e.g., similar, same, like) or *difference* (e.g., different, dissimilar, dissimilarity).

A comparison structure appears in chapter 14, section 1B in the geography textbook. In the first two paragraphs of this section, Mrs. Touré's students will read about the similarities and differences between ecosystems in two African regions. Students are already knowledgeable about the West and Central African ecosystem, having read about it in chapter 13, and now will use this knowledge to read and learn about the southern and eastern ecosystem in chapter 14.

The comparison structure in chapter 14, section 1B is shown below. The structure spans two paragraphs and focuses on the topic of regional ecosystems. The topic key word *ecosystems* and specific regional names appear in the section heading "Patterns of Ecosystems" and the first sentence of paragraph 1, respectively.

Similarities between the regions' ecosystems are presented in paragraph 1, signaled by the word *like*, and focus on details about equatorial span, the proximity of the Sahara Desert in the north, seasonal precipitation, and wind patterns. Differences follow in paragraph 2, signaled by the word *different*, and focus on details about elevation, temperature, and precipitation.

> Like West and Central Africa, Southern and Eastern Africa lie on both sides of the Equator. This region also has the Sahara in the north and wetter regions near the Equator. Wind patterns that cause seasonal rains in West and Central Africa also affect this region.
>
> However, there is a major difference between the two regions. Many parts of Southern and Eastern Africa have a higher elevation, or height, than West and Central Africa. This height means that areas near the Equator are less hot and wet than similar areas in West and Central Africa. For example, even though Mount Kilimanjaro and Mount Kenya are near the Equator, they are so high that snow caps their peaks year-round. (Chu et al. 2011, 532)

7. Evaluative structure

The evaluative structure offers two perspectives on the same thing, one perspective focusing on positive aspects and the other on negative aspects. The structure recognizes that most things in the world have positive and negative values and aims to answer the two-prong question: What is positive (helpful) about this topic, and what is negative (harmful)?

Evaluative structures typically span two paragraphs. The evaluated thing (i.e., evaluated topic) is explicitly identified in the first paragraph. Positive and negative evaluations (evaluative details) follow in the same or succeeding paragraph. Evaluative structures are signaled explicitly by words like *help*, *helpful*, *harm*, *harmful*, or *hurt*. Negative evaluations may also be signaled implicitly by words with negative connotations like the word *dangerous* (see example below). Transitions from one set of values to another (positive to negative or negative to positive) may be signaled by an adversative conjunction like *but*, *yet*, *on the other hand*, or *however*.

Mrs. Touré's students will encounter evaluative structures periodically in their course textbook. One of these structures appears in chapter 14, section 1C, "Riches from the Land." This section focuses on the economy in southern and eastern Africa, its mineral resources, mining, and farming. The evaluative structure shown below appears midway through the section and presents information about the positive and negative aspects of mining in the region.

> Mining helps countries like South Africa and Botswana build strong economies. It brings jobs to local people and it yields products to sell to people abroad. However, miners often work for long hours in poor conditions. Some underground mines are very dangerous. Many miners have lost their lives when mines collapsed or other accidents occurred.

Mining can also hurt the environment. Some types of mining leave large scars on the land. Mining can cause pollution. Air and water can be polluted when minerals are processed and when fuel is burned to run drills. (Chu et al. 2011, 534–35)

In this structure, positive aspects about mining are presented first, followed by negative aspects. Three positive aspects about mining are identified: mining builds stable economies, creates jobs for local people, and yields products for export. Two groups of negative aspects follow: mining is dangerous for miners (long hours, dangerous conditions, frequent accidents, loss of life), and it damages the environment (scars the land, causes water and air pollution).

The structure spans two paragraphs and is signaled explicitly by the words *help* and *hurt*. The evaluated topic, mining, is identified explicitly at the outset, and the transition from one set of values to the other (positive to negative) is signaled by the conjunction *however*.

8. Causal explanation structure

The causal explanation structure provides succinct details about the cause of an identified phenomenon. Causal explanations in the social sciences focus on social phenomena as opposed to those in the natural sciences, which focus on natural phenomena. One or several interrelated social phenomena (the paragraph topic) are explicitly identified in these structures, and the structure is signaled explicitly by the word *explain*, *because*, or *cause*. Causal explanations may span one or more sentences in a paragraph, are typically limited to a single paragraph, and may include multiple causes.

A causal explanation structure focusing on two interrelated social phenomena, high unemployment and poverty rates, appears in the first section of the Namibian article, "The History [of Land Ownership]." Shown below, the structure spans one full paragraph and is signaled by the words *explain* and *because*.

This explains the high unemployment and poverty rate in the country, because without any land of their own, the majority black population cannot be self-employed farmers; they have to be necessarily employed either in commercial agriculture or in the formal sector where jobs are not easy to come by. (Ankomah 2015, 12)

This explanatory structure is preceded by a sequence of paragraphs that provides two important statistical facts about landownership in Namibia and additional information about commercial agriculture. In these preceding paragraphs, readers first learn that 40 percent of the land is owned by absentee European landowners who use the land commercially (statistical fact 1), that

45 percent of Namibians occupy just 7 percent of Namibia's total territory (statistical fact 2), and that employment opportunities in the commercial agriculture sector are limited (additional information).

The explanatory structure then connects this information causally to the social phenomena of high rates of unemployment and poverty in Namibia, stating indirectly that these high rates of unemployment and poverty are caused by limited opportunities for native Namibians, one, to own land and earn a living by farming, and two, to find work that enables them to support themselves and their families.

9. Consequential explanation structure

The consequential explanation structure provides details about the effects of a particular action. The structure may be signaled explicitly by the word *effect* or *consequence* or a related word like *outcome, response, reaction*, or *repercussion*. More often than not, however, the structure is signaled implicitly by its elements, which include a precipitating action (action A→), actors and reactors, and a resulting action (action →B^{1-n}). Consequential explanation structures may span one or more paragraphs.

The consequential explanation structure shown below appears in chapter 4 of the specialized book about Kenya. The structure spans one full paragraph and is signaled implicitly by a precipitating action (some Kenyan communities resisted foreign rule), actors (native Kenyans, the Nandi and Giriama communities), reactors (British rulers, British soldiers), and a resulting action that focuses on death, loss of personal and communal possessions, loss of self-governance, and subjection to foreign laws.

> While some Kenyan communities reached peaceful agreements with the British, others fought foreign rule. During the 1890s and early 1900s, the Nandi, who lived in the western Rift Valley, resisted the British. So did the Giriama, who lived along the coast. To punish the Nandi for resisting the British takeover, British soldiers killed thousands of men and seized most of their livestock. They and other peoples lost their land to the British, as well as their political independence. Kenya officially became a colony under the control of the British. Local communities had to follow the laws created for them in Great Britain, rather than running their own affairs. (Burgan 2015, 52–53)

Type 3 Informational Writing Structures

Type 3 informational writing structures include the factorial explanation and fact stream structures. Both of these writing structures communicate information about section topics.

10. Factorial explanation structure

The factorial explanation structure provides information about several or more factors that contributed to a particular state or situation. The structure may be signaled explicitly by the word *factor* but is most often signaled implicitly by the delineation of factors that contributed to a state or situation identified at the outset. Factorial explanations typically span two or more paragraphs and often span whole sections of text.

A factorial explanation structure, too long to reproduce here, appears in chapter 13, section 3A in the geography textbook. The structure is signaled implicitly; spans the whole section, seven paragraphs in all; identifies a particular situation in paragraph 1 (the present poor state of the economy in West and Central African countries), and delineates three contributing factors in paragraphs 2–7 (colonialism, corruption, and poor-quality farmland).

11. Fact stream structure

The fact stream structure communicates a set of facts about a section topic in a single paragraph. Fact stream paragraphs like the example below consist of a simple stream (or flow) of facts—fact statements—about an identified section topic. Fact stream structures are signaled implicitly by the presence of fact statements and absence of a paragraph topic, main ideas, and supporting details, and largely appear in textbooks.

The fact stream structure shown below, whose facts are identified for illustrative purposes, appears in chapter 14, section 3A in the geography textbook. This section 3A fact stream paragraph presents current information about ethnic groups that reside in southern and eastern Africa. The information presented in the paragraph consists of some basic facts about these ethnic groups as well as information about the languages spoken in the region and regional religious practices.

> Some ethnic groups live in a single country [fact 1]. Others stretch across borders [fact 2]. Few countries are made up a single ethnic group [fact 3]. Some of the largest groups are the Zulu and Xhosa, who live in South Africa; the Kikuyu in Kenya; and the Hutu and Tutsi in Rwanda [fact 4]. In the past, different ethnic groups lived different lifestyles [fact 5]. For example, the Maasai, in Kenya and Tanzania, herded cattle [fact 5 example]. The Baganda in Uganda farmed and lived in large villages [fact 5 example]. However, today many people in the region live in cities [fact 6]. They no longer make a living in the ways that their ancestors did [fact 7]. (Chu et al. 2011, 544)

This fact stream structure includes seven fact statements. These facts flow from the section heading "Ethnic Groups" and focus on the residential location of regional ethnic groups (facts 1–2), the largest ethnic groups (facts 3–4), lifestyle differences (facts 5), residential relocations (fact 6), and lifestyle changes (fact 7).

Reading for Understanding and Text-Building Knowledge

In their assigned unit texts about Africa, Mrs. Touré's sixth grade students will encounter all but one of the informational writing structures delineated above, all but the numbered offset list structure. In middle grade social studies courses, students like Mrs. Touré's are best positioned to extract essential meanings from assigned course texts if they readily recognize the informational writing structures they encounter during reading and extract the intended meanings conveyed by these structures.

Proficient middle grade readers shift quickly and flexibly from one mode of meaning extraction to another while reading informational texts. They shift from their primary mode of meaning extraction, whose focus is the identification of a paragraph topic and main ideas, to a secondary mode, whose focus aligns with the intended meanings conveyed by a particular type of informational writing structure encountered in a text. For example, when encountering a causal explanation structure in a course textbook, proficient readers shift their meaning extraction focus from the identification of a paragraph topic and main ideas to an identified social phenomenon and explanatory details about the cause of this phenomenon.

Reading for Understanding and Auxiliary Paragraph Structures

Mrs. Touré's students will encounter two additional structures in their assigned unit texts: the embedded glossary structure and example structure. These two auxiliary paragraph structures convey information that helps readers to consolidate their understandings about a paragraph topic or main idea. Mrs. Touré's students will encounter both structures in their course textbook and the example structure in assigned supplementary texts. Embedded glossary and example structures may span one or more sentences.

Embedded glossary structures appear regularly in the geography textbook. Fifteen of these structures appear in chapter 14 alone. These structures identify a term that readers need to know to understand a paragraph topic or main idea, then explain the term in a brief interlinear note—a gloss. Glossed terms in chapter 14 include common nouns (e.g., ecotourism, apartheid) and proper nouns (e.g., Boers, African National Congress). Some of these glossed terms are identified as "key terms" at the beginning of all three sections in the chapter.

Embedded glosses are located within paragraphs and provide definitional, conceptual, or descriptive information about important terms that appear in boldface and yellow highlighting. Three examples from chapter 14 in the geography textbook follow. Definitional information is provided for the first glossed term, conceptual information for the second, and descriptive information for the third:

> However, **poaching**, or illegal hunting, is still a problem. (Chu et al. 2011, 533)

> Some [Kikuyu] began a movement called **Mau Mau** that decided to use force to end British rule in Kenya more quickly. (Chu et al. 2011, 542)

> One of Southern and Eastern Africa's unique features is the **Great Rift Valley**. This is a long, unusually flat area of land between areas of higher ground in Eastern Africa. (Chu et al. 2011, 530)

Example structures (i.e., examples) appear in each type of informational text selected by Mrs. Touré for her study of Africa. Examples appear in the course textbook, several articles, and both excerpted chapters from the specialized books about South Africa and Kenya. Most of these examples are signaled explicitly by the phrase *for example, for instance*, or *such as*, as illustrated by the following examples:

> Governments are making serious efforts to fight AIDS. For example, the Ugandan government sends text messages on mobile phones to educate people about the epidemic. (Chu et al. 2011, 549)

> Instead of dealing peacefully with their differences, the ruling government treated opposing leaders harshly. For instance in 1969, Tom Mboya, a popular leader and early supporter of independence, was assassinated. (Burgan 2015, 59–60)

> In South Africa and other countries, people grow many crops. They run large commercial farms or plantations. These farms grow crops such as sugarcane, cotton, avocados, and tropical fruits. (Chu et al. 2011, 535)

Goal-oriented and Purposeful Meaning Extraction

Proficient readers' efforts to extract essential meanings from assigned texts during reading are goal-oriented and purposeful. That is, their efforts to read for understanding are guided by a conscious effort to achieve their ultimate reading goal—of understanding the main ideas in a text and being able to use these ideas at a later date—and a conscious effort to achieve a specific topic-related reading purpose clarified before reading.

Similarly, Mrs. Touré's students are best positioned to extract essential meanings from assigned unit texts by consciously aiming to achieve their ultimate reading goal and specific topic-related reading purposes. When reading the Namibia article, for example, Mrs. Touré's students will be optimally positioned to extract essential meanings from the text by consciously aiming to achieve their ultimate reading goal and to extract essential meanings about landownership and the status of land negotiations between Namibians and their government, the article's topic.

INFERENCING

Statements and Target Questions

As noted earlier in this chapter, the identification of paragraph topics and main ideas in informational texts can be easy or challenging. When specific key words appear in a paragraph and signal a paragraph topic or main idea, the identification of a paragraph topic or main idea is relatively easy. But when key words are obscure or absent in a paragraph, as they frequently are in informational texts, the identification of a paragraph topic or main idea can be challenging.

In this second case, proficient readers make targeted inferences about key sentences in a paragraph in order to identify a paragraph topic or main idea. To make an inference means to reason from one thing to another (*OED Online* 2018). In the during reading phase of assigned school reading events, making inferences centers on the extraction of essential meanings from understated ideas in assigned texts. In this book, the during reading action of making inferences is delimited to the identification of paragraph topics and main ideas from obscure or absent paragraph topic or main idea key words.

This section addresses the following questions:

- How do middle grade students identify paragraph topics through inferencing?
- How do students identify main ideas through inferencing?
- How many words will students draw on in a paragraph to infer a paragraph topic, and where are these words typically located in a paragraph?

Paragraph Topic Inferencing

Many paragraph topics in the texts selected by Mrs. Touré for her sixth grade study of Africa are challenging to identify. In the specialized books and articles about Kenya, South Africa, Namibia, and Rwanda, many paragraph topic key words are obscure or absent. In order for Mrs. Touré's students to identify paragraph topics in such cases, they must infer relevant paragraph topic key words from key sentences in a paragraph at large and use these words to identify a paragraph topic. How do students accomplish this?

Paragraph topic inferencing is required for all three paragraphs in chapter 4, section G in the specialized book about South Africa. This same stretch of text was used earlier in this chapter to illustrate the two-way flow of meaning and easy identification of main ideas in informational texts. All but one main idea communicated in this stretch of text are easily identified, while all three paragraph topics, shown in outline form below, must be inferred. Let's look closely at the first two paragraphs in this section in terms of paragraph topic inferencing:

G. South Africa unions: 1910–1930

1. Union formations
2. Legislative restrictions on native South Africans
3. Living conditions for native South Africans

1. Paragraph 1: Union formations
(1) By the early twentieth century, Great Britain controlled much of the land that makes up what is now South Africa. (2) In 1910, Britain brought together four of the colonies in the region—Natal, Free State, Orange, and Transvaal—to **form** the **Union** of South Africa. (4) Full citizenship was limited mostly to whites. (5) A small number of black and Coloureds [*sic*] in the Cape had the right to vote, but the vast majority of blacks were denied the vote. (6) In 1912, black South Africans created the African National Congress (ANC) to fight for full citizenship. (Blauer and Lauré 2013, 53)

The topic of paragraph 1, union formations, is challenging to identify for four reasons. First, the paragraph topic key words *form* and *Union* appear in the second sentence rather than the first. Second, the first key word, *form*, must be transformed into a plural noun, *formations* (i.e., to form, form → formation + *s*). Third, the second key word, *union*, a common noun with a general meaning, must be derived from a proper noun, Union, whose meaning is specific. Fourth, the paragraph topic key words *form* and *Union* overlap with two of four main idea key words in this same sentence and clause (i.e., form, Union, South Africa).

To identify the topic of paragraph 1, union formations, students must: identify sentence 2 as a key sentence in the paragraph, a sentence that implicitly functions as the topic sentence in the paragraph; focus on two words in sentence 2, *form* and *Union*; transform the word *form* into *formations*; use their conceptual knowledge about nouns to identify the common noun *union* as a paragraph topic key word; and approach paragraph topic inferencing with the understanding that paragraph topic key words and main idea key words may overlap at times.

> 2. Paragraph 2: Legislative restrictions on native South Africans
> (1) The land's white rulers **legalized** the separation of whites and blacks. (2) In 1913, they enacted the Natives' Land Act. (3) This act **restricted** the areas of land that could be owned by black **South Africans**, who were referred to as "**natives**." (4) Blacks were not allowed to own land in most of the country, including all of the cities. (5) These were declared to be for the exclusive use of whites. (6) Blacks could only enter the cities to work for whites. (7) Otherwise, they were confined to crowded black townships. (8) In 1936, whites controlled 93 percent of the land. (9) They passed laws that eventually provided 13 percent of the land to blacks, who outnumbered whites by seven to one. (10) The land that blacks were allowed to own was the least useful: it was worst for growing crops. (Blauer and Lauré 2013, 53–54).

The topic of paragraph 2, legislative restrictions on native South Africans, is even more challenging to identify than the topic of paragraph 1, and there are five reasons for this. First, the paragraph topic key words *legalized, restricted, South Africans,* and *native* are distributed across three sentences in the paragraph, not just the first two sentences. Second and third, five key words are needed to identify the paragraph topic, and these words must be strategically grouped to render the noun groups *legislative restrictions* and *native South Africans.*

Fourth, three of the key words must be transformed to render the paragraph topic. The key words *legalized* and *restricted,* both past-tense verbs, must be transformed into an adjective and plural noun, respectively (i.e., legalized → legislative; restricted → restriction + s); and the key word *natives,* a plural noun, must be transformed into a singular noun (i.e., natives → native). The transformation of the key word *legalized* into *legislative* is particularly challenging, as the word *legislative* is not typically perceived as a derivative of the word *legalize* (or legal).

Fifth, many students will likely identify the word *black* as a paragraph topic key word rather than the word *native*. The word *black* (black, blacks) appears in sentences 1, 3–4, 6–7, and 9–10—seven times in all, whereas the word *native* (Natives', "natives") appears in sentences 2–3—only twice. On the whole, however, the paragraph aims to present information about newly enacted laws that restricted native South Africans—indigenous South Africans (the first people of South Africa)—from acquiring legal title to their own lands, their own ancestral lands.

To identify the topic of paragraph 2, legislative restrictions on native South Africans, students must: identify sentences 1 and 3 as key sentences in the paragraph; focus on five key words in these sentences; transform three of these key words into an adjective or noun (singular or plural); reorder and combine the words *native* and *South Africans* to form a single key word noun group; recognize the conceptual importance of the word *native* in the paragraph; and select key words that connect most meaningfully to the important information presented in the paragraph.

Main Idea Inferencing

Many main idea key words are likewise obscure or absent in the set of texts selected by Mrs. Touré for her unit on Africa. For paragraphs with obscure or absent main idea key words, students must infer key words from key sentences in these paragraphs and use these words to identify main ideas.

Main idea inferencing is required about as often as not for the book about South Africa. In chapter 4, section G, "Union Formations," both main ideas are easily identified in paragraph 1, whereas in section H, "Establishing Apartheid," main idea inferencing is required to identify all the main ideas. The easy identification of main ideas for paragraph 1 in section G was discussed earlier in this chapter. A partial outline for section H, paragraph 1 follows. In this paragraph, four main ideas (a–d) must be derived by inferencing. Let's examine each in turn:

H. Establishing Apartheid: 1948
1. New separation law enactment
   a. new lawmakers
   b. new law
   c. purpose of the new law
   d. new rules

1. Paragraph 1: New separation law enactment
(1) In 1948, **the National Party**, which represented the Afrikaners, won the general election. (2) This party quickly set about enacting **laws** to separate all the people in South Africa according to ethnic background. (3) This [new separation law] was called *apartheid*, a word that means separateness. (4) Apartheid was **intended** to separate the races in every aspect of daily life. (5) Beaches, park benches, and water fountains were segregated. (6) Blacks were forced to use separate doors to enter post offices, banks, and other buildings. (7) Apartheid established **rules** for where black people could live, go to school, get medical care, and work. (8) Blacks had to carry

passes to prove they had a job and a legal right to be in a city. (9) They also had to prove they had the right to live in a particular township. (10) The Afrikaners wanted to know exactly where all black South Africans lived. (Blauer and Lauré 2013, 55–56).

Sentences 1, 2, 4, and 7 are key sentences in this paragraph. They contain the main idea key words *the National Party*, *laws*, *intended*, and *rules*, all derived or confirmed by inferencing. The key word *new*, a paragraph topic key word derived by inferencing, repeats in all four main ideas. Its repetition is needed to ensure coherence, the logical and meaningful development of the paragraph topic.

Main idea 1, which includes the absent key word *lawmakers*, is derived from main idea key words in sentences 1–2. The first three key words, *the National Party*, appear as a noun group in sentence 1. The National Party became the new governing (lawmaking) party in South Africa in 1948. The fourth key word, *laws*, appears in sentence 2. As a singular noun, this key word (law) confirms the identification of lawmaking as a main idea key word and functions as a key word for main ideas 2–3.

Main idea 3, which includes the absent key word *purpose*, a noun, is derived from the past participle verb *intended*, which appears in sentence 4. The identification of the key word *purpose*, the best key word for main idea 3, is challenging for at least five reasons.

First, the subject of sentence 4, a thing—apartheid, the new separation law enacted by the new lawmaking party—is ascribed an intention. Intention, however, is not typically ascribed to things (like laws). Instead, second, intention or purpose should be ascribed to the new lawmakers, who—expressly aiming (intending) to separate South Africans, Afrikaners and native South Africans—passed a law that legitimated and legalized this separation.

Third, the noun *purpose* is not readily derived from the verb *intend* or noun *intention* but is more readily derived from the noun/verb *aim*. Fourth, passive sentences like sentence 4 with passive verbs (was intended) are not easily transformed into active sentences with active verbs (intend). Fifth, the restoration of the missing phrase *new separation law* in sentence 3 would make the identification of the key word *purpose* easier.

Main idea 4, which includes the key word *rules*, may be more or less challenging to identify for some of the same reasons given above. In sentence 7, as in sentence 4, the subject is a thing (apartheid, the name of the new separation law), and things are not typically perceived as agential. People (lawmakers) make things (like rules): the new lawmakers passed a law with new rules that restricted native South Africans in numerous ways. On the other hand, a simple transformation of the subject (Apartheid → The new apartheid law) would significantly reduce the challenge of identifying the word *rules* as a main idea key word.

To identify four main ideas in this paragraph, students must: identify four key sentences in the paragraph; focus on six key words in these key sentences; infer main ideas from multiple key words in one or more sentences, plural nouns, inanimate subjects, omitted subject words, a passive verb, and a past participle; and use a paragraph topic key word repeatedly.

Main idea inferencing is also required in chapter 14, section 2D, "The Rise and Fall of Apartheid" in the geography textbook. The last paragraph in this section focuses on the end of apartheid. While the topic of this paragraph (ending apartheid) is easily identified, the main ideas are challenging to identify. The paragraph contains five main ideas, and all must be derived by inferencing. The main ideas include key players, Mandela's role, de Klerk's role, unified action, and apartheid ends.

2. Paragraph 2: Ending apartheid
   (1) One man who **played** a **key role** in ending apartheid was **Nelson Mandela**. (2) He was an ANC leader who was jailed in 1962. (3) He continued to protest from his prison on Robben Island. (4) Another man who **played** a **role** was **F. W. de Klerk**, South Africa's president from 1989 to 1994. (5) Although he was white, de Klerk realized that apartheid was destroying South Africa. (6) In 1990, he released Nelson Mandela from prison. (7) **Together** Mandela and de Klerk **worked** to **end apartheid**. (8) In 1994, South Africans of all races voted together. (9) Mandela became president. (10) South Africa was truly independent. (Chu et al. 2011, 543)

Sentences 1, 4, and 7 are key sentences in this paragraph. They contain 12 main idea key words, including two repeated words and two synonyms, and two initials. Deriving main ideas from these key words and initials requires varying degrees of inferencing.

Main idea 1, key players, is derived from key words in sentences 1 and 4. The repeated key word *played*, a past-tense verb, must be transformed into *players*, a plural noun. The second key word *key*, an adjective that appears in sentence 1 and describes the (instrumental) role played by one native South African man in ending apartheid, must be used instead to describe two South African men—one native South African and one Afrikaner, identified in sentences 1 and 4, respectively—whose united action ended apartheid.

Main ideas 2–3, Mandela's role and de Klerk's role, follow logically from main idea 1 and are derived from the repeated key word *role* in sentences 1 and 4 and the names Nelson Mandela and F. W. de Klerk that first appear in sentences 1 and 4 and subsequently repeat. Only surnames are used as main ideas, and each surname is transformed into the possessive case (*'s*).

Main ideas 4–5, united action and apartheid ends, are derived from four key words that appear in sentence 7. These main ideas are challenging to identify for at least six reasons. First, two main ideas must be derived from one (the same) key sentence. Second, because of the brevity of the key sentence, one or both main ideas may be overlooked (only nine words appear in sentence 7, and four of these are main idea key words!).

Third, main idea 4, united action, a noun group that consists of an adjective (united) and noun (action), must be derived from key words that are neither adjectives nor nouns. One key word is an adverb (together) and the other is a past-tense verb (worked).

Fourth, main idea 5, apartheid ends, is derived from a complex verb group (worked to end), whose primary verb (worked) is used to infer main idea 4, and whose secondary verb (to end) is used to infer main idea 5. Fifth, the secondary verb in this complex verb group (to end) must be transformed into a third-person singular indicative verb (end + s). Sixth, main idea 5 can only be derived by reversing the verb (ends) and object (apartheid).

To identify five main ideas in this paragraph, students must: identify three key sentences in the paragraph; focus on 12 key words and a set of initials in these key sentences; infer main ideas from multiple key words in one or more sentences, a brief key sentence, repeated words, people's names, past-tense verbs, a complex verb group, an infinitive verb, and an adverb.

LOOKING BACK AND AHEAD

During reading, proficient readers engage in six mental actions that enable them to achieve their ultimate reading goal. In addition to visualizing and reading fluently, proficient readers also read for understanding and infer meanings from assigned texts.

Reading for understanding and inferencing involve the ongoing extraction of important information about prominent topics explored in assigned informational texts. During reading, proficient readers engage in purposeful meaning extraction and use their knowledge of words, concepts, and various text-building structures to read for understanding. They also engage in inferencing in order to extract important information from assigned texts, information that is absent or obscure.

During reading, proficient readers also engage in the actions of formulating and building coherence to achieve their ultimate reading goal. These two actions are examined next.

GROUNDING: DURING READING PHASE ACTIONS

This chapter is grounded in vocabulary processes (NRP 2000; Kuhn and Stahl 2013; Nagy and Scott 2013), text structures (Goldman and Rakestraw 2000; Unsworth 2001), text cohesion (Halliday and Matthiessen 2014; Halliday and Hasan 2014), and inferencing (Kintsch 2013; O'Brien, Cook, and Lorch 2017).

6

During Reading Actions III

Mr. Watson, a seventh grade social studies teacher in the West Huntington School District, is completing a master's degree in curriculum and instruction at Huntington Central University. The third course in his program focuses on middle level reading instruction. His course instructor, Dr. Sekibo (pronounced sŭ kē′ bō), is a visiting professor from Lockhart University in Australia, where he teaches middle grade literacy courses in the Graduate School of Education. Dr. Sekibo has taught courses in universities around the world and specializes in text comprehension, text cohesion, and text complexity.

Mr. Watson's midterm assignment focuses mainly on the during reading phase of a middle grade reading event and the action of building coherence. The assignment requires Mr. Watson to select and read two middle grade informational texts on the same topic. One text must come from a social studies textbook and the other a specialized book.

To complete the assignment successfully, Mr. Watson will:

1. *Complete a full set of before reading actions for the text*
2. *Identify the action of building a coherent text as a primary reading purpose*
3. *Read the text continuously for understanding*
4. *Create a two-level web that represents coherent idea development in the text*

Mr. Watson will also complete a written reflection that addresses two questions: What three insights about building a coherent text during reading did you gain from this experience, and how will these insights impact the reading instruction you provide in middle grade social studies courses?

Mr. Watson leafs through an advance copy of the myWorld American History textbook *(Davidson, Stoff, and Bertolet 2019)* and selects unit 7, chapter 3 as his first text. Unit 7 explores sociocultural developments in the 40-year period preceding the Civil War (1820–1860), and chapter 3 focuses specifically on the topic of slavery in the Old South. Mr. Watson's second text, which also focuses on the topic of slavery, is a previously published account of the life and adventures of a runaway slave named Robert Voorhis. This particular narrative is one of 12 that appear in the specialized book The Long Walk to Freedom *(Carbado and Weise 2012).*

Mr. Watson places the history textbook in front of him, opens to unit 7, chapter 3, and clarifies his reading goal aloud. "My ultimate reading goal," he reminds himself, "is to understand the main ideas in the text and be able to use these ideas at a later date." In his course notebook, he records the date, time, and title of this first text, "King Cotton and Life in the South." He leafs through the text quickly, noting each level one heading, then lists four reading objectives for today's first reading event. While reading chapter 3, Mr. Watson aims to:

1. Learn about the cotton industry in the South prior to the Civil War
2. Learn about plantation life from the perspective of slaves
3. Acquire specific terminology related to the plantation system and slavery
4. Build a coherent text

Leaving his notebook open to these four reading objectives, Mr. Watson sets his notebook aside and leafs through the chapter again several times, noting the level two headings, highlighted terminology, section images (photographs, artwork, graphs), paragraph density, and the average paragraph length in each section, A–F. Highlighted key terms in the chapter include the terms cultivate, cash crop, *and* slave codes. *Other important terms not highlighted in the chapter, which Mr. Watson records in his notebook, include the terms* patent, plantation, cotton production, dominate, revolt, expansion, spirituals, rebellion, *and* revenge.

Mr. Watson spends several minutes viewing the chapter's images, thinking aloud about them, and connecting their content to forthcoming ideas he will encounter in the text. He then takes less than a minute to activate his knowledge about the chapter topic. His knowledge of life in the Old South (1820–1860), cotton plantations, and slavery is extensive. He promptly brings to mind his knowledge of the cotton gin, its impact on the cotton industry, and plantation life from the perspective of owners and slaves.

One task remains before Mr. Watson is ready to read the text. He needs to prepare a web that, when added to during reading and ultimately com-

pleted, will represent his understandings about chapter 3 as a coherent whole. At the center of a sheet of white paper, turned sideways, he records the chapter topic KING COTTON & LIFE IN THE SOUTH. During reading, he will stop briefly at the end of each section, A–F and branch out from the central topic coherently and logically. Each brief stop should take less than 10 seconds, he thinks.

His first stop, however, lasts much longer than 10 seconds. More than 10 minutes pass while Mr. Watson attempts to understand the connection between the first section's headings, paragraph topics, and main ideas. Only after rereading the section several times in whole and in part and revising his web does he produce a coherent representation of the ideas presented in section A. His resulting web, shown in figure 6.1, includes the branched first- and second-level ideas cotton kingdom, cotton planting, cotton cleaning, and need for a slave.

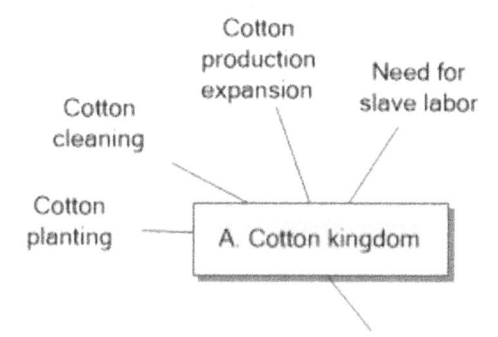

KING COTTON & LIFE IN THE SOUTH

Figure 6.1. Unit 7, Chapter 3A Web

Before moving on, Mr. Watson generates an outline for section A in his notebook. Shown below, this short outline consists of the chapter title (III), level one heading (A), and three level two headings (1–3). He places his section A outline and web side by side and compares them. The differences between these two representations for this same stretch of text astonish him.

III. King Cotton and Life in the South

    A. The South's cotton kingdom

        1. Eli Whitney invents the cotton gin
        2. The cotton kingdom and slavery
        3. How did the North and West promote slavery?

COTTON PLANTATIONS & LIFE IN THE OLD SOUTH

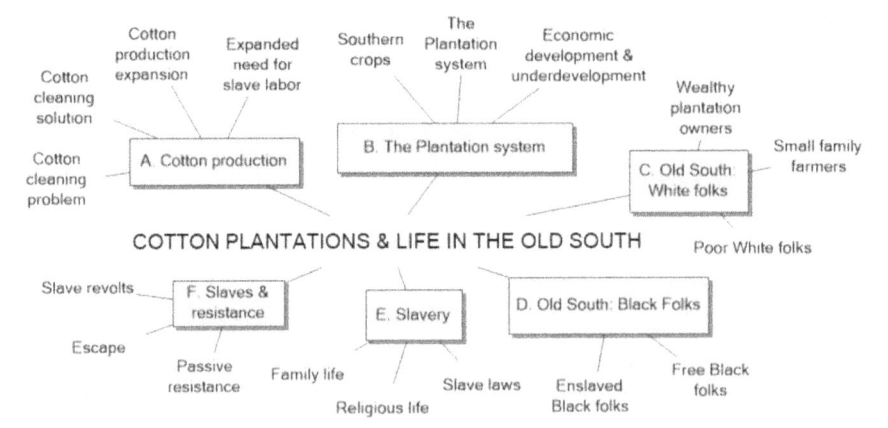

[Concept web with the following nodes and connections:]

- A. Cotton production
  - Cotton cleaning problem
  - Cotton cleaning solution
  - Cotton production expansion
  - Expanded need for slave labor
- B. The Plantation system
  - Southern crops
  - The Plantation system
  - Economic development & underdevelopment
- C. Old South: White folks
  - Wealthy plantation owners
  - Small family farmers
  - Poor White folks
- D. Old South: Black Folks
  - Free Black folks
  - Enslaved Black folks
- E. Slavery
  - Slave laws
  - Family life
  - Religious life
- F. Slaves & resistance
  - Slave revolts
  - Escape
  - Passive resistance

Figure 6.2. Unit 7, Whole Chapter 3 Web

A half hour later, having produced the two whole representations of unit 7, chapter 3 shown in figure 6.2 and textbox 6.1, Mr. Watson is newly astonished by the persistent differences between the branched and outlined ideas in these two representations.

TEXTBOX 6.1.
Unit 7, Whole Chapter 3 Outline

III. King Cotton and Life in the South
    A. The South's cotton kingdom
        1. Eli Whitney invents the cotton gin
        2. The cotton kingdom and slavery
        3. How did the North and West promote slavery?
    B. Reliance on plantation agriculture
        1. Limited southern industry
        2. Southern cities
        3. Economically dependent
    C. What were the characteristics of White Southerner society?
        1. The "Cottonocracy"
        2. Small farmers
        3. Comparing northern and southern whites
    D. What was life like for African Americans in the South?
        1. Free African Americans
        2. Enslaved African Americans
    E. Slavery in the South
        1. Slave codes
        2. Family life
        3. Religion offers hope
    F. How did enslaved African Americans resist their enslavement?

Some weeks later, Mr. Watson listens intently while his university colleagues share their experiences with him and their professor in a retrospective midterm assignment segment focusing on the during reading action of building coherence. When Mr. Watson is called on to share his experiences, he identifies his topic, grade focus, and text (the textbook chapter), then looks directly at his professor and tells him sincerely that his experience was profound.

Mr. Watson distributes copies of his web, "Cotton Plantations and Life in the Old South," points to the first branched level one idea, "Cotton Production," and tells his colleagues candidly that he struggled a good deal with this first section, trying to understand it as a whole. "The headings and paragraphs each made sense to me on their own," says Mr. Watson, "but I couldn't make sense of the section as a whole: it didn't cohere."

Now pointing to the second branched level one idea on his web, he says, "The text started to cohere for me here. As soon as I struck out the level one idea 'Reliance on Cotton' and replaced it with 'Plantation System' (which already appeared on my web as a level two idea), the text started to make sense to me. That was my first insight: that the section headings were getting in the way, making it harder for me to build a coherent text."

"Paradoxically so," interjects his professor, "as all of you noted in your reflections."

"My second insight is harder to share, harder to put into words," says Mr. Watson in a softer tone, glancing down at his web. A moment later he continues. "I completed this web at my dining room table. I had just finished transferring it to a clean sheet of paper and was checking it for accuracy. Then I put my draft aside and looked closely at my finished product, this one, the web you have in front of you. I followed the branched ideas outward from the center, round my web clockwise, and suddenly felt an overwhelming sense of—what I can only describe as a sense of—wholeness."

Mr. Watson glances at his web again, is silent for a moment, then continues, "I never felt that way before about a text, least of all a textbook chapter, and am astonished that I did. I never thought about a textbook chapter or any of my assigned course texts being whole or my students gaining whole understandings about the texts I assign. It never occurred to me to think about that."

Dr. Sekibo looks directly at Mr. Watson and nods his head.

"Ordinarily, for a textbook chapter like this," continues Mr. Watson, "I introduce the text, talk about it briefly, and assign a few questions for homework. I've always focused on several major ideas presented in the text, usually two or three. And my students rightly predict that similar questions to the ones they respond to for homework will appear on a forthcoming test."

Mr. Watson pauses briefly then continues. "That's the thing," he says. "I've never given my students the opportunity to experience a whole text as I did for this assignment, having created this web. I've focused too narrowly on parts of the texts at the expense of the whole and students' whole understandings about a text. I need to give my students the opportunity to understand a text as fully as I understand the text reflected here in this remarkable web."

INTRODUCTION: DURING READING PHASE ACTIONS

Proficient readers engage in six coordinated mental actions during reading. Four of these actions were explored at length in preceding chapters. These first four actions include visualizing, reading fluently, reading for understanding, and inferencing. This chapter focuses on the last two during reading actions, of formulating and building coherence.

Like the actions of reading for understanding and inferencing, discussed in chapter 5, the actions of formulating and building coherence essentially focus on meanings: one on smaller units of meaning and the other on larger units of meaning.

Additional chapters from the *myWorld American History* textbook (Davidson, Stoff, and Bertolet 2019), the same textbook used by Mr. Watson in the opening vignette, are featured in this chapter. All these chapters appear in unit 7, "Society and Culture Before the Civil War." This chapter also features chapters from two specialized books and an autobiography: *The Rise and Fall of American Slavery* (McNeese and Gates 2004), *Our Song, Our Toil: The Story of American Slavery as Told by Slaves* (Stepto 1994), and *Thirty Years a Slave* (Hughes 1897).

FORMULATING

Statements and Target Questions

During reading, while reading for understanding, all of us continuously register important ideas encountered in a text. That is, all of us note particular ideas that strike us as important. As we read on, this cache of ideas changes and grows and at some point takes the shape of a text. That is, all of us use our cache of ideas to formulate a tentative text. The action of formulating refers to the during reading process of producing a tentative text from cached ideas.

This section addresses the following questions:

- How can a text taking shape in a reader's head be represented?
- When, during reading, do readers first begin to register ideas encountered in a text?

- Do readers register more ideas from some paragraphs than others?
- Are readers more likely to register nouns than verbs during reading?
- Do readers register adjectives and adverbs during reading?
- What role do section headings play in the action of formulating a text?

Formulating a Text: "King Cotton and Life in the South"

Mr. Watson's midterm assignment in the opening vignette, whose primary focus was the action of building a coherent text, might also have focused in part on the action of formulating a text. The assignment might have included, for example, an initial set of tasks that required Mr. Watson to read the first few pages of a text and record the ideas that struck him as important. Had he done this for chapter 3: "King Cotton and Life in the South," in the *myWorld American History* textbook (Davidson, Stoff, and Bertolet 2019, hereafter referred to as the history textbook) and read to the end of the first section in this text, he might have produced the cache of ideas shown in table 6.1.

Table 6.1. Cached Ideas for Section A in "King Cotton and Life in the South"

§	¶	Cached Ideas	Note
	1	cotton plantations + slave system +	introductory ¶
A	2	increased demand + cleaning cotton +	introductory ¶
A1	3		
	4	cotton gin +	
	5	economic growth +	
A2	6		
	7		
	8		
	9	(cotton) belt +	
	10	(spreading) slavery +	
A3	11	slave labor +	

Nine ideas from section A in Mr. Watson's history textbook chapter "King Cotton and Life in the South" appear in table 6.1. Two of these ideas are encountered in introductory paragraphs and the others in paragraphs 4–5 and 9–11. Most of these ideas appear in the table exactly as they do in the text, verbatim. Economic growth, for example, appears in the table exactly as it does in paragraph 5: "As a result, this new technology [the cotton gin] brought economic growth" (Davidson, Stoff, and Bertolet 2019, 432).

Two ideas, however, appear in a qualified form in table 6.1. These two ideas, belt and slavery, whose sentence contexts are shown below, are encountered in paragraphs 9 and 10 and rendered more substantive when qualified by the words *cotton* and *spread[ing]*, both of which are present in the original sentence context and shown parenthetically in the table.

By the 1850s, cotton plantations extended in a belt from South Carolina to Texas. (Davidson, Stoff, and Bertolet 2019, 432)

Tragically, as the Cotton Kingdom spread, so did slavery. (Davidson, Stoff, and Bertolet 2019, 432)

The action of formulating a text may be represented in a tabular form, as in table 6.1, or in a linear form, as shown below. In a linear representation, each notable idea encountered in a text is added in turn to an evolving cache of ideas whose final formulation may or may not reflect the development of major ideas within or across paragraphs or a text's essential meanings. An addition symbol (+) appears before each newly cached idea.

cotton plantations + slave system + increased demand + cleaning cotton + cotton gin + economic growth + (cotton) belt + (spreading) slavery + slave labor

Formulating Texts: Two Book Chapter Representations

Let's suppose that Mr. Watson did in fact produce the two representations above for his history textbook chapter "King Cotton and Life in the South" as part of his midterm assignment for Dr. Sekibo, then in a follow-up assignment produced linear representations for several book chapters he plans to use in a forthcoming seventh grade study of American slavery and abolitionism. One chapter comes from the specialized book *The Rise and Fall of American Slavery* (McNeese and Gates 2004) and the other a biography, *Thirty Years a Slave* (Hughes 1897).

First Book Chapter Representation: "The Slave Trade"

The first eight paragraphs in chapter 2 of "The Slave Trade," from *The Rise and Fall of American Slavery* (McNeese and Gates 2004), are reproduced below. This stretch of text includes an introductory paragraph and two full sections of the chapter. The underlined ideas were noted and cached by Mr. Watson as he engaged in the during reading action of formulating (a text).

THE SLAVE TRADE

Slavery—an <u>economic system</u> in which people own other people as property—is an extremely <u>old institution</u>. People in ancient cultures, living thousands of years go, kept people as slaves. From Egypt to Sumeria; Babylonia to Assyria; Persia to India; classical Greece to imperial Rome, slavery was a <u>system of labor</u>. While many people today think of slavery as something associated with black Africans, ancient slaves came from any and <u>all races</u> and ethnic groups. By the time of the Middle Ages, a new type of slavery was being created. This system of forced labor was the beginning of black African slavery.

Slavery in the New World

Fifty years before Christopher Columbus discovered the Americas in 1492, Portuguese seamen were cautiously establishing trade connections with African coastal ports. Typically, these Portuguese explorers and traders were seeking such precious items as gold, ivory, and spices. But they soon realized the value and availability of black slaves. In 1441, a Portuguese seaman, Antam Goncalvez, carried two West Africans back to his homeland as a gift to a local prince. This opened the door for a "raid and trade" system of removing Africans from their homelands and shipping them off to labor in communities in Europe or European-controlled islands in the Mediterranean and the eastern Atlantic. During the 1440s, the black slave trade between Africa and Europe took root.

Many of the African slaves the Portuguese brought to Europe were put to work on sugar plantations. By the 1500s, sugar production had become an important part of the economy of Portuguese islands in the Atlantic. Because sugar production required great amounts of labor, the number of African slaves continued to rise.

Beginning with Columbus's first voyage in 1492, Europeans were slowly introduced to the New World, which consisted of North America, South America, and the Caribbean. Sugar production spread to the New World and encouraged the expansion of slavery at an even greater pace. Soon, cane production was one of the most important parts of the European economic system in the Americas. The climate and soil of Brazil proved ideal to sugar production. Later, production developed in the Caribbean.

European Competition for Colonies

The first African slaves were imported to the New World within a decade of Columbus's 1492 voyage to America. By 1600, twenty-five thousand African slaves were working and dying on sugar plantations from Cuba to Hispaniola to Brazil. Such slaves represented a cheap labor force for the Spanish and Portuguese colonizers in the Americas. The labor required of the average African field hand on sugar plantations and in sugar mills was extremely strenuous. Most Africans died only four or five years after their delivery to the New World. Sugar planters had to buy new slaves to replace those who died. But the profits from sugar were so high the slave owners could afford to buy new workers. After all, the owners were not paying the slaves for their work.

For the first century of African slavery in the Americas, the Portuguese controlled much of the human trade system. While the Portuguese had led the way among Europeans, other European powers also became involved in the slave trade. As other Europeans established new colonies in the Americas, slavery soon became part of their economic systems. As early as the 1500s, English traders and shippers were heavily involved in the slave trade. In 1655, the British seized the large island of Jamaica and began organizing their own sugar plantations and mills.

By the 1700s, slaves had become a significant part of English trade. In the seventeen century, English ships delivered no more than ten thousand slaves during any single decade. But after the turn of the century, the number of

English-shipped Africans <u>increased</u> by several times. During the 1730s, for example, Englishmen carried more than <u>forty thousand</u> slaves across the Atlantic to the Americas. The following decade, the number increased by 50 percent. By the 1760s, the figure stood at <u>seventy thousand</u>.

It was only a matter of time until the Caribbean and Brazil were supporting hundreds of thousands of African slaves. Historians estimate that Europeans <u>shipped</u> <u>12 million</u> Africans for service in the New World as slaves between 1500 and 1850. Of that number, approximately <u>2 million died</u> while <u>onboard</u> slave ships somewhere in the Atlantic. (McNeese and Gates 2004, 18–22)

At the end of this second section, Mr. Watson stopped reading, recorded the underlined ideas in his notebook, one by one or by twos, as he encountered them in the text, and thus produced a linear representation of the first part of this chapter and the beginnings of a text taking shape in his head.

Shown below, Mr. Watson's linear representation for the first two sections of chapter 2: "The Slave Trade," includes all the ideas he noted as important during reading and underlined in his copy of the text. Some of these ideas have been qualified or slightly reworded—strenuous (labor) and increased (shipping)—thousands of African slaves (thousand African slaves) and heavy involvement (heavily involved).

> economic system + old institution + system of labor + all races + Portuguese explorers and traders + raid and trade + sugar plantations + (spreading) sugar production + expansion of slavery + thousands of African slaves + cheap labor + strenuous (labor) + died + Portuguese control + heavy involvement + increased (shipping) + forty thousand + seventy thousand + 12 million (shipped) + 2 million died (onboard)

Second Book Chapter Representation: "Life on a Cotton Plantation"

The first nine paragraphs in chapter 1, "Life on a Cotton Plantation," from *Thirty Years a Slave* (Hughes 1897), the second text used by Mr. Watson in his follow-up assignment for Dr. Sekibo, are reproduced below. Mr. Watson downloaded a full PDF version of the book from archive.org, read the first nine paragraphs in chapter 1, six sections in all, and used the underlining tool to note the striking ideas he encountered.

CHAPTER I.

LIFE ON A COTTON PLANTATION.

Birth–Sold In A Richmond Slave Pen.

I was <u>born</u> in Virginia, in <u>1832</u>, near Charlottesville, in the <u>beautiful valley</u> of the Rivanna River. My <u>father</u> was a <u>white</u> man and my <u>mother</u> a <u>negress</u>, the slave of one John Martin. I was a mere child, probably not more than <u>six</u> years of age, as I remember, when my mother, two brothers and myself were <u>sold</u> to Dr. Louis, a practicing <u>physician</u> in the village of Scottsville. We remained with him about five years, when he died, and, in the settlement of his estate, I was <u>sold</u> to one Washington Fitzpatrick, a <u>merchant of the</u> village. He kept me a short time when he took me to Richmond, by way of canal-boat, expecting to sell me; but as the market was dull, he brought me back and kept me some three months longer, when he told me he had hired me out to work on a canal-boat running to Richmond, and to go to my mother and get my clothes ready to start on the trip. I went to her as directed, and, when she had made ready my bundle, she bade me <u>good-by</u> with tears in her eyes, saying: "My son, <u>be</u> a <u>good</u> boy; be polite to every one, and always behave yourself properly." It was sad to her to part with me, though she did not know that she was never to see me again, for my master had said nothing to her regarding his purpose and she only thought, as I did, that I was <u>hired to work on the canal-boat</u>, and that she should see me occasionally. But alas! We <u>never met again</u>. I can see her form still as when she bade me good-bye. That parting I can never forget. I ran off from her as quickly as I could after her parting words, for I did not want her to see me <u>crying</u>. I went to my master at the store, and he again told me that he had hired me to work on the canal-boat, and to go aboard immediately. Of the boat and the trip and the scenes along the route I remember little–I only thought of my mother and my leaving her.

When we arrived at Richmond, George Pullan, a "nigger-trader," as he was called, came to the boat and began to question me, asking me first if I could remember having had the chickenpox, measles or whooping-cough. I answered, yes. Then he asked me if I did not want to take a little walk with him. I said, no. "Well," said he, "you have got to go. Your master sent you down here <u>to be sold</u>, and told me to come and get you and take you to the trader's yard, ready to be sold." I saw that to hesitate was useless; so I at once obeyed him and went.

A Slave Market.

The trader's establishment consisted of an office, a large <u>show-room</u> and a yard in the rear enclosed with a <u>wall</u> of <u>brick</u> fifteen feet high. The principal men of the establishment were the proprietor and the foreman. When slaves were to be exhibited for sale, the foreman was called to the office by means of a <u>bell</u>, and an order given him to bring into the show-room work of but a few minutes, and the <u>women</u> were <u>placed</u> in a row on one side of the room and the <u>men</u> on the other. <u>Persons</u> desirous of <u>purchasing</u> them passed up and down between the lines looking the poor creatures over, and <u>questioning</u> them in about the following manner: "What can you do?" "Are you a good cook? seamstress? dairymaid?"–this to the women, while the men would be questioned as to their line of work: "Can you plow? Are you a blacksmith? Have you ever cared for horses? Can you pick cotton rapidly?" Sometimes the slave would be required to open his mouth that the purchaser might <u>examine</u> the teeth and form some opinion as to his age and physical soundness; and if it was suspected that a slave had been beaten a good deal he would be required to step into another room and undress. If the person desiring to buy found the slave badly scarred by the common usage of whipping, he would say at once to the foreman: "Why! this slave is not worth much, he is all scarred up. No, I don't want him; bring me in another to look at." Slaves without scars from whipping and looking well physically always sold readily. They were never left long in the yard. It was expected that all the slaves in the yard for sale would be neatly dressed and clean before being brought into the show-room. It was the foreman's business to see that each one was presentable.

Slave Whipping As A Business.

Whipping was done at these markets, or trader's yards, all the time. People who lived in the city of Richmond would send their slaves here for punishment. When any one wanted a slave whipped he would send a note to that effect with the servant to the trader. Any petty offense on the part of a slave was sufficient to subject the offender to this brutal treatment. Owners who affected culture and refinement preferred to send a servant to the yard for punishment to inflicting it themselves. It saved them trouble, they said, and possibly a slight wear and tear of feeling. For this service the owner was charged a certain sum for each slave, and the earnings of the traders from this source formed a very large part of the profits of his business. The yard I was in had a regular whipping post to which they tied the slave, and gave him "nine-and-thirty," as it was called, meaning thirty-nine lashes as hard as they could lay it on. Men were stripped of their shirts in preparation for the whipping, and women had to take off their dresses from the shoulders to the waist. These whippings were not so severe as when the slaves were stripped entirely of their clothes, as was generally the case on the plantations where slaves were owned by the dozen. I saw many cases of whipping while I was in the yard. Sometimes I was so frightened that I trembled violently, for I had never seen anything like it before.

Sold In The Market.

I was only in the yard a short time before I was bought by one George Reid who lived in Richmond. He had no wife, but an old lady kept house for him and his three sons. At this time he had a place in the post office, but soon after I came there he lost it. He then moved into the country upon a farm of about one thousand acres, enclosed by a cedar hedge. The house was a plain frame structure upon a stone basement and contained four rooms. It was surrounded with shrubbery, and was a pleasant country seat. But I did not like it here. I grieved continually about my mother. It came to me, more and more plainly, that I would never see her again. Young and lonely as I was, I could not help crying, oftentimes for hours together. It was hard to get used to being away from my mother. I remember well "Aunt Sylvia," who was the cook in the Reid household. She was very kind to me and always spoke consolingly to me, especially if I had been blue, and had had one of my fits of crying. At these times she would always bake me an ash cake for supper, saying to me: "My child, don't cry; 'Aunt Sylvia' will look after you." This ash cake was made of corn meal and water, a little salt to make it palatable, and was baked by putting it between cabbage leaves and covering it with hot ashes. A sweeter or more delicious cake one could not desire, and it was common upon the tables of all the Virginia farmers. I always considered it a great <u>treat</u> to get one of these cakes from "Aunt Sylvia."

The <u>appellations</u> of "aunt" and "uncle" for the older slaves were not only <u>common</u> among the blacks, but the whites also addressed them in the same way.

On The Auction Block

I was <u>sick</u> a great deal–in fact, I had suffered with chills and fever ever since Mr. Reid bought me. He, therefore, concluded to <u>sell me</u>, and, in November, 1844, he took me back to Richmond, placing me in the Exchange building, or auction rooms, for the sale of slaves. The sales were carried on in a large hall where those interested in the business sat around a large block or stand, upon which the slave to be sold was placed, the <u>auctioneer</u> standing beside him. When I was placed upon the block, a Mr. McGee came up and felt of me and asked me what I could do. "You look like a right smart nigger," said he, "Virginia always produces good darkies." <u>Virginia</u> was the <u>mother of slavery</u>, and it was held by many that she had the best slaves. So when Mr. McGee found I was born and bred in that state he seemed satisfied.

The bidding commenced, and I remember well when the auctioneer said: "<u>Three hundred eighty dollars</u>–once, twice and sold to Mr. Edward McGee." He was a <u>rich cotton planter</u> of Pontotoc, Miss. As near as I can recollect, I was not more than <u>twelve</u> years of age, so did not sell for very much.

Price Of Slaves.

Servant <u>women sold for $500</u> to $700, and sometimes as high as $800 when possessing extra qualifications. A house maid, bright in looks, strong and well formed, would sell for $1,000 to $1,200. Bright mulatto girls, well versed in sewing and knitting, would sometimes bring as high as <u>$1,800</u>, especially if a Virginian or a Kentuckian. Good <u>blacksmiths</u> sold for $1,600 <u>to $1,800</u>. When the slaves were put upon the block they were always sold to the highest bidder. Mr. McGee, or "Boss," as I soon learned to call him, <u>bought</u> sixty other slaves before he bought me, and they were started in a <u>herd</u> for Atlanta, Ga., on foot. (Hughes 1897, 5–12)

Mr. Watson's linear representation of these six sections from chapter 1 in *Thirty Years a Slave* (Hughes 1897) is shown below. Here again, as in his previous representations, all the ideas Mr. Watson noted and underlined in the text are included in the representation, and many are qualified. That the qualifier *being* appeared so often in this particular representation surprised Mr. Watson at first but on second thought made sense, given that the text, an

126   Chapter 6

autobiography, recounts the lived experiences, thoughts, and feelings of the author, Louis Hughes.

> born (1832) + beautiful valley + (white) father + (negress) mother + (sold to) physician + (then to a) merchant + good-bye (to mother) + (told to be) good + (being) sad + hired to work on canal boat + never met (mother) again + (being) sold (in a) showroom + (with a brick) wall + bell (ringing) + men (and) women (placed on block) + (being) questioned (and) examined + (some) badly scarred (but) presentable + whipping markets + (whipping) note (for) petty offense + servant (sent) + certain sum + whipping post + thirty-nine lashes + stripped + (being) frightened + (sold to) post office (clerk) + plain house + grieving (for my mother) + (kind) cook (with) treats + common appellations (of aunt) + (often) sick + (being) sold (again) + auctioneers + Virginia (the motherland of) slavery + (sold for) $348.00 + (purchased by a) rich cotton planter + (being) 12 + women sold for $500 (to $1800) + blacksmiths (up to $1800) + bought (many) + herded (home)

Observations

Mr. Watson's astute observation about the qualifier *being* and its frequent appearance in this second book chapter representation inspired him to compare his representations of all three texts and record his observations. Mr. Watson's recorded observations, enumerated below, focus on first ideas, paragraph length, word class, qualification, and headings.

1. First cached ideas
Ideas are cached from the first paragraph in all three texts. Two ideas are cached from the first sentence in each book chapter and one idea is cached from the last sentence in the introductory paragraph of the textbook chapter.

> Slave Trade: economic system, old institution
> Life on a Cotton Plantation: born (1832), beautiful valley
> King Cotton: cotton plantations

2. Paragraph length
Both book chapters contain longer paragraphs than the textbook chapter, and these longer paragraphs contribute more ideas to their respective representations than shorter ones.

3. Cached ideas: Word class
Cached ideas more often take the form of a noun or verb than another class of word. Not surprisingly, classified nouns appear in the representations of all

three texts (e.g., economic system, sugar plantations, cotton production, slave system, cotton gin, whipping post). Nor is it surprising that verbs appear more often in the representation of the autobiographical chapter than in the other representations; and many of these verbs, including *sold, questioned, examined, bought,* and *herded,* all convey significant meanings about the author's personal experiences as a slave.

Cached verbs in the other two representations and adjectives in all three representations appear more so parenthetically, as qualifiers (or qualified), than as self-supporting ideas.

King Cotton: cleaning cotton; spreading slavery
Slave Trade: (spreading) sugar production; strenuous (labor)
Life on a Cotton Plantation: bell (ringing); (being) frightened

4. Qualification

Qualified ideas appear in all three representations. In two representations, those of "King Cotton and Life in the South" and "The Slave Trade," ideas are qualified by nouns, adverbs, and verbs. In the representation of "Life on a Cotton Plantation," ideas are qualified additionally by prepositions, conjunctions, adverbs, phrases, numeratives, and numbers. The age and genre of the text may account for the extended range of qualification observed in its representation.

Qualification in "King Cotton and Life in the South" and "The Slave Trade"

nominal qualification: (cotton) belt
adverbial qualification: two million died (onboard)
verbal qualification: (spreading) slavery, increased (shipping)

Additional Qualification in "Life on a Cotton Plantation"

prepositional qualification: (sold to) physician
conjunctive qualification: questioned (and) examined
adverbial qualification: (often) sick
phrasal qualification: Virginia (the motherland of) slavery
numerative qualification: bought (many)
numerical qualification: born (1832)

5. Impact of section headings

Mr. Watson's last observation focused on the section headings in each of the three texts and their likely impact on the ideas he noted and cached during reading. That is, he wondered if any of these headings had impelled him to note and cache particular ideas. Suspecting that they had, he reviewed each set of headings and rated its impact on him as high or low.

The section headings in both informational texts rated low for Mr. Watson in terms of their impact on him during reading, while those in the autobiographical text rated high. Key words in all six section headings in the autobiographical text "Life on a Cotton Plantation" appear verbatim, slightly modified, or as details in Mr. Watson's representation of the text, as shown below:

Birth, Sold: born (1832), (sold to) physician
Market, whipping markets
Whipping, whipping posts
Sold (sold to) post office (clerk)
Auction, auctioneers
Price (sold for) $348.00, women sold for $500 (to $1800)

BUILDING COHERENCE

Statements and Target Questions

As reported in the opening vignette, Mr. Watson's main midterm assignment task was to create a two-level web that represented the coherent development of ideas in a whole text. To complete this task, Mr. Watson used unit 7, chapter 3, "Cotton Kingdom and Life in the South," in the *myWorld American History* textbook (Davidson, Stoff, and Bertolet 2019). His representation of this chapter, as a two-level web, was shared in the opening vignette (see figure 6.2 above).

Web representations of whole texts like the one produced by Mr. Watson illustrate (i.e., make visible) the during reading action of building coherence. Proficient readers build coherence during reading by modeling a text in their heads as they read for understanding. The action of building coherence is an intentional action that focuses on essential meanings conveyed by a text. Mental models of texts, produced during reading, cohere inasmuch as their constitutive ideas hang together logically and cohesively.

This section addresses the following questions:

- How do the actions of formulating and building coherence compare? How can these two during reading actions be represented visually?
- How do readers build coherent texts? What role do paragraph topics play in the mental modeling of a text?
- What insights can readers gain about a text by engaging in the action of building coherence during reading?
- What insights can teachers gain about assigned unit texts by exploring their development collaboratively?

Two Scenarios, Two Actions

In the second half of his graduate course with Dr. Sekibo, Mr. Watson pairs up with his classmate Mrs. Carter to complete an in-class exercise focusing on the during reading actions of formulating and building coherence. Mrs. Carter also teaches seventh grade social studies courses but in a different district than Mr. Watson. The partnership has been charged with the task of producing two representations for the first part of chapter 6 in *The Long Walk to Freedom* (Carbado and Weise 2012), a text selected by Mr. Watson for his midterm assignment.

Mr. Watson and Mrs. Carter will produce representations of this text as though they were actual students in the classes they teach. Mr. Watson teaches a boy named Mark and Mrs. Carter a girl named Tiffany, both seventh graders. Mr. Watson and Mrs. Carter will read the first part of the text—the same stretch of text—twice, first as Mark then as Tiffany—and produce a linear representation as one and web representation as the other. In this way, they aim to better understand the differences between the during reading actions of formulating and building coherence.

The Selected Text: Chapter 6, First 10 Paragraphs

Chapter 6 reproduces the autobiographical account of Robert Voorhis, first published in pamphlet form as the *Life and Adventures of Robert, The Hermit of Massachusetts* (Voorhis 1829). In this brief autobiographical account, Voorhis (1770–1832) recalls his life as a slave: his childhood and his various imprisonments, enslavements, and efforts to obtain freedom. At age sixty, when his autobiography was published, Voorhis lived reclusively on the outskirts of Providence, Rhode Island, in a dwelling he constructed himself out of stones.

Voorhis's autobiographical account spans 14 pages in chapter 6 (Voorhis 1829, 97–111) and is preceded by a short introduction provided by the editors Carbado and Weise. Mr. Watson has brought two copies of the chapter. He and his partner skim the chapter quickly and decide to use the first 10 paragraphs for their in-class exercise.

Formulating, as Mark

Focusing exclusively on the during reading action of formulating, Mr. Watson and Mrs. Carter read the first part of chapter 6 as Mark and produce the following linear representation collaboratively.

Born (Princeton, 1769) + mother (in bondage) + father (white) + one sister + conveyed (to Georgetown, at 1) + never (saw mother and sister again) + (at) 14

130   Chapter 6

or 15 (apprenticed to Shoemaker) + (worked at) gardening (until 10) + (met) young female (Alley) + wanted me (as life partner) + my first love + master (unwilling to grant freedom) + willing (to sell me, Fifty Pounds) + (borrowed money from) good friend + (became friend's) lawful property + JAMES BEVINS + good fortune + joy + married + three years (passed) + (blessed) with two children + refunded (a good) portion of fifty pounds (to Bevins) + (no) receipts + error + late one evening + seized (by Bevins) + (pronounced) a liar + dragged (away secretly, at night) + (put in) irons + addressed (Bevins) + (put in) hold + (no) sleep + imagining (poor wife and children) + (spent) three days (in irons, eating moldy bread) + reached (Charleston) + (spent five days in) solitude (in prison) + conducted (to public auction) + (purchaser) granted (indulgence, to walk around unguarded) + (without) a pass + (sought) to escape + death (better than) slavery + strolled about the wharves + found a Sloop (bound for Philadelphia) + (ready to) haul (out) + secreted myself between two casks in the hold + (with) fairer prospects of regaining my liberty + (felt) secret joy + divine providence (delivering me)

Building Coherence, as Tiffany

After a short break, Mr. Watson and Mrs. Carter complete the second part of their in-class exercise. Now focusing exclusively on the during reading action of building coherence, they read the same set of paragraphs, as Tiffany this time; and in a short time, following their professor's advice about limiting their webbing time to 10 minutes and spending no longer than a minute on each branched set of ideas, produce the two-level web representation shown in figure 6.3.

At the center of this web is the chapter topic MY LIFE AS A SLAVE, derived from key words that appear in the chapter's title and introductory paragraphs—*life* and *slave*. Branched out from the chapter topic are seven level one ideas, all paragraph topic key words that appear in paragraphs 1–3

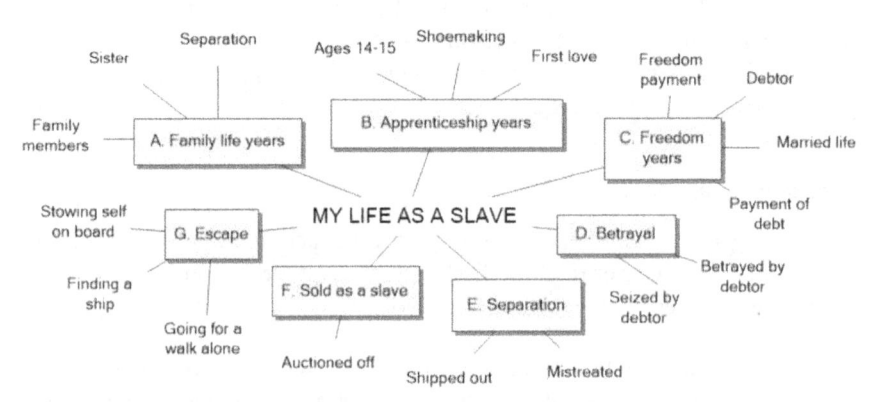

Figure 6.3.   My Life as a Slave Web

or 5–9; and branched out from each of these ideas are one to four level two ideas, all main idea key words that appear in paragraphs 1–10. The reverse flow of meaning from smaller to larger ideas is shown below:

MY LIFE AS A SLAVE ← life, slave
Family life years ← life, years, family
Apprenticeship years ← apprenticed (years)
Freedom years ← freedom (years)
Betrayal ← injustice, seized
Spirited away ← dragged (away), hurried on board a Schooner, (in) irons
Sold as a slave ← disposed of at public auction
Escape ← liberty, regain

Two significant differences between the during reading actions of formulating and building coherence are revealed by a comparison of the linear and web representations produced by Mr. Watson and Mrs. Carter for the first part of the Voorhis text. Formulating is an additive action, focusing primarily on smaller units of meaning (main ideas, details). In contrast, building coherence is a configurative action, focusing primarily on larger units of meaning (paragraph topics). Moreover, the action of formulating is less likely to yield a unified and durable mental model of a given text than the action of building coherence.

Building a Coherent Text: "The Slave Trade"

A linear representation for part of chapter 2: "The Slave Trade" was presented above. You will recall that Mr. Watson selected the chapter as an assigned text for his forthcoming seventh grade unit on slavery and abolitionism and used the chapter in a follow-up midterm assignment in his graduate course with Dr. Sekibo to better understand the action of formulating. The first eight paragraphs of the chapter were reproduced above (see 121–22).

Chapter 2: "The Slave Trade" appears in the specialized book *The Rise and Fall of American Slavery* (McNeese and Gates 2004). The chapter focuses on African American slavery (circa 1480–1720) and presents historical information about indigenous slave trading practices in Africa, the trans-Atlantic slave trade, and the transportation of African slaves to American markets. The chapter consists of six sections (labeled here for convenience as A–F) whose headings include: "Slavery in the New World," "European Competition for Colonies," "African Origins of Slavery," "Transatlantic Slavers," "The Middle Passage," and "Reaching the New World."

On Mr. Watson's recommendation, Mrs. Carter included the chapter as an assigned text in her own seventh grade study of American slavery. She bought a copy of the McNeese and Gates book online, read the book eagerly front to back, returned to chapter 2, and generated questions that would guide her students' understanding of the major ideas presented in the chapter. She reduced her questions to four, worded them carefully, and shared them with Mr. Watson. Shown below, her finalized set of questions focus on slave trade practices and the implications of these practices for captured African people:

> How were slave trading practices similar and different in and beyond Africa?
> How did African people respond to being enslaved?
> How were enslaved African people transported to the Americas?
> In what ways were African people's transportation experiences dehumanizing?

By including this new set of questions and new text in her unit on American slavery, Mrs. Carter believes that her students' learning experiences and the overall impact of her unit will be enhanced. Mrs. Carter, however, has another enhancement in mind for her unit. Given her new understandings about reading and the during reading action of building coherence, she wants to guide her students' efforts to build a coherent text using chapter 2: "The Slave Trade."

Toward this end, Mrs. Carter reads chapter 2 again, as if for the first time, aiming to understand the chapter as a whole and to determine the kind of support her students will need to build a coherent text. Her rereading of the chapter and efforts to build a coherent text herself yield the web representation shown in figure 6.4.

Figure 6.4. Web Representation for Chapter 2

Shared Observations

Several similarities between her web representation for chapter 2 and the original text strike Mrs. Carter immediately when she compares chapter 2 and her finalized web side by side. First, the chapter topic SLAVE TRADE, which appears at the center of her web, reproduces the chapter's title verbatim. Second, the number of branched level one ideas in her web matches the number of sections in the chapter, six and six. More so, however, Mrs. Carter is struck by the different meanings conveyed by one and the other, her web and the text.

Mrs. Carter shares her web and webbing observations with Mr. Watson when they meet for coffee on Saturday afternoon. Mr. Watson has agreed to collaborate with her to enhance both of their units on slavery by guiding their students' efforts to build coherence during reading. Mrs. Carter has provided Mr. Watson with copies of her web and webbing observations as well as an annotated copy of chapter 2. Mrs. Carter first shares her observations about level one ideas then level two ideas. Mr. Watson listens attentively, studies the web himself, and shares several observations of his own.

Level One Observations

Mrs. Carter's observations about level one ideas focus on wording, the repetition of certain words, and three essential topics.

1. Wording

Only one level one item reproduces verbatim the corresponding heading in the original text: branch F, "Reaching the New World."

2. Repeated words

The words *New World*, *origins*, and *trade* (trade, traders, trading) are all repeated in level one ideas: *New World* appears in branches A, B, and F; *origins* in branches A and C; and *trade* in branches B–D. These repeated words help to unify the text.

3. Essential topics

Level one ideas (i.e., section topics in the original text) essentially focus on the topics of slave trade, slave traders, and slaves themselves. The slave trade is the focus of branches A, C, and D; slave traders branch B; and slave themselves branches E and F.

Here Mr. Watson interjects, reaching across the table with his pen, and pointing excitedly at Mrs. Carter's copy of the web, at level one branches A and B. "These ideas are paired," says Mr. Watson excitedly. "All six ideas are paired: AB, CD, and EF. First we learn basic information about New World

134   *Chapter 6*

slave trading and traders (text sections A and B). Then we learn about slave trading practices in and beyond Africa (text sections C and D). Then we learn about the transportation of African slaves to New World slave markets in the Americas—their departure for and arrival at these New World markets (text sections E and F)."

Both Mrs. Carter and Mr. Watson record this new observation in their notes, agreeing to call it idea development.

4. Idea development
Section topics in the original text, as revealed by the web representation, are developed coherently in pairs: AB → CD → EF.

Level Two Observations

Mrs. Carter's observations about level two ideas in her web follow neatly from and extend Mr. Watson's observations about the paired development of section topics in chapter 2. Mrs. Carter now shares her next set of observations with Mr. Watson:

1. Number of branches
The number of level two branches ranges from 2 to 7. Branch set F has the least number of branches (2) and branch set E the greatest (7).

2. Starred ideas
Mrs. Carter directs Mr. Watson to put a star beside four level two ideas in the web: B1 Portuguese control, C1 West African origins, D4 Slave trade justification, and F2 Selling slaves at auction. These particular ideas are developed in two paragraphs each in the original text. All the other ideas are each developed in one paragraph only.

3. Unifying level two elements
Particular elements in each branched set of level two ideas play a notable role in unifying the text in part or in whole. The elements expansion and need in branches A3, B3, A2, and B4 play notable roles in unifying the first two sections of the text, sections A and B. Other elements, shown in table 6.2, play notable roles in unifying several or more sections of the text.

Table 6.2. Unifying Elements in Branched Set of Level Two Ideas

Section	Unifying Element
AB	Expansion; need
ABD	Portuguese (involvement)
ABCD	European (involvement)
DE	slave (D) → slave (E)

The elements *Portuguese* and *European* in branch sets A, B, C, and D play a role in unifying the first four sections of the text, sections A–D. The element *Portuguese* in branches A1, B1, and D1 plays an explicit role in unifying these four sections. The element *European(s)* appears explicitly in branches C3 and D2 and implicitly in branches A1, B1, B2, and D1 (Europeans ← Portuguese and British Europeans) and plays a concurrent role in unifying these same four sections. In the second half of the text, the element *slave* in branches D3, E1–3, and E5, referring specifically to slaves themselves, plays a notable role in unifying sections D and E.

All that Mr. Watson can add to Mrs. Carter's insightful set of level two observations is an observation about the weighting of content in the web and original text. He calls his observation content weighting.

4. Content weighting

As revealed by the web, more content is presented in sections D and E than in other sections of the text. In other words, sections D and E, which focus more so on the experiences of slaves than the slave trade itself, have weightier content than sections A–C and F. "The chapter seems to swell in these two sections," adds Mrs. Carter, "and then, not so gently, subside."

Unit Enhancement: Building Coherence

Agreeing that the foregoing discussion about chapter 2 and Mrs. Carter's web has helped each of them to better understand the chapter as a whole, Mrs. Carter and Mr. Watson return to the key question that brought them together today: How can they guide their students' efforts to build a coherent text using this new chapter about the slave trade?

They discuss the question at length and agree that the following mediational actions will enhance the impact of their units and their students' learning experience:

1. Mrs. Carter will prepare a web starter template for the chapter. She will provide the chapter topic, all level one and two branches, all the level one ideas, and roughly half of the level two ideas. She will send a copy of the template to Mr. Watson.
2. She and Mr. Watson will review the starter template with their students in the before reading phase and explain its purpose. Their students will aim to build coherence during reading by completing the template section by section independently in real time.
3. She and Mr. Watson will require their students to mentally register the next level one idea before reading the corresponding section in the text. For example, students will not proceed to section C, "African Origins of Slavery," until they have mentally registered the web idea for this section,

branch C, "African slave origins and the emerging trans-Atlantic trade." Students will also ensure that they have supplied all missing level two ideas or elements before proceeding to the next section.
4. She and Mr. Watson will collect their students' completed webs, review them together over coffee, and discuss the results.

LOOKING BACK AND AHEAD

During reading, all readers register important ideas encountered in a text, and some readers expressly aim to understand the ways these ideas cohere and produce a whole text. These two actions, formulating and building coherence, were the focus of this chapter.

All six during reading actions, when skillfully executed, enable readers to achieve their ultimate reading goal. By visualizing, reading fluently, reading for understanding, inferencing, formulating, and building coherence, readers—middle grade readers—are optimally positioned to cache and retain essential meanings conveyed by assigned unit texts, understand how these meanings interrelate, and use these meanings productively in new contexts.

This concludes our exploration of the during reading phase. Next we turn our attention to the final phase of a reading event, the after reading phase.

GROUNDING: DURING READING PHASE ACTIONS

This chapter is grounded in cognitive processing theory (Samuels 2013; Rummelhart 2013) and text comprehension (Britton and Graesser 2014; Kintsch 2013).

7

After Reading Actions

Mr. Takahasi teaches seventh and eighth grade social studies courses at New Horizons Public Charter School in Boise, Idaho, and has taught at the school since it opened four years ago. New Horizons Public Charter School, situated in the southeastern corner of the city, is 130 miles northwest of Minidoka War Relocation Center, one of 10 Japanese American internment camps established by the United States government during World War II.

War Relocation Centers like Minidoka were established by executive order in February 1942, three months after the attack on Pearl Harbor. Mr. Takahasi's grandfather and great-aunt were interned at the Minidoka camp as children from 1942 to 1945. They were among the roughly 9,400 Japanese American children and adults interned at the camp during its three-year operation.

The Minidoka camp officially closed in 1946, but was subsequently designated a National Historic Site and partially restored. Mr. Takahasi worked at the restored camp as a guide for four summers while completing his teaching degree at Idaho State University in Pocatello.

In his eighth grade American history course, in his unit on World War II (Modern America, 1935–1945), Mr. Takahasi spends several weeks on the topic of War Relocation Camps, and the Minidoka camp in particular, then takes his students for a tour of the Minidoka National Historic Site. Aiming to teach his students about the impact of the Pearl Harbor attack on Americans like his late grandfather and great-aunt, who were children at the time, he poses the question: What was the war experience like for Japanese American parents and their children?

To answer this question, Mr. Takahasi's students will draw on knowledge they acquired with him a year ago in their seventh grade world history unit, "The Two Great Wars."

One of the first texts that Mr. Takahasi assigns his students in his eighth grade unit on World War II is an excerpt of a memoir written by Monica Sone, which appears in the book Japanese American Internment Camps *(Grapes 2001). In the chapter "Evacuation Day," Mrs. Sone recalls her first experiences as an internee: helping her parents to close the family home in Seattle, tagging their suitcases and coats with a special registration number, traveling south from Seattle aboard a special evacuation bus, and arriving at their first destination: Camp Harmony Assembly Center in Puyallup.*

"You read and responded to this chapter by Monica Sone for homework," says Mr. Takahasi. "I want to do two rounds of sharing this morning, one round for each question you responded to in your history journal. I'll call on some of you in the first round and others in the second. Paraphrase your response. I don't want you reading it directly from your journal."

The first round of sharing begins. Students called on share details about one evacuation day experience recounted by Mrs. Sone in the chapter and its possible long-term impact on her. Four students share their responses before the first round ends and the second begins.

"You may have found this second question harder to respond to than the first," says Mr. Takahasi, crossing the room. "This question too was a two-part question: What was your personal purpose for reading this text, and to what extent did you achieve that purpose? I'm also curious to know, as many of you are too, how you achieved your reading goal if you achieved it. Share that with us too."

Mr. Takahasi calls on Arianna to begin the second round of sharing.

"I recorded two purposes in my journal before reading the chapter," says Arianna. "I aimed to read the chapter attentively and to read it all the way to the end in one sitting. I shut myself in my room on the weekend and read the chapter straight through to the end, all in one sitting. It took me less than an hour. You made me interested to read about Mrs. Sone, who lived to be 92 and became a psychologist after the war."

Mr. Takahasi calls on Brooke to share next.

"I aimed to read attentively too," says Brooke. "I also aimed to learn as much as I could about Mrs. Sone's experiences as an internee and to care about her experiences. I wondered what it was like growing up in Seattle and having parents that owned a hotel. I found some pictures of Mrs. Sone online, one of her as a child, sitting beside her mother, smiling and happy; and one of her many years later, on her 90th birthday, so old. It must have been very hard for Mrs. Sone to relive her experiences as a prisoner of war. I kept this in mind, reading the chapter."

INTRODUCTION: AFTER READING PHASE ACTIONS

Middle grade students engage in the after reading action of assessing, as demonstrated by Arianna and Brooke in the opening vignette, by reflecting on the actions they took before or during reading. Assessing is one of four after reading actions proficient readers engage in to achieve their ultimate reading goal of understanding the main ideas in a text and being able to use these ideas at a later date. Other after reading actions proficient readers engage in include summarizing, reconfiguring, and clarifying. These four after reading actions are the focus of this chapter.

In the before reading phase of a reading event, proficient readers look ahead to the after reading phase and plan to spend 20–30 minutes after reading summarizing, reconfiguring, assessing, and clarifying. The first two actions focus on the assigned text as a whole, and the last two actions on specific before or during reading actions or specific ideas encountered in the text.

Many of the assigned texts used by Mr. Takahasi in his eighth grade American history unit on World War II are used to illustrate the four after reading actions in this chapter. All of these texts focus on Japanese Americans' internment experiences during World War II and are full-length chapters that appear in the specialized books *Japanese American Internment Camps* (Grapes 2001), *I am an American* (Stanley 2006), *Life in a Japanese American Internment Camp* (Yancey 1998), and *Imprisoned: The Betrayal of Japanese Americans During World War II* (Sandler 2013).

SUMMARIZING

Statements and Target Questions

After reading an assigned text, proficient readers spend several minutes or longer summarizing it. To summarize a text means to state its substance in a condensed form (*AHD Online* 2018). Some readers prefer to summarize a text mentally or verbally, while others prefer to list the most important ideas presented in a text in a print or digital format or to produce a written account of a text in one or two paragraphs.

This section addresses the following questions:

- What is the purpose of summarizing?
- How do middle grade students produce summaries? Will these students focus on smaller or larger units of meaning to produce a summary?
- What summarizing options do students have? What factors will guide their selection of one option over another?

Summarizing Texts

By engaging in the action of summarizing, middle grade students aim to recall important information presented in an assigned text. Four summarizing options are available for students. Depending on the length and complexity of any given text, students may elect to produce a simple mental summary of that text using key words or more substantive verbal or written summaries. For book chapters like those selected by Mr. Takahasi for his unit on World War II, students are best positioned to achieve their ultimate reading goal by producing written statements or paragraph summaries.

An example of each summarizing option and summary follows. Mr. Takahasi produced these examples himself and uses them as summarizing exemplars in his unit. All of these examples are based on the chapter about removal centers in *Imprisoned: The Betrayal of Japanese Americans During World War II* (Sandler 2013). The chapter spans 24 pages of continuous text (without sections) and includes offset quotations, photographs with captions, a table, and a special feature about an internment camp photographer.

1. Simple recall exemplar

Mr. Takahasi shares this exemplar verbally with his students but first makes it clear that this particular summarizing option is predominantly a mental action. Then, to demonstrate this option, he leafs through the chapter to remind himself of the ideas he encountered during reading and simply recalls these ideas using paragraph key words.

Simple Recall Exemplar for "The Removal Centers"

unpleasant surprises, desert camps, swampy camps, ailments, emotional stress, coping, educational programs, leaving the camp

2. Numbered key word list exemplar

Mr. Takahasi shares both verbal and written exemplars of this second summarizing option, as some of his students will prefer to verbalize their numbered key word list rather than recording it in their social studies journal. From his own experience, Mr. Takahasi has learned that recorded vertical lists result in better long-term recall than horizontal or verbal key word lists.

Numbered Key Word List Exemplar for "The Removal Centers"

1. unpleasant surprises
2. desert camps
3. swampy camps
4. ailments
5. emotional stress

6. coping
7. educational programs
8. leaving the camp

3. Numbered statements exemplar

For this summarizing option too, Mr. Takahasi shares two versions of his exemplar. But first he distinguishes this third option from the second and fourth, telling his students that a numbered statements summary is more expansive than a numbered key word summary but not as specific nor as coherent as a paragraph summary. Mr. Takahasi then shares his written exemplar with students and reviews each statement in turn, while leafing through the chapter as before and singling out particular paragraphs that contain corresponding ideas in his statements. This exemplar includes one less item than the previous exemplars, as statement 2 contains two ideas (deserts, swamplands).

Numbered Statements Exemplar for "The Removal Centers"

1. The location and appearance of relocation centers were surprisingly inhospitable.
2. Some relocation centers were located in deserts or swamplands.
3. Internees often became sick because of overcrowding.
4. Internees often experienced emotional stress as a result of their internment.
5. Internees found various ways to cope with their internment.
6. School-age children were required to attend internment camp schools.
7. Some internees were given special permission to leave internment camps.

4. Paragraph summary exemplar

Mr. Takahasi provides his students with a one-sided handout (in the landscape mode) that includes his numbered statement exemplar on the left side and his paragraph summary exemplar on the right. He and his students review the handout together and note the differences between the exemplars in terms of specificity and coherence.

Paragraph Summary Exemplar for "The Removal Centers"

Many internment camps were located in uninhabitable areas of the United States. Several camps were located in desert regions where sandstorms were common and temperatures soared to 100 degrees or more during the day. One internment camp was located in the swamplands of Arkansas, where internees had to deal with large pools of stagnant water and daily swarms of mosquitoes. Overcrowding at these camps often led to outbreaks of diseases such as dysentery, typhoid, and tuberculosis, and many older internees experienced emotional stress as well, being treated like prisoners with limited freedom.

To boost morale at these camps, internees engaged in various recreational activities—creative activities and sports. They beautified their surroundings, made things like baskets and jewelry, and competed in sports like baseball, Ping-Pong, and boxing. School buildings had not been included in the original internment camp plans but soon were provided at parents' insistence. These buildings were not properly equipped and teachers were often in short supply, but internee children made do. In February 1943, internees ages 17 and older were permitted to leave their camps permanently if they agreed to resettle in a different part of the country or serve in the military.

That the two exemplars on their handout differ in terms of specificity is readily apparent to Mr. Takahasi's students. His students note that the paragraph summary includes more specific information about internment camps than the numbered statements summary. For example, the paragraph summary identifies specific diseases that broke out in these camps and lists various activities that internees engaged in to boost morale.

The degree to which the summaries differ in terms of coherence is not readily apparent to his students, so Mr. Takahasi highlights certain elements in each summary to help his students to judge its coherence. These highlighted elements are reproduced below:

Highlighted Elements in Numbered Statements Summary
the location and appearance of relocation centers were → some location centers were located → internees often became → internees often experienced → internees found → school-age children were required to → some internees were given

Highlighted Elements in Paragraph Summary
many internments camps were located → several camps were located → one internment camp was located → overcrowding at these camps often led to → to boost morale, internees engaged in → school buildings had not been included . . . but were provided → and internee children made do → in February 1943, internees age 17 and older were permitted to leave

With Mr. Takahasi's guidance, his students judge the paragraph summary to be more coherent than the numbered statements summary. Information about internment camps in the paragraph summary flows continuously from one idea to the next—from location to location and the conditions internees were confronted with in these locations—to the activities they engaged in and the opportunities offered to them in terms of education and release. In contrast, information in the numbered statements summary is presented more as a discrete set of facts about internment camps and internees.

RECONFIGURING

Statements and Target Questions

During reading, proficient readers tentatively model a text in their heads as they read for understanding; and after reading, they reconfigure the model to better reflect the essential meanings conveyed by a text. To reconfigure a text after reading means to remodel it in whole or part, mentally or materially. Tentatively modeled texts and reconfigured texts often differ markedly in terms of the arrangement and wording of ideas.

This section addresses the following questions:

- What is the purpose of reconfiguring?
- What reconfiguring options do middle grade students have? How does each option differ from the other? What factors will guide students' selection of one option over another?
- How do modeled and remodeled texts differ in terms of the arrangement and wording of ideas?

Reconfiguring Texts

By engaging in the action of reconfiguring, middle grade students aim to reshape an assigned text and produce a retrospective model of that text as a coordinated whole that reflects its essential meanings. Reconfigured texts take the form of a web or outline. Examples follow. A reconfigured web and outline for one chapter, respectively, in the books *I Am an American: A True Story of Japanese Internment* (Stanley 2006) and *Life in a Japanese American Internment Camp* (Yancey 1998) are used by Mr. Takahasi as reconfiguring exemplars in his unit on World War II.

1. A reconfigured web for chapter 6: "Sorting Out"

Stanley's book *I Am an American* (2006) presents the personal reflections of Shi Nomura about his internment at the Manzanar War Relocation Center in Owens Valley, California, roughly 200 miles north of Los Angeles. Mr. Nomura's reflections are embedded in a larger discourse on the Japanese American internment experience during World War II. Chapter 6: "Sorting Out," focuses on Mr. Nomura's return to Manzanar after a brief furlough in northern Montana working on a farm and his subsequent application for permission to leave Manzanar permanently.

A during reading visual representation for chapter 6 focusing exclusively on Mr. Nomura's personal reflections is shown in figure 7.1. This web representation simulates the during reading action of building coherence and was

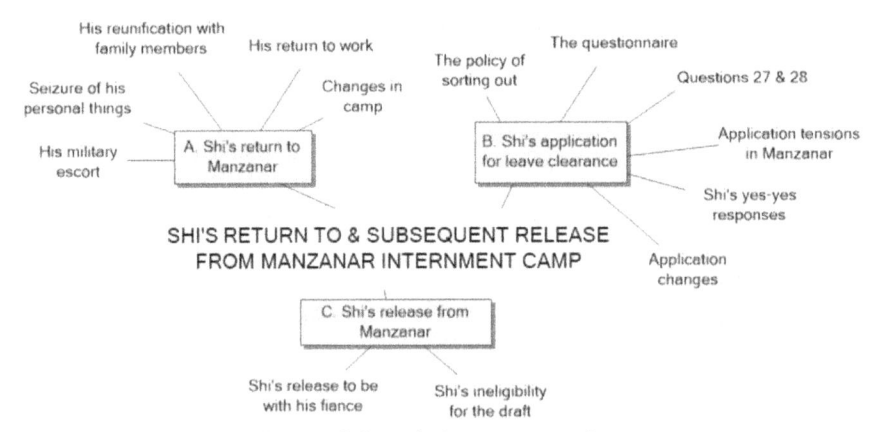

Figure 7.1. During Reading Modeling of Chapter 6: "Sorting Out"

developed collaboratively by Mr. Takahasi and his students while reading four of the 19 paragraphs in the chapter, paragraphs in which Mr. Nomura is explicitly named. In this during reading modeling of chapter 6, branches A–C all focus on Mr. Nomura's personal internment experiences: his return to Manzanar, his application for permanent leave, and his subsequent release from Manzanar.

A reconfigured web for chapter 6, produced by Mr. Takahasi and his students after reading the chapter in its entirety, is shown in figure 7.2. In this after reading reconfiguration of chapter 6, branches A–C all focus on release opportunities offered to Japanese American internees in the fall and winter of 1942–1943. Each branch in this reconfigured web focuses on a different release opportunity. Internees were given opportunities to attend

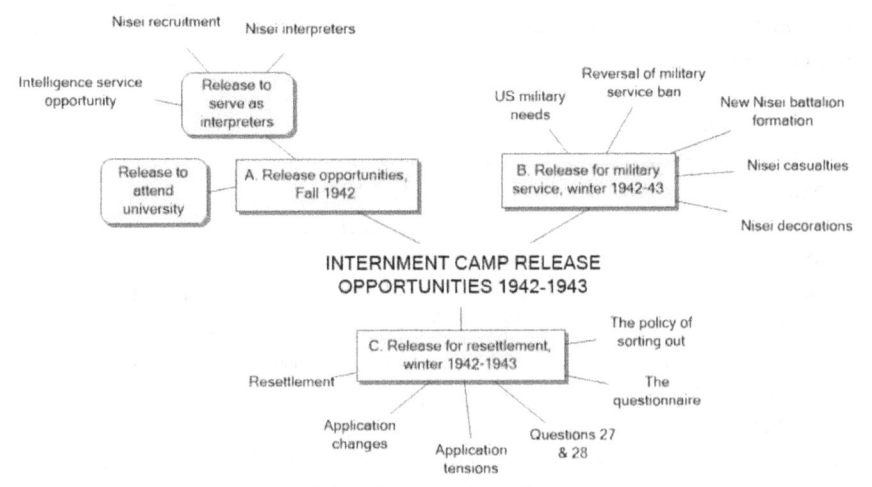

Figure 7.2. Retrospective Web for Chapter 6: "Sorting Out"

After Reading Actions 145

university, serve as interpreters or soldiers, or resettle themselves in an eastern or midwestern state.

2. A reconfigured outline for chapter 4: "Creating Communities"

Chapter 4 in Yancey's book *Life in a Japanese American Internment Camp* (1998) focuses exclusively on everyday life in an internment camp and topics related to governance, education, employment, and more. The chapter is divided into 11 sections. Before reading the chapter, Mr. Takahasi, as he commonly does for sectioned chapters like this, labels the sections with letters A–K and produces the prefigured outline shown on the left in table 7.1.

Table 7.1 also shows a second outline, a reconfigured outline for chapter 4 produced by Mr. Takahasi after reading that differs from the first in substantial ways. Some of these differences are immediately apparent to Mr. Takahasi's students when he presents the outlines to them on a handout. The second outline has a more specific title than the first, one that explicitly

Table 7.1. Prefigured and Reconfigured Outlines for Chapter 4: "Creating Communities"

Prefigured Outline	Reconfigured Outline

IV. Creating communities
  A. Newfound leisure
  B. Teaching by instinct
  C. "A shortage beyond comprehension"
  D. Expressions of faith
  E. Concerned outsiders
  F. Councils and controversy
  G. Jobs for low pay
  H. Farms in the desert
  I. Clinics in horse barns
  J. The lighter side
  K. Quality of life
	IV. Internment life
	  A. Internment pastimes (53, 61–63)
	    1. Building things
	    2. Gardening
	    3. Playing games and sports
	    4. Reading and writing
	  B. Internment schools (53–55)
	    1. The purpose of schools
	    2. Internment schoolteachers
	    3. School initiatives
	    4. Challenges
	  C. Internment worship (55–56)
	    1. Buddhist worship
	    2. Christian worship
	  D. Internment leadership (57–58)
	    1. Community council formation
	    2. Leadership eligibility
	    3. Support and resistance
	  E. Internment employment (59–60)
	    1. The importance of working
	    2. Camp employment opportunities
	    3. Entrepreneurial opportunities
	    4. Agricultural initiatives
	  F. Internment health care (60–61)
	    1. Professional services
	    2. Facilities and conditions

relates to the title of the book. Fewer section topics appear on the second outline; the word *internment* appears in all of them; and most of these topics are labeled differently than they are on the first. But the most obvious difference between the outlines is the appearance of level two (paragraph) topics on the second, which lengthens it considerably.

There are other differences as well between the two outlines that Mr. Takahasi shares with his students. Section topics B and E in the reconfigured outline, which focus on internment schools and employment, include ideas presented in two sections each in the chapter, the sections labeled B and C and G and H in the prefigured outline. "This is what you do when you reconfigure a text after reading," says Mr. Takahasi. "You move ideas around, reconstitute them, merge them." Section A as well in the reconfigured outline includes ideas presented in other sections of the chapter, most notably the sections labeled J and K in the prefigured outline.

"And only the most important ideas are represented in this second outline," says Mr. Takahasi. "I might have included a section on visitors, concerned outsiders, and additional level two topics in several sections of the outline—and originally I did, but ended up deleting them. Less is more, as they say."

ASSESSING

Statements and Target Questions

After reading, in addition to summarizing and reconfiguring an assigned text, proficient readers also assess their overall comprehension of a text, their understanding of specific words or ideas, and the effectiveness of their actions before and during reading. The after reading action of assessing is a two-prong action that includes reflection and evaluation.

This section addresses the following questions:

- How is the action of assessing commonly understood by middle grade teachers and students? How is the action modeled in this book?
- What is the purpose of assessing?
- Which before and during reading actions might students reflect on after reading?
- What insights might students gain about their efficacy as readers by reflecting on the actions they took before and during reading?
- What scheme might students use to value their overall comprehension of assigned texts?
- What might students aim to clarify for themselves after reading?

The After Reading Action of Assessing

If middle grade students were asked to picture themselves engaging in the after reading action of assessing, many of them would picture themselves writing a test. And if then they were asked why they were writing a test, many would undoubtedly say, "To get a good grade." But in this book, the action of assessing has nothing to do with testing or grades and everything to do with students becoming better readers.

Put simply, by engaging in the after reading action of assessing, as modeled in this book, students aim to better understand themselves as readers and read more effectively. They do this in large part by evaluating the effectiveness of specific actions they engaged in before and during reading that helped them to achieve their reading goal.

Two middle grade students demonstrated the action of assessing in the opening vignette. After reading a personal account of evacuation day during World War II, Mr. Takahasi's students Arianna and Brooke reflected on their before reading actions of clarifying purpose and developing topic knowledge and reported the effectiveness of their actions in specific ways.

Middle grade students like Arianna and Brooke benefit by reflecting on the effectiveness of all four before reading actions including clarifying one's reading purpose, generating expectations, activating topic knowledge, and developing topic knowledge. They also benefit by reflecting on the effectiveness of three during reading actions: reading for understanding, inferencing, and building coherence. And as will be shown in forthcoming examples, middle grade students benefit by reflecting on specific challenges they encountered and overcame during reading.

But the after reading action of assessing involves more than just reflecting on the effectiveness of one's actions before and during reading and specific challenges one encountered during reading. It also involves a quick evaluation of one's overall comprehension of the text and one's need for clarification.

Two Illustrations: Reflecting

First Illustration: Reflecting on the Before Reading Action of Generating Expectations

Before reading the chapter on internment life in Yancey's book *Life in a Japanese American Internment Camp* (1998), Mr. Takahasi's students generate expectations about the chapter with an assigned partner and record these expectations as bulleted points in their history journals. Mr. Takahasi gives his students four minutes to do this: two minutes to leaf through the chapter with their partner, and two minutes to record their expectations in their journals.

After reading the chapter for homework, Mr. Takahasi's students then assess the extent to which their expectations for the chapter align specifically with information presented in the chapter. Mr. Takahasi projects the question: What did you end up reading about (or not reading about) that you expected to read about in the chapter? He gives his students 15 minutes to record a response in their journals and several minutes to share their response in groups of four. Momentarily, when his students have returned to their seats, he shares his own response with his students.

"I expected to read about children's experience in internment schools," says Mr. Takahasi, glancing at his response but paraphrasing it. "I expected to read about the different clubs children could join as internees, clubs like Girl Scouts or Boy Scouts, but further along in the chapter I didn't expect to read much about children because children don't appear in later pictures in the chapter. I heard some of you say a moment ago, while I was listening in on your conversations, that you expected to read a lot about internees' recreational activities. I did too. Baseball especially."

Many of his students nod their heads in agreement, then Mr. Takahasi laughs. "But I didn't expect to read about horses; did you? Never mind. Best to keep that one private. Although I do understand why some of you might have been led to think that, given the section heading on page 60, 'Clinics in Horse Barns.' "

Mr. Takahasi holds up his journal and points to his list of expectations for the chapter. "I generated most of these expectations from four or five pictures in the chapter. I didn't find the headings very helpful. But now to the heart of the matter," says Mr. Takahasi, lowering his journal, then continuing.

"I didn't end up reading very much at all about children beyond the first few pages in the chapter. I read that children were affectionate and devoted, according to one of their teachers, and that older children like yourselves could belong to Boy Scouts, Girl Scouts, various athletic clubs, and honor societies. Some internee students even started a school newspaper. I didn't expect to read about that, and I didn't expect to read so much about educational obstacles in internment schools. School buildings themselves, for example, were poorly built and noisy. Teachers were hard to come by. Classes were jammed together. But many students persevered."

Mr. Takahasi closes his journal and puts it aside. Before moving on, he tells his students that in hindsight and given more time he might have done two things to better prepare himself for the ideas he encountered in the chapter. "I might have been more attentive to the pictures of adults. That's one thing. And the other is: I might have read the introductory paragraph, picked out words like *organizations*, *school*, *church*, and *government*, related them to the word *communities* in the chapter title, and asked myself: What would I expect to go on in an internment community?"

Second Illustration: Reflecting on the During Reading Action of Reading for Understanding

For homework that night, Mr. Takahasi's students focus on one section in the chapter, read that section again, and respond to one of the following questions in their journals: To what extent were you able to track important ideas in this section? Or, what challenges did you encounter and overcome while reading this section? Mr. Takahasi collects the responses the next day, reads them with great interest, and selects two as future exemplars. The first response focuses on the section "The Lighter Side" and the second response on the section "Councils and Controversies."

Exemplar 1: Tracking Important Ideas During Reading

I reread the section called "The Lighter Side," the second to last section in the chapter, and had no trouble tracking important ideas in this section. The section gives information about the different recreational opportunities internees had at these camps. Internees could participate in outdoor or indoor activities. The first and second paragraph focus on outdoor activities—holiday activities, sports, playground activities, and gardening—and the third paragraph focuses on indoor activities like reading, putting on plays, playing music, or watching movies.

I didn't realize that I had been reading specifically about outdoor activities in the first two paragraphs until I got to the third paragraph and saw the word *indoor* in the very first sentence. The section as a whole is very organized. I realize that now. First you read about outdoor activities and then about indoor activities. Internees had more indoor activities to choose from, I guess, because the third paragraph is the longest. Main ideas are easy to spot everywhere in the section. You'll see a lot of them at the start of a sentence, holidays, sports, playgrounds, theater (theatrical), music (musicians), and classes.

Exemplar 2: Overcoming Challenges During Reading

The section called "Councils and Controversies" is the most challenging section to read in the chapter. It challenged me last night reading it the first time and challenged me again tonight. So what's confusing about this section?

I read the section again tonight and put numbers beside the sentences that confused me. When I was done, only three sentences had numbers beside them. I had numbered both sentences in paragraph 1 and the fourth sentence in paragraph 3. So I went to work trying to figure out why these sentences were confusing.

The first word in paragraph 1 was new to me, the word *self-government*. When I came to the word last night, I didn't know what it meant but kept on reading, hoping to learn its meaning later in the section. But when I reached the end of the second sentence, I was totally confused. That was last night. Tonight I looked hard at this sentence and realized that the sentence has so many words in it (37) that I'm not surprised I got confused. I also realized that the end of the sentence is the really important part. The last 9 words help you to understand two things: the meaning of the word *self-government* and the meaning of the paragraph as a whole.

Tonight I also looked hard at paragraph 3 and the sudden appearance of the word *ban* in the fourth sentence. In paragraph 2, you read about internee campaigns for positions on the community council, then begin to read about internee support for these councils in paragraph 3, when suddenly you're blindsided by the word *ban*. Tonight, after going back to the start of the paragraph and rereading the first three sentences, I finally understood that the government banned a certain group of internees from being council members, those that were born in Japan.

Illustrations: Evaluating

After reading each assigned text in their unit on World War II, Mr. Takahasi's students evaluate their overall comprehension of the text and their need for clarification about words or ideas encountered in the text.

Evaluating One's Overall Comprehension of the Text

In seventh grade, Mr. Takahasi taught his students to rate their comprehension using a four-point scale: 4—excellent, 3—good, 2—not so good, and 1—help! When he calls for their ratings now for the chapter "Creating Communities," his students quickly display their ratings on their chests with an appropriate number of fingers—4, 3, 2, or 1. Mr. Takahasi scans the room, takes note of each rating—especially those that are low—and directs his students to record their ratings in their journals.

Evaluating One's Need for Clarification

Also in seventh grade, Mr. Takahasi taught his students to annotate texts lightly during reading: to mark texts sparingly in pencil—lightly and slightly—using check marks for important ideas, uppercase *T*'s for important words, and minus signs for unknown words and confusing ideas. These annotations help his students to evaluate their need for clarification after reading.

Mr. Takahasi prompts his students to review their annotations for the chapter "Creating Communities" and record a quick clarification note in their journals. He anticipates from his own annotations for the chapter and students' recent reflections in their journals that a good number of students will need to clarify their understanding of community councils and words like *Caucasian*, *denominations*, *non-denominational*, and *rationale*, which he elected not to review or teach before assigning the text for homework.

CLARIFYING

Statements and Target Questions

After reading an assigned text, proficient readers clarify their understanding of particular elements in the text. In chapter 3, the action of clarifying was defined as the action of making clear or setting forth clearly. Proficient readers engage in the action of clarifying before and after reading. Before reading, they clarify their reading goal and purpose. After reading, they clarify their understandings about specific words and ideas encountered in the text.

This section addresses the following questions:

- What is the purpose of clarifying?
- What will middle grade students aim to clarify for themselves after reading?
- What clarifying options do students have? What factors will guide their selection of one option over another?
- Why is it helpful for students to reach the end of a text before returning to particular paragraphs to clarify words and ideas?

The After Reading Action of Clarifying

Having annotated an assigned text during reading and marked particular words and ideas as confusing, students now return to the text after reading and engage in one of four clarifying actions that will help them to better understand the text in part or in whole. Four clarifying options are available to students. These four options, shown in table 7.2, include rereading, cross-referencing, enhanced annotating, and questioning.

Table 7.2. Clarifying Options

Option	Description
Rereading	Reading paragraphs or sections in an assigned text again in whole or part to resolve confusions about words or ideas presented in the text
Cross-referencing	Using a source of information other than an assigned text to resolve confusions about words or ideas presented in the text
Enhanced annotating	Adding to existing annotations in the text for the purpose of clarifying meanings
Questioning	Resolving confusions about words or ideas presented in an assigned text by posing and answering one's own questions

Mr. Takahasi prompts his students in both seventh and eighth grades to use the options in table 7.2 to clarify their understanding of words and ideas in assigned unit texts. Depending on the length and complexity of the text, his students' familiarity with the topic, and available time, Mr. Takahasi prompts his students to use one or more clarifying options. But more often than not, his students need to use multiple clarifying options for the same text and aim to clarify their understandings about ideas in individual or multiple sentences and paragraphs.

Three Students in Action: Clarifying

Throughout his unit on World War II, while his students are actively engaged in clarifying their understandings about confusing words or ideas encountered in a text, Mr. Takahasi visits his students at their seats, observes them in action, and assists them as needed. At different points in his unit, Mr. Takahasi observes three particular students, Amida, Kiana, and Delroy, clarifying their understanding about specific words or ideas in assigned chapters about evacuation day and removal centers.

Amida and Kiana both seek to clarify their understanding about a specific word or idea in the evacuation day chapter. Delroy, on the other hand, seeks to clarify his understanding about one whole paragraph in the removal centers chapter. As the following illustrations will show, each student engages in one, two, or three clarifying actions to resolve confusions about a text.

Amida: Clarifying by Cross-Referencing, Rereading, and Enhanced Annotating

Amida aims to clarify her understanding about the words *grace* and *dignity*, which appear on pages 105 and 106, respectively, in the chapter "Evacuation Day" (Sone 2001). The word *grace* appears in the section "Fast and Furious Order" and the word *dignity* in the section "Family 10710." During reading, Amida marked both words with a minus sign and *T* (-*T*).

Amida enters the word *grace* in her online dictionary and quickly rules out the first two meanings shown by rereading the original sentence with each meaning in mind. In the original sentence, Monica Sone writes that "A thousand and one details must be attended to in this one week of grace" (Sone 2001, 105). Here, the word *grace* does not mean 1. a smooth way of moving or 2. polite behavior, but rather 3. more time. The dictionary provides the example of a person being given a grace period (more time) to do something important.

Amida writes this simple definition, "more time," in the margin of her text and draws a line (a branch) from it to the word *grace* in the original sentence.

After rereading the sentence and confirming to herself that the sentence makes sense, she moves on to the next word, *dignity*.

Kiana: Clarifying by Cross-Referencing

Kiana aims to clarify her understanding about a small town in Washington State called Puyallup, mentioned several times in the chapter "Evacuation Day" (Sone 2001). Monica Sone and her family were moved to Puyallup on May 1, 1942, but little information about the town is given in the chapter. When annotating the text during reading, Kiana marked the word *Puyallup* twice as confusing. By clarifying her understanding of the word, she expects to better understand the town's significance for Mrs. Sone and her family members.

Kiana searches online for information about Puyallup and learns in several minutes that Puyallup (pronounced pyū ăl' əp) is a city in Washington State located 35 miles south of Seattle. The Puyallup fairgrounds, home of the annual Washington State Fair, were used as an assembly center during World War II. The city is named after the Puyallup people, members of the Coast Salish Nation, who first settled the region. In the Coast Salish language the word *Puyallup* refers to the Puyallup people themselves and their generous and welcoming nature.

This information about Puyallup, provided by the clarifying action of cross-referencing, helps Kiana to better understand Mrs. Sone's relocation experiences during World War II. Kiana now understands that Mrs. Sone and members of her family traveled 35 miles by bus south of their home in Seattle to the city of Puyallup, where thousands of Japanese Americans like themselves were assembled before being relocated to internment camps. "No wonder Puyallup seemed like a small town to Mrs. Sone," says Kiana to her teacher. "She grew up in Seattle."

Delroy: Clarifying by Rereading and Questioning

Delroy aims to clarify his understanding of one paragraph in chapter 5, "The Removal Centers," from Sandler's book *Imprisoned* (2013). In the last part of the chapter, you read about a questionnaire that internees were required to complete in 1943 that determined their eligibility for permanent release. The last six paragraphs in the chapter focus entirely on this questionnaire and its effects on internees. Delroy, while reading the chapter, marked one of these paragraphs as confusing and has returned to it now after reading, aiming to understand it by engaging in the clarifying actions of rereading and questioning.

Delroy reads all six paragraphs again and confirms to himself—then to his teacher, who is standing by, ready to assist him—that he understands all but the one paragraph he marked as confusing, the fourth paragraph in the set. "Focus on that one then," prompts his teacher, "and ask yourself this: Do any important words appear in the first sentence?"

The first sentence is short. Delroy reads it quickly and reports to his teacher that two words are important, the words *question* and *dilemma*. To which his teacher replies, "Good. That's your starting point, Delroy. Now ask yourself this: What question, and whose dilemma?"

"Question 28 in the questionnaire," replies Delroy quickly; he then skims the paragraph immediately above and reports to his teacher that question 28 asked internees if they were willing to swear allegiance only to the United States and forswear their allegiance to Japan, the emperor of Japan, and the Japanese government. To which his teacher returns, "Good. Now who experienced a dilemma trying to answer this question, and why?"

Delroy can answer the first part of the question now—who? the Issei—but has to read further along, about halfway through the paragraph, before he can answer the second part of the question. So he reads the first half of the paragraph again with his teacher's question in mind and suddenly understands that the Issei felt trapped by question 28. Delroy tells his teacher that he gets it now, that the Issei weren't American citizens and couldn't legally swear allegiance to the United States. "And if they gave up their allegiance to Japan, where they were born, they would have lost the only citizenship they had."

"That's a serious dilemma," says his teacher. "I understand why the Issei felt trapped by the question. I wonder how the Nisei felt, but I see we're about to find out. Look at the second half of the paragraph. See what I mean?"

Delroy does see what his teacher means. The words *Nisei*, *question 28*, and *problem* all appear in a middle sentence in the paragraph, where the second half of the paragraph begins. The whole paragraph makes sense to him now. He reports to his teacher that the Nisei felt insulted by question 28. They were American citizens and already swore allegiance to the United States. "And many Nisei were even outraged by the question," adds Delroy. "You read about that here in the next paragraph."

"You can change that minus sign to a plus sign now in your text, and do it proudly," says his teacher, patting him on the back.

All Students in Action: Clarifying

Having learned from a show of hands that the majority of his students were confused by the section on community councils in the Yancey text, Mr. Takahasi has reproduced the section on a handout that he will use this morning to help all of his students to clarify their understandings about the section.

The section "Councils and Controversies" consists of four paragraphs. Mr. Takahasi has numbered these paragraphs on his handout 1–4 for easy reference and marked them as his students did in their original texts with check marks, uppercase *T*'s, and minus signs. Aiming to clarify his students' understanding of the text mainly by enhanced annotating, Mr. Takahasi has also marked the text with paragraph topics, underlining, and a branched gloss.

Paragraph 1 from the handout is shown in figure 7.3. The paragraph is numbered. The paragraph topic appears flush right above the paragraph. The term *self-government* is highlighted, marked with a plus sign and *T* (*T*+), and glossed. Each main idea key word is underlined in the text and noted to the right of the paragraph with a check mark.

an organization controlled by its own members

Community councils

¶1 Self-government was another aspect of center life designed to increase organization and stability. In the first months of internment, the WRA announced that elected community councils would be allowed to act as spokes-persons and liaisons between internees and staff, with the goal of encouraging the smooth running of the centers.

+T

✓✓

✓

Figure 7.3. Enhanced Annotations for Confusing Section in a Chapter

Mr. Takahasi reminds his students that for challenging sections like this they should first identify as many paragraph topics as possible and record them neatly in the text. "The first three paragraph topics, community councils, campaigning, and weakened support, are easy to identify, but the fourth one is tricky," says Mr. Takahasi. "I inferred the word actions in council actions, the fourth paragraph topic, from the list of matters council members had to respond to (e.g., recreation, food quality, education). In other words, they had to act on these matters."

Mr. Takahasi directs his students' attention back to paragraph 1. He suspects that all of his students struggled to understand this particular paragraph, asks for a show of hands, and confirms his suspicions. He tells his students that he struggled with the paragraph too and had to annotate it with greater care than the other three paragraphs to understand it.

"This first paragraph is about internment camp community councils," says Mr. Takahasi. "A community council is an organization controlled by its members, a form of self-government. You can see that I glossed the term self-government in the text."

Mr. Takahasi takes a short pause, then continues. "We need to know three things about these councils," says Mr. Takahasi. "One. The War Relocation Act (WRA) allowed internees to form these councils (✓). Two. Council members acted as spokesmen and liaisons for internees (✓). Three. A council's goal was to run a smooth camp (✓). And all of these ideas are represented by my enhanced annotations—my recorded paragraph topic, branched gloss, plus sign, and underlined main idea key words. Now, let's annotate the third paragraph together."

LOOKING BACK AND AHEAD

After reading assigned texts in social studies courses like Mr. Takahasi's, middle grade students benefit by engaging in all four reading actions examined in this chapter. Students benefit by summarizing the major ideas presented in these texts; reconfiguring their understandings about these texts; assessing their overall comprehension of these texts and the effectiveness of their actions before and during reading; and clarifying their understanding of specific words and ideas encountered in the text during reading. These four after reading options will likely take students 10–60 minutes to complete or longer depending on the particular options selected.

This concludes our exploration of the three phases of a reading event and the distinctive set of actions proficient readers engage in. In the final chapter of this book, we explore mediational practices that help students to read more effectively in middle grade social studies courses.

GROUNDING: AFTER READING PHASE ACTIONS

This chapter is grounded in metacognition and reading processes (Baker and Brown 1984), interactive models of reading development (Brown, Palincsar, and Armbruster 2013), secondary school reading (Alvermann and Moore 1991; Taylor and Beach 1984; Armbruster, Anderson, and Ostertag 1987), and text comprehension (Britton and Graesser 2014; Kintsch 2013).

8

Mediational Practices

Middle grade social studies teachers like Mr. Takahasi in the previous chapter enhance their students' understanding of course content by helping their students to read assigned unit texts proficiently.

In chapter 7, Mr. Takahasi provided specific instructional support that helped his eighth grade students take appropriate actions after reading assigned texts about Japanese Americans' internment experiences during World War II. In chapters 3–6, Mrs. Harper, Mrs. Touré, Mr. Rivera, Mr. Watson, and Mrs. Carter all helped their sixth, seventh, or eighth grade students take appropriate actions before or during reading to enhance their students' understandings about early people, criminal justice, specific regions of Africa, or American slavery.

All middle grade social studies teachers can enhance their students' understanding of course content and support their students' development as proficient readers by providing instructional support that explicitly and strategically aims to help students to take appropriate actions before, during, and after reading.

In chapter 3, Mrs. Harper explicitly and strategically helped her sixth graders to generate expectations about an assigned textbook chapter about early people using the mediational practice of image previewing. In chapter 6, Mr. Watson and Mrs. Carter explicitly and strategically helped their seventh graders to develop a coherent understanding about an assigned book chapter about American slavery using the mediational practice of chapter webbing.

Throughout this book, we have seen middle grade social studies teachers use a variety of mediational practices to enhance their students' understanding of assigned unit texts and support their students' development as proficient readers. These practices include written previews, guided questioning, thinking aloud, enhanced annotating, exemplars, journaling, and more. This chapter recalls these and other mediational practices you read about in previous chapters and presents additional practices that you can use in your own classroom.

The chapter is divided into five sections. Mediational practices showcased in previous chapters are recalled in the first section of the chapter. In the next three sections, mediational practices that specifically aim to help students to take appropriate actions before reading, after reading, and in all three phases of the same reading event are described and illustrated in turn. Much of the chapter focuses on a limited number of mediational practices, so the last section of the chapter provides a guide that can help you to select other practices not explored in this book that will enhance your students' reading experiences.

This chapter addresses the following questions:

- What mediational practices did showcased teachers use in previous chapters that helped their middle grade students to take appropriate actions before, during, and after reading?
- What additional mediational practices could you use to support your students' development as proficient readers?
- What guiding questions can help you to determine the appropriateness of an instructional practice for use in a middle grade social studies classroom?

PREVIOUSLY SHOWCASED PRACTICES

Mediational practices showcased in previous chapters are shown in table 8.1. Middle grade social studies teachers in chapters 1, 3, 4, and 7 used one or more of these practices to help their students to take appropriate reading actions in one or two phases of a reading event. These practices were showcased in each chapter's opening vignette or elsewhere in the chapter, and only one practice—the written preview—is revisited in this chapter.

Table 8.1. Previously Showcased Practices

Chapter	Phase	Practices
1, 3	Before	the written preview, assigned reading objectives, guided viewing, the knowledge activation guide
7	After	a cloze task, exemplars, journaling, enhanced annotating
3, 7	Before and After	word classification, topic outlining, topic webbing
4, 7	During and After	the note-making table, the metalinguistic discussion

Note. The metalinguistic discussion focuses specifically on English-language structures and functions and aims to develop students' knowledge about the way language works—the way it is used—in written texts. Throughout chapter 4, beginning in the opening vignette, Mr. Rivera used metalinguistic discussions in his seventh grade civics course to help his students to read assigned texts proficiently. His metalinguistic discussions focused on smaller and larger linguistic units: phonemes, morphemes, individual words, word groups, clauses, and whole sentences.

Other mediational practices were used by middle grade social studies teachers throughout this book to enhance their students' reading experiences and support their students' development as proficient readers. The practices of demonstrating, guiding, prompting, annotating, discussing, and the written summary, showcased throughout this book, may be used before, during, or after reading to help students to engage in a specific reading action.

BEFORE READING MEDIATIONAL PRACTICES

Four practices are described and illustrated below. These practices include image previewing, the written preview, teacher-directed closed word sorts, and terminology cubing. All of these practices help middle grade students to take one or more actions before reading that help them to achieve their ultimate reading goal for assigned reading events.

Image Previewing

Basic Information about Practice

Many assigned texts contain photographic images of real people and things that aim to enhance students' overall reading experience and their understanding of course content. Image previewing, used extensively by Mrs. Harper in chapter 3 to prepare her sixth grade students for an assigned text about early people, enables middle grade students to share their observations with others about particular images that appear in an assigned text.

> *Targeted reading actions*: generating expectations, activating relevant topic knowledge
> *Preferred texts*: textbooks, book chapters, and articles (all with images)
> *Preferred images*: photographs of people and things
> *Grouping*: whole class, partnerships
> *Time allocation*: 20 minutes

Implementation of Practice

Having previously demonstrated and guided the process of image previewing with their students, teachers assign students to partnerships, identify required materials, project the same set of questions used by Mrs. Harper in chapter 3, reproduced below, and review these questions with their students before proceeding.

Image Previewing Questions

1. What type of image am I looking at?
2. (a) What do I see in the image? (b) What people do I see? (c) What do they look like? (d) What are they doing? (e) What things do I see? (f) What do they look like? (g) How they are used?
3. What will I likely read about in the text that relates to this image?

Teachers then complete six steps to implement the practice with their students:

1. State the purpose of the practice
2. Guide students' selection of an image in the assigned text
3. Direct students to examine and share their observations about this image with their partners using questions 1–2 (above)
4. (a) Call on several partnerships to share their observations with everyone (b) remind students to share expansively, and (c) pose questions to help students share expansively
5. Reiterate students' responses to question 3 (above)
6. Direct students to read the assigned text

Example

In chapter 3, at the beginning of her sixth grade study of early people, Mrs. Harper directed her students to work collaboratively with a partner to generate expectations about the content of chapter 1 in their course textbook. Two of her students, Kim and Erin, were eager to share their observations about the image on page 68.

Kim and Erin told their teacher and classmates that the image, a photograph, was very mysterious and that neither of them understood what they were seeing at first. But then they spotted a baby, a girl, looking back at them in the picture. The girl was with her dad—and both were wearing hats—they were going somewhere, the girls reported. "The girl is bundled up in the saddle, holding on to two posts. Erin called them saddle posts," reported Kim.

"The dad is making sure that the saddle doesn't move and the girl is safe," reported Erin. "They're taking their pots and food. That's their food in that gray bag tied to the post. I bet there's water in that metal container."

And when Mrs. Harper asked them what they expected to read about in that part of the chapter, Erin and Kim responded: people on the move, and their reasons for moving.

Written Previews

Basic Information about Practice

Written previews introduce students to assigned unit texts. A written preview is prepared by the teacher and presented verbally to students immediately before they read an assigned text on their own in class. All written previews include four basic elements: an identification of the text's topic, a statement of relevance, a summary of the text, and guiding questions.

Targeted reading actions: clarifying purpose, generating expectations, activating relevant topic knowledge
Preferred texts: textbooks (if suitable), book chapters, articles
Materials: one copy of written preview prepared by the teacher in advance
Grouping: whole class
Time allocation: 10 minutes

A Four-Paragraph Preview

In a four-paragraph written preview, as in the forthcoming example, the first paragraph presents the topic and a brief statement about the relevance of the topic for students. The next two paragraphs present a brief description of the assigned text. The last paragraph presents key questions that students will aim to answer during reading.

Implementation of Practice

Teachers prepare a written preview for an assigned unit text then complete four steps to implement the practice with students:

1. (a) Identify the assigned text, and (b) connect it to the current unit of study
2. (a) Read first paragraph to students, and (b) engage students in brief discussion about the topic and its relevance
3. Read second, third, and fourth paragraphs to students
4. Direct students to read the assigned text

Example

The following four-paragraph written preview was created for chapter 3: "Why Are Juveniles Incarcerated?" in the information book *Youth in Prison* (Smith and McIntosh 2007).

Written preview: "Why Are Juveniles Incarcerated?" (Book Chapter)

Teenagers are sentenced to juvenile prisons to stop them from hurting themselves or others and to discourage them from committing crimes. A tenth grade classmate of mine in high school was sentenced to juvenile prison for robbing a convenience store. Crime, even juvenile crime, impacts all of us at one or more points in our lives.

In 2007, when this chapter was written, four teenagers ages 13–17 were sentenced to juvenile prison, one for theft and three for murder. You'll read about these teenagers first thing in the chapter and be disturbed, even shocked by their personal situations and crimes. One of them shot and killed his girlfriend accidentally and another stabbed and killed her best friend's brother. You'll learn that all four teenagers came from troubled homes, and that this is a common denominator among most juvenile offenders.

Did you know that Latin and African American youth and youth from poor families are more likely to be incarcerated than youth from white middle-class families? And did you know that many incarcerated juveniles experienced severe emotional or psychological distress growing up? This was certainly the case for the young people you meet at the start of the chapter, Tomás, Daniel, and Stacey. All came from troubled homes. Tomás and Daniel both couldn't bear to live at home. Tomás ran away and lived on the streets for a while, and Daniel joined a gang. And Stacey's home life was abusive and violent.

While reading this chapter on juvenile incarceration, think about the following questions:

1. Why are so many minority boys from poor neighborhoods incarcerated?
2. What personal factors often lead to juvenile delinquency and incarceration?
3. Are more young people arrested for violent or nonviolent crimes?

Suggestions

Read the assigned text yourself several times before developing a written preview. Consider limiting your written preview to four paragraphs in the interests of time and convenience. Articulate the topic clearly and succinctly in your first paragraph, and limit your discussion about the topic and its relevance to five minutes. You will find that discussions longer than five minutes often lessen students' enthusiasm to read an assigned text.

When describing the text in your second and third paragraphs, focus on highly relevant and engaging information, and define key terms used in your description. Limit the questions you pose in your fourth paragraph to three, and focus on essential meanings conveyed by the text.

Another Example

In chapter 1, we met Mr. Buckley, a seventh grade history teacher, who prepared a written preview for two sections in a chapter about different forms of government in ancient Greece. Sections 3 and 4 in Mr. Buckley's course textbook focused on democracy in Athens and oligarchy in Sparta. Mr. Buckley read the full chapter carefully, determined its suitability for a written preview, and prepared a written preview for the last two sections in the chapter. He prepared his preview as a handout, which he distributed and read to his students.

Mr. Buckley's written preview for two sections of a chapter in his course textbook includes the four basic elements in all written previews—an identification of the text's topic, a statement of relevance, a summary of the text, and guiding questions. For this particular written preview, Mr. Buckley preferred to summarize the text in bulleted points and presented his guiding questions earlier in the preview. He also included a set of directions for reading the assigned sections in the textbook and provided the preview to students in the form of a handout.

Teacher-Directed Closed Word Sorts

Basic Information about Practice

Teacher-directed closed word sorts help students to anticipate and identify important words and ideas they will soon encounter in an assigned text. In groups of two or three, students sort roughly 20 words into categories provided by their teacher. The sort is closed in the sense that the teacher has closed the option for students to provide their own categories. Word sorts that enable students to provide their own categories are called open sorts.

> *Targeted reading actions*: generating expectations
> *Preferred texts*: textbooks, book chapters, articles
> *Materials*: word and category cards prepared by teacher in advance
> *Grouping*: partnerships, whole class
> *Time allocation*: 30 minutes

Implementation of Practice

Teachers select roughly 20 words from an assigned unit text and group them in meaningful categories. Teachers prepare these words and categories as a handout, assign students to groups of two or three, and distribute a handout to each group. Teachers then complete six steps to implement the practice with students:

1. (a) Identify the assigned text, and (b) connect it to the forthcoming word sort
2. State the purpose of the word sort
3. Review word sorting tasks and expectations
4. Direct students to complete the sort collaboratively with group members
5. (a) Project your own sorted word set, and (b) share your sorting rationale, if needed
6. Direct students to read the assigned text

Example

The following teacher-directed closed word sort materials were prepared using chapter 1, "Early People," in Pearson's *myWorld History* textbook (Karpiel et al. 2012).

1. Word set

   Table 8.2. Word Set Selected by Teacher

anthropologist	archaeologist	Ardi	beliefs	art
Homo habilis	skeletons	kinship	Lucy	teeth
Geologist	storytelling	*Homo sapiens*	fossils	tools
Donald Johanson	Mary Leakey	Neanderthal	pottery	values
Louis Leakey	fragments	humanoid	botanist	

2. Categories

   Artifacts
   Cultural elements
   Evolutionary development
   Specialists
   Notable individuals

3. Sorted word set

   Table 8.3. Word Set Sorted by Teacher

CATEGORY	SORTED WORDS
Artifacts	skeletons, fossils, tools, pottery, fragments, teeth
Cultural elements	beliefs, kinship, art, values, storytelling
Evolutionary development	*Homo sapiens*, Neanderthal, *Homo habilis*, humanoid
Specialists	archaeologist, geologist, anthropologist, botanist
Notable individuals	Louis Leakey, Mary Leakey, Donald Johanson, Lucy, Ardi

Terminology Cubing

Basic Information about Practice

Terminology cubing helps students to develop understandings about key terms they will encounter in an assigned text. In partnerships, students explore six facets of an assigned term using a special die prepared by their teacher. Each partnership records information about the assigned term in their vocabulary notebook, then shares this information with classmates.

Targeted reading actions: generating expectations, developing topic knowledge
Preferred texts: textbooks
Materials: terminology cube (see figure 8.1)
Grouping: partnerships, whole class
Time allocation: 20 minutes

Terminology Cube Preparation and Storage

Teachers prepare one terminology cube for each partnership using the template shown in figure 8.1. Students assemble their partnership cube, use the cube to learn about their assigned term, then return the cube to their teacher who stores it for later use.

Vocabulary Learning Tasks

Partners take turns rolling their cube and work together to complete each task specified. Partners are ready to share information about their assigned term with others when they have described the term structurally, defined the term formally in a comprehensible way, associated the term with other terms or words they know, pronounced and spelled the term, and used the term appropriately in a real-world context.

Implementation of Practice

Having previously demonstrated and guided the process of terminology cubing with their students, teachers assign students to partnerships, direct them to prepare a new cubing entry in their vocabulary notebooks, assign a term to each partnership, supply each partnership with a cube, and review each cube-face task with students before proceeding. Teachers then complete five steps to implement the practice with students:

1. (a) Identify the assigned text, and (b) connect it to the current unit of study
2. Review the full set of assigned terms with students
3. Direct students to cube and record information about their assigned terms
4. Call on partnerships to share information about their assigned terms
5. Direct students to read the assigned text

Cubing Template

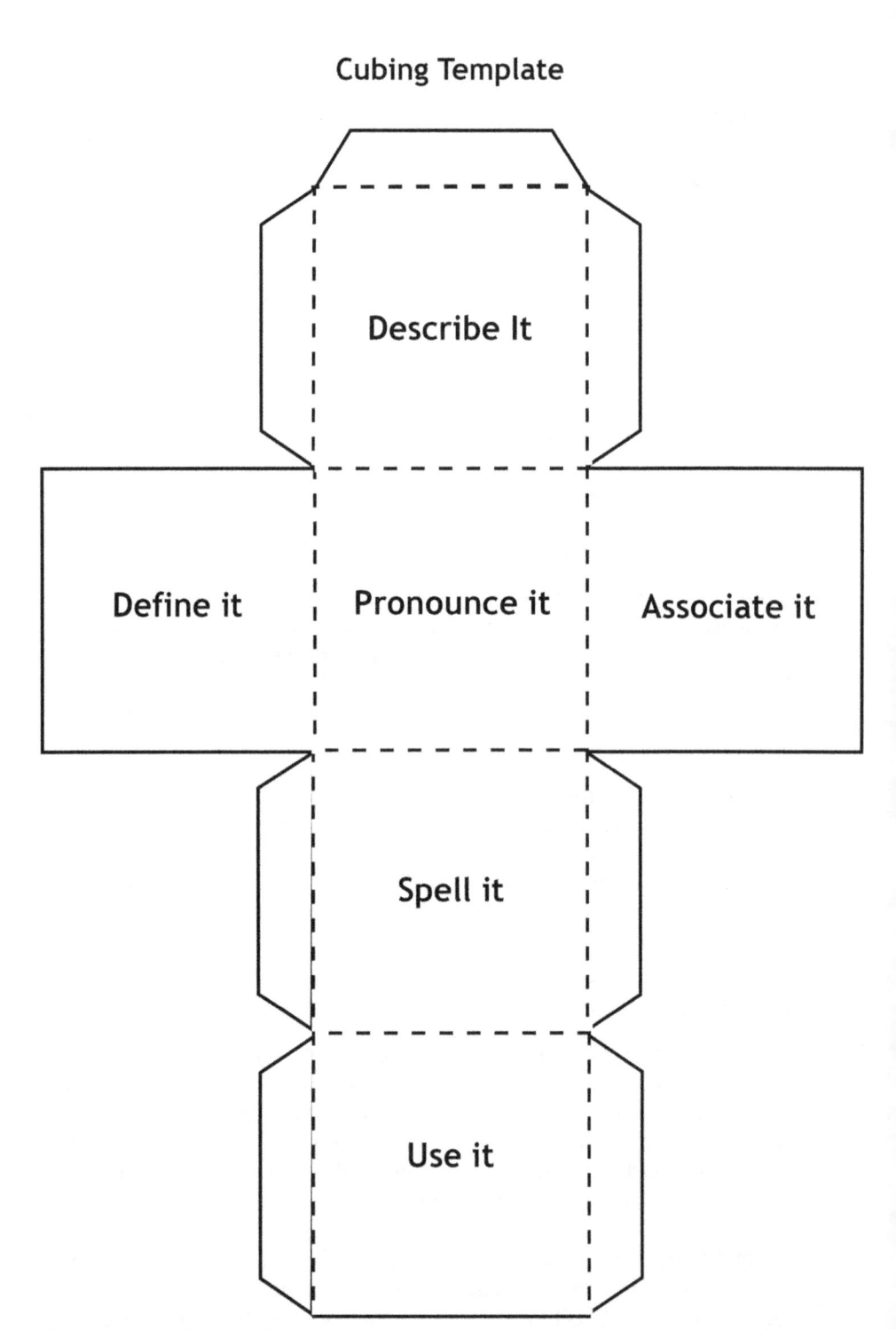

Describe It

Define it | **Pronounce it** | **Associate it**

Spell it

Use it

Figure 8.1. Cubing Template

Example

The following information about the term *rehabilitation*, obtained by terminology cubing, was shared by two students in Mr. Rivera's seventh grade civics class (see chapter 4 above). The term appears in chapter 20, section 2, "The Criminal Justice System," in the *Prentice Hall Civics* textbook (Davis, Fernlund, and Woll 2009).

> Assigned word: rehabilitation
>
> > **DESCRIPTION**: rehabilitate (base word, v.), -tion (suffix)
> > **PRONUNCIATION**: /rē hə bĭl ə tā´ shən/
> > **SPELLING**: re·ha·bil·i·ta·tion; 6 syllables
> > **DEFINED**: the act or process of rehabilitating (rehabilitate, to help someone newly released from prison to readapt to life outside of prison)
> > **ASSOCIATED WITH**: crime, imprisonment, sentence, release, freedom, new life
> > **USED**: Some people believe that rehabilitation programs lower crime rates.

AFTER READING MEDIATIONAL PRACTICES

Introduction

The after reading mediational practices of the concept of definition map and after reading survey are examined below. These two practices help middle grade students, respectively, to clarify their understandings of particular words and ideas presented in a text and to consolidate their understandings about a text by engaging in all four after reading actions.

Concept of Definition Maps

Basic Information about Practice

Concept of definition maps help students to clarify their understandings of important words or terms encountered recently in assigned texts. In groups of four, students select one of five to eight words or terms provided by their teacher, discuss the word or term with group members, and complete their own copy of the template.

> *Targeted reading actions*: clarifying meanings (words or terms)
> *Preferred texts*: textbooks, book chapters, articles
> *Materials*: concept of definition map (see figure 8.2)
> *Grouping*: groups of four
> *Time allocation*: 15–20 minutes

168   *Chapter 8*

Template Organization and Completion

The concept of definition template, shown in figure 8.2, consists of four main sections. In the middle and upper sections, respectively, students will record the selected word or term and its definition. In the side and lower sections, respectively, students will respond to the questions: *What is it like?* and *What are some examples of it?*

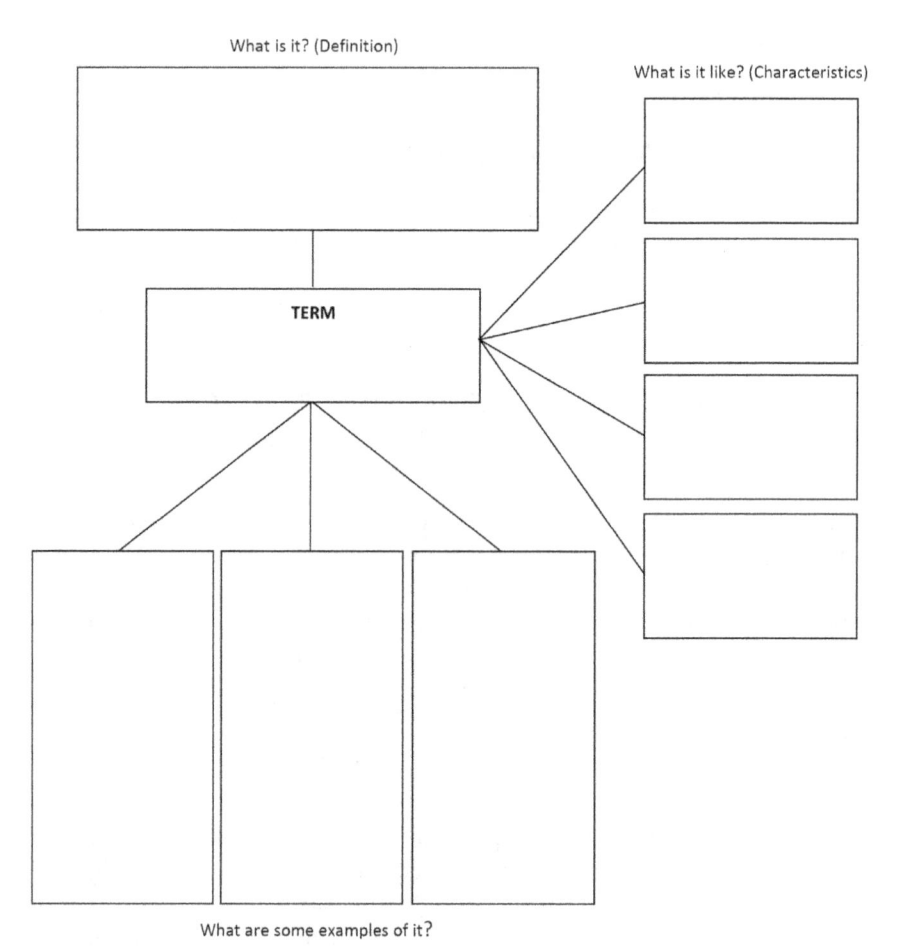

Figure 8.2. Concept of Definition Map Template

Implementation of Practice

Having previously demonstrated and guided the process of completing a concept of definition map with their students, and having listed five to eight important words or terms from a recently read text, teachers assign students to groups of four, provide each group member with a concept of definition map template, and review each template section with students. Teachers then complete five steps to implement the practice with students:

1. (a) Project all five to eight words or terms in your list, (b) identify the source text, and (c) read each word or term aloud
2. (a) Direct students to discuss the list of words or terms with group members, (b) select one word or term to map, and (c) report their selection to you
3. (a) State the purpose of the concept of definition map, and (b) connect the practice to the after reading action of clarifying
4. Direct students to map their selected word or term substantively
5. (a) Collect completed maps, (b) review, and (c) return

Example

A concept of definition map for the term *memorial service*, completed by four students in Mr. Takahasi's eighth grade American history class (see chapter 7 above), is shown in figure 8.3. The term *memorial service*, as indicated at the top of the figure, appears in the last chapter of the autobiography *Looking Like the Enemy* (Gruenewald 2005). Details about the chapter and book and a chapter summary were provided by Mr. Takahasi.

After Reading Surveys

Basic Information about Practice

After reading surveys prompt students to engage in three after reading actions and prepare to engage in the fourth. Survey questions and directives prompt students to summarize an assigned text, reflect on the text as a coherent whole, evaluate their overall understanding of the text and the effectiveness of their before or during reading actions, and identify particular elements in the text that need clarification. The after reading survey takes the form of a template that students can complete independently for any assigned unit text.

Targeted reading actions: summarizing, reconfiguring, assessing, clarifying meanings (words, terms, or ideas)
Preferred texts: textbooks, book chapters, articles
Materials: survey handout prepared by the teacher in advance
Grouping: whole class
Time allocation: 10 minutes

Concept of Definition Map

Source book: Looking Like the Enemy
Chapter or section title: "Return to Minidoka"
Summary: In July 1944, Mary Matsuda Gruenewald, her brother, and her parents arrived at the Minidoka internment camp in southern Idaho after previous relocations to internment camps in northern California and Wyoming. The Matsudas were among 120,000 Japanese Americans who were evacuated from their homes by Presidential Order and relocated to internment camps. Now 18, Mrs. Gruenewald was given permission to leave the Minidoka camp to join the United States Cadet Nurse Corps in Clinton, Iowa. More than 60 years later, Mrs. Gruenewald returns to the Minidoka camp with other internees and writes about this experience in the last chapter of her book.

What is it? (Definition)

What is it like? (Characteristics)

- a special service that honors the life and death of one or more people
- attended by surviving family members and special guests
- is a formal event marked with music and speeches
- includes moments of silence to honor the dead
- helps people to feel connected and valued

WORD OR TERM
memorial service

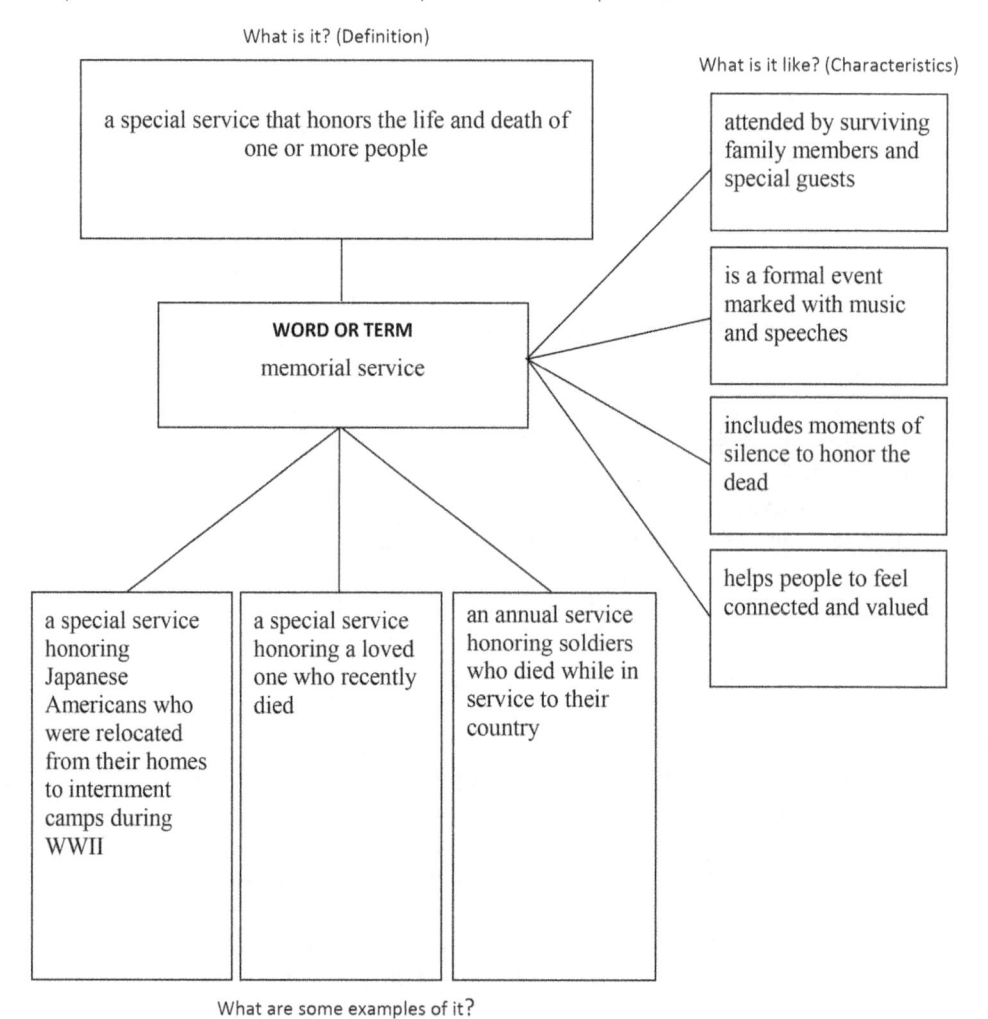

Examples:
- a special service honoring Japanese Americans who were relocated from their homes to internment camps during WWII
- a special service honoring a loved one who recently died
- an annual service honoring soldiers who died while in service to their country

What are some examples of it?

Figure 8.3. Concept of Definition Map: *Memorial Service*

Survey Organization and Completion

The after reading survey consists of four main sections numbered 1–4. Survey questions and directives for each section are shown below. To complete the survey, students first record information about the assigned text, then respond to each survey question or directive in turn. Students will complete the survey individually, then proceed to clarify their understandings about particular textual elements identified in the survey.

1. Summarizing
   Summarize the text using a numbered key word list. Did the introductory section prepare you for the important ideas you encountered in the text?
2. Reconfiguring
   Did the headings help you to read for understanding? Would reorganizing these headings help you to better understand the text and retain important ideas?
3. Assessing
   On a 4-point scale, rate each of the following: your overall understanding of the text, the quality of your generated expectations, your identification of unknown words, your reading speed, your attentiveness, and your identification of important ideas.
4. Clarifying
   What sections in the text will you seek to clarify for yourself? What words, terms, or ideas in the text will you seek to clarify for yourself?

Implementation of Practice

Having previously guided their students' completion of an after reading survey for several assigned unit texts, teachers distribute the survey template and complete five steps to implement the practice with students:

1. Remind students about the purpose of the after reading survey
2. Direct students to complete the survey independently and thoughtfully
3. Provide assistance as needed
4. (a) Collect and (b) review completed surveys
5. (a) Return surveys to students with commendations, and (b) oversee their storage in students' binders

Example

The after reading survey shown in figure 8.4 was completed for chapter 7, "The Juvenile Justice System Should Address Racial Inequalities," in the book *Juvenile Crime* (Gerdes 2012).

Chapter 8

AFTER READING SURVEY

Text: "The Juvenile Justice System Should Address Racial Inequalities"
Number of sections: 6
Date: January 16, 2019

1. Summarizing
    a. Summarize the text using a numbered key word list.
    b. Did the introductory section prepare you for the important ideas you encountered in the text?

Numbered Key Word List Summary	Introductory Section
1. Jurisdictional explanation 2. Arrest procedures 3. Automatic transfer laws 4. Racial bias 5. Solutions	Yes. The introductory paragraphs mention specific minority groups, the harsher treatment they received in the juvenile justice system, and several explanations for this unequal treatment. But it doesn't mention anything about solutions.

2. Reconfiguring
    a. Did the headings help you to read for understanding? Headings A and D-F helped, but headings B and C didn't.
    b. Would reorganizing these headings help you to better understand the text and retain important ideas? Yes. I would organize the chapter in two parts: Explanations and Solutions.

3. Assessing
   On a 4-point scale, rate each of the following:

3	your overall understanding of the text	
3	the quality of your generated expectations	4 = excellent 3 = good 2 = so-so 1 = help!
3	your identification of unknown words	
3	your overall reading speed	
4	your attentiveness	
3	your identification of important ideas	

4. Clarifying
    a. What sections in the text will you seek to clarify for yourself? E. Federal Solutions
    b. What words or terms in the text will you seek to clarify for yourself?
       jurisdictional, adjudication, reauthorization, disparities

Figure 8.4.   Completed After Reading Survey

MULTIPHASE MEDIATIONAL PRACTICES

Introduction

Three multiphase practices are described and illustrated below. The first practice, the think-aloud, has been showcased extensively throughout this book in chapter vignettes and elsewhere and helps middle grade students—by teacher modeling—to take appropriate actions before, during, and after reading.

The other two practices, both reading guides, prompt students selectively and strategically before, during, and after reading to clarify their reading objectives, generate expectations about forthcoming ideas and words in a text, read fluently and for understanding, and clarify their understandings of specific words and ideas encountered during reading.

The Think-Aloud

The think-aloud, as a mediational reading practice, is a metacognitive action rendered verbally that helps students to understand a specific before, during, or after reading action and use that action effectively on their own. Reading actions are commonly modeled during guided reading instruction in a think-aloud in response to specific annotations in a text. A think-aloud may be delivered before, during breaks in, or after reading; may be planned or improvised; and is equally effective with one or many students.

Targeted reading actions: any before, during, or after reading action
Preferred texts: textbooks, book chapters, articles
Time allocation: varies according to purpose

Implementation of Practice

Teachers complete five steps before, during, or after reading to implement the practice with students:

Before Reading Implementation

1. Identify the assigned text
2. Identify the specific reading action you will engage in
3. (a) Engage in that action, and (b) report your engagement verbally
4. (a) Call on students to engage in that same reading action and (b) report their engagement verbally
5. State the benefits of engaging in that reading action

During Breaks in or after Reading Implementation

1. Direct students' attention to a specific location in the assigned text
2. Provide information about this specific location in the text
3. (a) Identify a specific reading action that you will engage in, (b) state your purpose for engaging in this action, and (c) connect the action to the specific location in the text you previously identified
4. (a) Engage in that action, and (b) report your engagement verbally
5. State the benefits of engaging in that reading action

Two Examples

Previously in this book, middle grade social studies teachers Mrs. Harper and Mr. Takahasi used the mediational reading practice of the think-aloud to demonstrate the actions of proficient readers before and after reading that help them to achieve their ultimate reading goal of understanding the main ideas in a text and being able to use these ideas at a later date. These two teachers used a think-aloud, respectively, to demonstrate the action of generating expectations about an assigned text before reading and clarifying one's understanding about an assigned text after reading.

Example 1: A Before Reading Think-Aloud

As reported earlier in this chapter, sixth grade teacher Mrs. Harper used the mediational practice of image previewing to help her students to generate expectations about the content of a chapter on early people. Before implementing the practice with her students, she demonstrated it using a think-aloud focusing on the image of a skull on page 58 in the chapter.

> MRS. HARPER: This is a photograph of an actual human skull. But it's not a complete skull. Parts of it are missing. Parts are missing on the side of the skull. [She feels around her ears.] The ear will be missing of course, because our ears are not made out of bone and don't last long after we die. There should be more bone around the ear, here, around the ear hole. And part of the forehead is missing above the left eye. Come to think of it, that's a pretty odd looking forehead. It doesn't come down straight like ours. It's slanted. [She feels her own forehead and nods her head.]
>
> The jaw is missing too. If this is an early human skull, it has to have a jaw. Can you imagine not having a jaw? How could you eat your food? How could you chew it? [She opens her mouth wide then laughs.] Sorry about that. I can't help laughing, thinking about my throat starting right here, just under my top lip. That doesn't make sense. I wonder what the jaw in this skull looked like. I wonder if it held as many teeth as ours. And some top teeth are missing too in this skull.
>
> But it's not an original skull. I mean, it's not an actual skull. I couldn't help noticing the word *fossil* in the caption. The caption is so close to the image and so short that it's hard not to skim it. Of course this skull is a fossil. Even made of bone, a skull can't last forever; and this skull looks like a rock, a rusty rock. And the more I look at it, the whole thing looks pieced together. I wonder if somebody found the skull in pieces and glued it together like this.
>
> Okay. So in this first part of the chapter, I expect to read about this skull and the skulls of early people, if they're found in certain locations, how old they are, and what they tell us about the lives of early people.

Example 2: An After Reading Think-Aloud

In chapter 7, Mr. Takahasi used a think-aloud to help his eighth grade students to resolve their confusions about internee self-government in Japanese internment camps. You will recall that many of Mr. Takahasi's students struggled to understand a section in Yancey's (1998) book about community life and the establishment of community councils. In response to his students' confusion, Mr. Takahasi performed a think-aloud using an annotated copy of that one section of text that confused his students.

Mr. Takahasi reminded his students that for challenging sections like this they should first identify as many paragraph topics as possible and record them neatly in the text, as he did on his annotated copy. He told his students candidly that he struggled to identify the fourth paragraph topic himself and had to infer the paragraph topic key word actions from the list of matters that appears at the bottom of the paragraph. And that, he told his students, was the first thing he did to clarify his understandings about this challenging section: he enhanced the annotations he made during reading, recording all four paragraph topics directly in his text.

Then he told his students, returning to paragraph 1, that this first paragraph had completely stumped him; and now, having read the paragraph again several times, he understood that the paragraph was about internment camp councils and that a community council was an organization controlled by its members, a form of self-government. So he glossed the term *self-government* directly in the text—his second enhanced annotation.

Mr. Takahasi went on to think aloud about his other enhanced annotations for the first paragraph then helped his students to think through and annotate another confusing paragraph in the section.

Selective Reading Guides

Basic Information about Practice

Selective reading guides help students to extract essential meanings from assigned texts. They help students to prepare to read assigned texts; to read texts fluently for understanding; and to clarify their understandings about important information presented in texts. Students familiarize themselves with a guide before reading; use the guide to understand a text during reading; then consolidate their understandings about that text after reading by sharing their responses to certain questions in the guide in a whole class review.

> *Targeted reading actions*: clarifying purpose, generating expectations, reading fluently, reading for understanding, formulating, building coherence, and clarifying meanings (words, terms, and ideas)

Preferred texts: textbooks, book chapters, articles
Materials: reading guide prepared by teacher in advance
Preferred length of guide: more or less half a page
Time allocation: 10 minutes before reading, 10–30 minutes after reading

Guide Preparation

Read the assigned text and annotate it with the express purpose of developing a highly selective guide that will help your students to extract essential meanings from the text during reading. Your annotations will expressly focus on important content, images, and terms.

Use the following partial template to develop a full-length guide for any assigned unit text. Insert the chapter title and text genre first, then use your annotated text to complete the first main entry in your guide. As shown in the partial template, each main entry will include a section heading, page and paragraph numbers, and at least one of the following elements: a statement, question, or directive. For optimal readability, subentry information will be offset by indentation or em dashes.

Partial Template for a Selective Reading Guide

Selective Reading Guide: "Chapter Title" (Text Genre)

HEADING

PAGE NUMBER. Paragraph number. Statement. Question. Directive. Note.

First question.
Additional questions.
What did this individual recall about their enslavement?
— Definition.
— Additional statements, directives, or notes.

Implementation of Practice

Having used selective reading guides in the past, teachers simply provide their students with the new guide, identify the corresponding assigned text, and direct students to read the guide silently. Teachers then complete seven steps before and after reading to implement the practice with students:

Before Reading

1. State the purpose of the guide
2. Clarify students' understanding of particular guide items
3. Remind students to read the assigned text at an optimal speed
4. Direct students to read the assigned text using the guide

After Reading

5. (a) Call on students to share their responses to certain questions in the guide, and (b) provide guidance that helps students to respond substantively to these questions
6. (a) Reiterate important ideas shared by students, and (b) direct all students to record these ideas on their guides in a highly readable way
7. Oversee students' storage of the guide in their binders

Example

The following selective reading guide was developed for chapter 4: "The Work of Slavery" in the book *Our Song, Our Toil* (Stepto 1994). Chapter 4 offers various perspectives on American slavery: the perspectives of early Puritans, slaveholders in northern and southern colonies, and actual slaves who published books about their experiences.

Selective Reading Guide: "The Work of Slavery" (Book Chapter)

INTRODUCTION
PAGE 41. Introductory paragraph. Slavery is compared to legal robbery, and slaveholders are charged with stealing labor from their enslaved workers. Is this a fair comparison? Think about an answer. Be prepared to share this answer verbally with classmates when directed.

IN THE NORTH
PAGES 41–42. Paragraphs 1–2. I inferred the topics for these paragraphs as Puritan colonies and northern colonies.
— Indentured: bound by a legal contract.
— Tanning: the process of turning an animal hide into leather.

IN THE SOUTH
PAGES 42–43. Paragraph 3. What kinds of skilled work were large plantation owners able to offer slaves that small farmers couldn't offer?
PAGE 43. Image. Can you spot slaves picking cotton, gathering cotton, loading cotton, and transporting cotton?
PAGES 43–49. Three subsections: introduction and personal accounts. The experiences of three former slaves are recounted in the last part of this chapter. As you read about each individual, Solomon Northup, Frederick Douglass, and Mary Prince, ask yourself the following questions:

Where was this individual born?
Where in the South was this individual enslaved?
What did this individual recall about their enslavement?— All three individuals wrote books about their experiences as slaves. What makes their experiences believable? What makes these experiences remarkable?

— Many period words are defined in the margins. Use these definitions to help you to understand each individual's personal account of being enslaved.

Comments

This example includes all the elements delineated in the guide preparation section. It includes statements, questions, and directives both as inset and offset elements, and each offset element is marked by indentation or an em dash. Statements and directives end with periods, and all questions end with a question mark. This particular guide includes more WH-type questions than YES/NO-type questions. Both types of questions are appropriate. A statement consists of one or more declarative sentences, and all directives begin with an imperative verb. One or more guide entries may direct students to skim parts of a text or to avoid reading certain parts entirely.

Nonhierarchical Reading Guides

Basic Information about Practice

Like selective reading guides, nonhierarchical reading guides help students to extract essential meanings from assigned texts and provide specific reading support for students before, during, and after reading. Students review the guide before reading; use the guide to understand a text during reading; then consolidate their understandings about that text after reading by sharing their responses to certain questions in the guide in a whole class review.

Nonhierarchical reading guides are expressly designed for informational texts and are longer and more comprehensive than selective reading guides. *Nonhierarchical* reading guides differ from *hierarchical* reading guides in fundamental ways. These differences are shown in table 8.4.

Table 8.4. Reading Guides Compared

Nonhierarchical Reading Guides	Hierarchical Reading Guides
Have an explicit reading focus	Have an explicit learning focus
Are intended to be used by readers before, during, and after reading	Are intended to be used by readers after reading to enhance vertical learning (see Bloom 1956)
Reflect the organization of the associated text	Use a three-part structure
Follow the order of ideas presented in the corresponding text	Group entries by levels of mental processing required for learning: Part 1 Literal comprehension Part 2 Interpretation Part 3 Application

Targeted reading actions: clarifying purpose, generating expectations, reading fluently, reading for understanding, formulating, building coherence, and clarifying meanings (words, terms, and ideas)
Preferred texts: textbooks, book chapters, articles
Materials: reading guide
Preferred length of guide: 1–2 pages
Time allocation: 10 minutes before reading, 20–30 minutes after reading

Guide Preparation

Read the assigned text, and annotate it with the express purpose of developing a nonhierarchical reading guide that will help your students to extract essential meanings from the text during reading. Like your annotations for the selective reading guide, your annotations for this guide will expressly focus on important content, images, and terms.

Use the following partial template to develop a full-length guide for any assigned unit text. Insert the topic and title of the text and relevant page numbers, customize the directions (see forthcoming example), then use your annotated text to complete each section and set of prompts. For each section heading and prompt, include a parenthetical page and paragraph/image reference, and highlight the latter element for clarity and easy reference.

Partial Template for a Selective Reading Guide
Topic: Chapter topic
Text title: Chapter number and title
Relevant page numbers: Page range

Directions: In chapter (insert chapter number), sections (insert section labels A–n), you will read important information about (insert the topic). You will read about (insert a simple list of section topics, separated by commas). Read each section continuously without stopping. At the end of each section, stop, and complete that section in the guide. Most items in the guide will take you 5–20 seconds to answer. Items that will take you longer to answer are marked with an asterisk. Skip any item without an asterisk that takes you too long to answer.

A. Insert section topic (page range, ¶numbers 1-n, relevant figures or maps)

  1. Insert prompt. (page number, ¶number)
  2. Insert prompt. (page number, ¶number)
  3. Insert prompt. (page number, ¶number)
  4. Insert prompt. (page number, ¶number)
  5. Insert prompt. (page number, ¶number)

The nonhierarchical reading guides you develop for unit texts in middle grade social studies courses will typically include as many sections as appear in the corresponding text. Limit the number of prompts you include in each section to eight, and prompt students to complete a range of actions that include filling in blanks, providing single word answers or simple phrases, circling, drawing, listing, matching, labeling, ordering, selecting, striking out, shading, and more. Very few prompts will take students longer than 20 seconds to complete.

Nonhierarchical reading guides, like all reading guides, are most effective when they focus on highly relevant information presented in a text and are comprehensible, consistently formatted, highly readable, straightforward, interesting, and purposeful.

Implementation of Practice

Having used nonhierarchical reading guides in the past, teachers simply identify the assigned text, provide students with the corresponding guide, review the organization of the guide, and direct students to read the guide silently. Teachers then complete the same seven steps for the selective reading guide to implement the practice with students (see 176–77).

Example

A partial nonhierarchical reading guide follows for chapter 13, section 1, "Chapter Atlas" in the *myWorld Geography* textbook (Chu et al. 2011). Chapter 13, section 1 focuses on West and Central Africa and consists of five level one sections (A–E). A complete guide was developed for this section in the chapter, but in the interest of space, only part of the guide appears below. Spaces for students' responses to prompts A5 and B2 are excluded from this example.

> Nonhierarchical Reading Guide: Chapter 13, section 1, "Chapter Atlas" (Textbook Chapter)
> Topic: West and Central Africa
> Text title: Chapter 13, section 1, "Chapter Atlas"
> Relevant page numbers: 504–11
>
> **Directions**: In chapter 13, sections 1A–E, you will read important information about West and Central Africa. You will read about the region's physical features, climate, natural resources, population, and problems. Read each section continuously without stopping. At the end of each section, stop, and complete that section in the guide. Most items in the guide will take you 5–20 seconds to answer. Items that will take you longer to answer are marked with an asterisk. Skip any item without an asterisk that takes you too long to answer.
>
> A. Physical Features (504–5, ¶1–5, map)
>   1. The rich and varied physical features of this region range from vast _____ to dense _____ . (504, ¶1)

2. This landform is the most common in the region. (504, ¶2)
   a. mountains
   b. desert
   c. plateau
   d. rainforest
3. West and Central Africa have some of the largest drainage basins of any region on earth. A drainage basin is an area of land where rainfall flows into a river or lake. What two drainage basins are located on the map on page 505? (505, map)
   _____ and _____
4. Which drainage basin is located on the Prime Meridian? (505, map)
   _____
5. Two of the three basins you read about are named after rivers. These two basins are named after the _____ and _____ Rivers. A third basin, the one you read about first, is not named after a river. Why? (505, ¶3–5)
   *(Respond in 1–2 sentences)

B. A Variety of Climates (506–7, ¶1–8, map, graphs)
   1. What is the air doing in the intertropical convergence zone? (506, ¶2)
      a. circling
      b. rising
      c. falling
   Use the climate map and graphs on p. 507 to answer questions 2–6.
   2. *Draw a rough line map of the African coast. Draw the equator and label it. Now label the ITCZ on your line map.
   3. What labels are included on the climate graphs? Circle one.
      a. temperature, climate zone, elevation
      b. temperature, rainfall, month of the year
      c. temperature, climate zone, country name
   4. Name two countries that are located mostly in the arid and semiarid zones.
      _____ and _____
   5. The Democratic Republic of the Congo is located in these three climate zones:
      _____, _____, and
      _____.
   6. Roughly how much rain does Kinshasa receive in January? _____ inches

E. The Problem of Disease (511, ¶1–5)
   1. _____ (T or F) Malaria is spread by tsetse fly parasites. (511, ¶1)
   2. _____ (T or F) Sleeping sickness affects people and animals. (511, ¶2)
   3. _____ (T or F) Many people do not have the money to protect themselves from treatable and preventable diseases. (511, ¶3)
   4. _____ (T or F) Dr. Miri tells people that preventing disease in rural parts of West and Central Africa has work-related benefits. (511, ¶3–5)

SELECTION GUIDE AND FURTHER READING

Orientation

The end of this book is near. The final section in this chapter offers a guide for selecting additional mediational practices for middle grade social studies courses and a set of suggested readings that will clarify or extend your understanding about particular practices explored in this chapter.

Selection Guide

Five questions will help you to determine whether a practice not explored in this book will likely enhance your students' reading experiences in a middle grade social studies course. All are YES/NO-type questions; and for questions 2 and 3, one or more specific phases and actions targeted by the practice should be identified. A practice that returns yes to all five questions and specifies a targeted phase and action will likely be suitable for mediational purposes in your course.

1. Does this practice aim to help students to read proficiently, skillfully, or strategically?
2. Does this practice aim to enhance students' reading experience in one or multiple phases of a school reading event?
3. Does this practice aim to help students to engage in one or multiple before, during, or after reading actions, as these actions are understood in this book?
4. Is this practice intended to be used with informational texts?
5. Is this practice appropriate for middle grade social studies texts and content?

Use your discretion to evaluate prospective mediational practices that do not explicitly aim to help students to read proficiently, skillfully, or strategically and are not specifically intended to be used with informational texts.

Further Reading

For further reading about the practices described in this chapter, see books or articles by Tierney and Readance (2005); Bear, Invernizzi, Templeton, and Johnston (2016); Templeton, Bear, Invernizzi, Johnston, Flanigan, Townsend, Helman, and Hayes (2015); Neeld (1990); McKenna and Robinson (2014); Graves, Prenn, and Cooke (1985); and McCormick (1989). Full bibliographic information for these sources follows in the references.

References

Alexander, Patricia A., and Emily Fox. 2013. "A Historical Perspective on Reading Research and Practice, Redux." In *Theoretical Models and Processes of Reading*, edited by Donna E. Alvermann, Norman J. Unrau, and Robert B. Ruddell, 3–46. Newark, DE: International Reading Association.

Alvermann, Donna E., and David W. Moore. 1991. "Secondary School Reading." In *Handbook of Reading Research*, edited by Rebecca Barr, Michael L. Kamil, Peter Mosenthal, and P. David Pearson, 951–83. New York: Longman.

AHD Online (*American Heritage Dictionary*). 2018. Boston: Houghton Mifflin Harcourt.

Anderson, Richard. 2013. "Role of the Reader's Schema in Comprehension, Learning, and Memory." In *Theoretical Models and Processes of Reading*, edited by Donna E. Alvermann, Norman J. Unrau, and Robert B. Ruddell, 476–88. Newark, DE: International Reading Association.

Ankomah, Baffour. 2015. "Mercury Rising! Namibia: Land of the Brave?" *New African* (May): 10–15.

Armbruster, Bonnie B., Thomas H. Anderson, and Joyce Ostertag. 1987. "Does Text Structure/Summarization Instruction Facilitate Learning from Expository Text?" *Reading Research Quarterly* 22: 331–46.

Armour, Jeff, and Sarah Hammond. 2012. "The Juvenile Justice System Should Address Racial Inequalities." In *Juvenile Crime*, edited by Louis Gerdes, 155–62. Detroit: Greenhaven Press.

Armstrong, Diane P., Judythe Patberg, and Peter Dewitz. 1988. "Reading Guides—Helping Students Understand." *Journal of Reading* 31: 532–41.

Ash, Gwynn Ellen, and James F. Baumann. 2017. "Vocabulary and Reading Comprehension: The Nexus of Meaning." In *Handbook of Research on Reading Comprehension*, 2nd ed., edited by Susan E. Israel and Gerald G. Duffy, 335–52. New York: Guilford Press.

References

Baker, Linda, and Anne L. Brown. 1984. "Metacognition and the Reading Process." In *Handbook of Reading Research*, edited by P. David Pearson, Rebecca Barr, Michael L. Kamil, and Peter Mosenthal, 353–94. New York: Longman.

Ball, Edward, and Wayne Lawrence. 2015. "Slavery's Trail of Tears." *Smithsonian* 46: 58–78.

Barrett, T. C. 1972. Taxonomy of Reading Comprehension. *Reading 360 Monograph*. Lexington, MA: Ginn & Co.

Bear, Donald R., Marcia Invernizzi, Shane Templeton, and Francine R. Johnston. 2016. *Words Their Way: Word Study for Phonics, Vocabulary, and Spelling Instruction*, 6th ed. Boston: Pearson.

Blauer, Ettagale, and Jason Lauré. 2013. *South Africa*. New York: Children's Press.

Bloom, Benjamin S. 1956. *Taxonomy of Educational Objectives: The Classification of Educational Goals. Handbook 1*. London: Longman Group.

Britton, Bruce K., and Arthur C. Graesser. 2014. *Models of Understanding Text*. Hoboken: Taylor and Francis.

Brown, Ann L., Annemarie Sullivan Palincsar, and Bonnie B. Armbruster. 2013. "Instructing Comprehension-Fostering Activities in Interactive Learning Environments." In *Theoretical Models and Processes of Reading*, edited by Donna E. Alvermann, Norman J. Unrau, and Robert B. Ruddell, 780–809. Newark, DE: International Reading Association.

Burgan, Michael. 2015. *Kenya*. New York: Children's Press.

Carbado, Devon W., and Donald Weise. 2012. *The Long Walk to Freedom: Runaway Slave Narratives*. Boston: Beacon Press.

Chu, Gregory, Susan Wiley Hardwick, Donald Holtgrieve, and Grant Wiggins. 2011. *myWorld Geography*. Boston: Pearson.

Davidson, James W., Michael B. Stoff, and Jennifer L. Bertolet. 2019. *myWorld American History*. Boston: Pearson.

———. 2016. *American History*. Boston: Pearson.

Davis, James E., Phyllis Maxey Fernlund, and Peter Woll. 2009. *Prentice Hall Civics: Government and Economics in Action*. Boston: Pearson Prentice Hall.

Deng, Alephonsion, Benson Deng, Benjamin Ajak, with Judy A. Bernstein. 2005. *They Poured Fire on Us from the Sky*. New York: PublicAffairs.

Ember, Carol R., and Melvin Ember. 2015. *Cultural Anthropology*. 14th ed. Boston: Pearson.

Fountas, Irene C., and Gay Su Pinnell. 2006. *Teaching for Comprehending and Fluency: Thinking, Talking, and Writing about Reading, K–8*. Portsmouth, NH: Heinemann.

Fox, Emily, and Patricia A. Alexander. 2017. "Text and Comprehension: A Retrospective, Perspective, and Prospective." In *Handbook of Research on Reading Comprehension*, 2nd ed., edited by Susan E. Israel and Gerald G. Duffy, 335–52. New York: Guilford Press.

Gerdes, Louise I. 2012. *Juvenile Crime*. Detroit: Greenhaven Press.

Goldman, Susan R., and John A. Rakestraw. 2000. "Structural Aspects of Constructing Meaning from Text." In *Handbook of Reading Research*, edited by Michael L. Kamil, Peter Mosenthal, P. David Pearson, and Rebecca Barr, 311–35. New York: Longman.

Grapes, Bryan J. 2001. *Japanese American Internment Camps*. San Diego: Greenhaven Press.

Graves, Michael F., Cheryl L. Cooke, and Michael J. Laberge. 1983. "Effects of Previewing Difficult Short Stories on Low Ability Junior High School Students' Comprehension, Recall, and Attitudes." *Reading Research Quarterly* 18, no. 3: 262–76.

Graves, Michael F., Maureen C. Prenn, and Cheryl L. Cooke. 1985. "The Coming Attractions: Previewing Short Stories." *Journal of Reading* 28, no. 7: 594–98.

Gruenewald, Mary Matsuda. 2005. *Looking Like the Enemy: My Story of Imprisonment in Japanese-American Internment Camps*. Troutdale, OR: NewSage Press.

Halliday, M. A. K., and C. M. I. M. Matthiessen. 2014. *Halliday's Introduction to Functional Grammar*. Milton Park, Abingdon, Oxon, UK: Routledge.

Halliday, M. A. K., and Ruqaiya Hasan. 2014. *Cohesion in English*. New York: Routledge.

Haugen, David M. 2013. *Juvenile Justice*. Detroit: Greenhaven Press.

Hughes, Louis. 1897. *Thirty Years a Slave: From Bondage to Freedom*. Milwaukee: South Side Print Company.

Karpiel, Frank, Kathleen Krull, George F. Sabato, and Michael Yell. 2012. *myWorld History*. Boston: Pearson.

Kintsch, Walter. 2013. "Revisiting the Construction-Integration Model of Text Comprehension and Its Implications for Instruction." In *Theoretical Models and Processes of Reading*, edited by Donna E. Alvermann, Norman J. Unrau, and Robert B. Ruddell, 807–839. Newark, DE: International Reading Association.

Kress, Gunther R., and Theo Van Leeuwen. 2006. *Reading Images: The Grammar of Visual Design, 2nd ed.* London: Routledge.

Kubakura, Wanjohi. 2015. "Floods Everywhere and Not a Drop to Drink." *New African* (June): 52–53.

Kuhn, Melanie R., and Steven A. Stahl. 2013. "Fluency: Developmental and Remedial Practices." In *Theoretical Models and Processes of Reading*, edited by Donna E. Alvermann, Norman J. Unrau, and Robert B. Ruddell, 385–411. Newark, DE: International Reading Association.

Lapp, Diane. 1989. *Content Area Reading and Learning*. Englewood Cliffs, NJ: Prentice Hall.

Lasky, Jack. 2016. *America's Prisons*. Detroit: Greenhaven Press.

McCormick, Patrick T. 2013. "Juveniles Should Not Be Tried or Sentenced as Adults." In *Juvenile Justice*, edited by David Haugen, 70–79. Detroit: Greenhaven Press.

McCormick, Sandra. 1989. "Effects of Previews on More Skilled and Less Skilled Readers' Comprehension of Expository Text." *Journal of Reading Behavior* 21: 219–39.

McKenna, Michael C., and Richard D. Robinson. 2014. *Teaching through Text: Reading and Writing in the Content Areas*. Boston: Allyn & Bacon.

McNeese, Tim, and Henry Louis Gates. 2004. *The Rise and Fall of American Slavery: Freedom Denied, Freedom Gained*. Berkeley Heights, NJ: Enslow.

Ministry of Education. (1992). *Joint College Entrance Examination*. Taipei, Taiwan.

Nagy, William E., and Judith A. Scott. 2013. "Vocabulary Processes." In *Theoretical Models and Processes of Reading*, edited by Donna E. Alvermann, Norman J. Unrau, and Robert B. Ruddell, 458–75. Newark, DE: International Reading Association.

National Reading Panel (NRP). 2000. *Teaching Children to Read: An Evidence-Based Assessment of the Scientific Research Literature on Reading and Its Implications for Reading Instruction.* Washington, DC: National Institute for Literacy.

Neeld, Elizabeth Cowan. 1990. *Writing.* Glenview, IL: Scott, Foresman/Little, Brown Higher Education.

O'Brien, Edward J., Anne E. Cook, and Robert F. Lorch Jr. 2017. *Inferences During Reading.* New York: Cambridge University Press.

OED Online (Oxford English Dictionary). 2018. Oxford: Oxford University Press.

Paterniti, Michael. 2017. "Should We Kill Animals to Save Them?" *National Geographic* (October): 70–99.

Pressley, Michael, and Peter Afflerbach. 1995. *Verbal Protocols of Reading: The Nature of Constructively Responsive Reading.* Hillsdale, NJ: Lawrence Erlbaum Associates.

Royte, Elizabeth. 2017. "The Gorillas Dian Fossey Saved." *National Geographic* (September): 110–27.

Rubalcaba, Jill, and Peter Robertshaw. 2010. *Every Bone Tells a Story: Hominin Discoveries, Deductions, and Debates.* Watertown: Charlesbridge.

Ruddell, Robert B., and Norman J. Unrau. 2013. "Reading as a Motivated Meaning-Construction Process: The Reader, the Text, and the Teacher." In *Theoretical Models and Processes of Reading*, edited by Donna E. Alvermann, Norman J. Unrau, and Robert B. Ruddell, 1015–68. Newark, DE: International Reading Association.

Rummelhart, David E. 2013. "Toward an Interactive Model of Reading." In *Theoretical Models and Processes of Reading*, edited by Donna E. Alvermann, Norman J. Unrau, and Robert B. Ruddell, 719–47. Newark, DE: International Reading Association.

Samuels, S. Jay. 2013. "Toward a Theory of Automatic Information Processing Reading, Revised." In *Theoretical Models and Processes of Reading*, edited by Donna E. Alvermann, Norman J. Unrau, and Robert B. Ruddell, 698–718. Newark, DE: International Reading Association.

Sandler, Martin W. 2013. *Imprisoned: The Betrayal of Japanese Americans During World War II.* New York: Walker Books.

Schunk, Dale H. 2016. *Learning Theories: An Educational Perspective.* Morrisville, NC: Pearson.

Smith, Roger, and Marsha Mcintosh. 2007. *Youth in Prison.* Philadelphia: Mason Crest Publishers.

Sone, Monica. 2001. "Evacuation Day." In *Japanese American Internment Camps*, edited by Bryan Grapes, 104–13. San Diego: Greenhaven Press.

Spears, Richard A. 2006. *McGraw-Hill's Dictionary of American Idioms and Phrasal Verbs.* New York: McGraw-Hill.

Stanley, Jerry. 2006. *I Am an American: A True Story of Japanese Internment.* New York: Crown Books.

Stepto, Michele. 1994. *Our Song, Our Toil: The Story of American Slavery as Told by Slaves.* Brookfield, CT: Millbrook Press.

Taylor, Barbara M., and Richard W. Beach. 1984. "The Effects of Text Structure Instruction on Middle-Grade Students' Comprehension and Production of Expository Text." *Reading Research Quarterly* 19: 134–46.

Templeton, Shane, Donald R. Bear, Marcia Invernizzi, Francine R. Johnston, Kevin Flanigan, Dianna R. Townsend, Lori Helman, and Latisha Hayes. 2015. *Vocabulary Their Way: Word Study with Middle and Secondary Students*, 2nd ed. Boston: Pearson.

Tierney, Robert J., and John E. Readence. 2005. *Reading Strategies and Practices: A Compendium*, 6th ed. Boston: Pearson.

Unsworth, Len. 2001. *Teaching Multiliteracies Across the Curriculum: Changing Contexts of Text and Image in Classroom Practice*. Maidenhead, Berkshire, UK: Open University.

Voorhis, Robert. 1829. *Life And Adventures of Robert Voorhis, The Hermit of Massachusetts, who has lived 14 years in a cave, secluded from human society*. Providence, RI: Printed for H. Trumbull.

Yancey, Diane. 1998. *Life in a Japanese American Internment Camp*. San Diego: Lucent Books.

Index

abstract subjects, 51, 53–54, 60
accuracy, 19, 21, 26, 59, 63, 77, 117
activated knowledge, 45–48
activating knowledge, xii, 16–18, 33, 45–48, 147, 159, 161
activating relevant topic knowledge. *See* activating knowledge
adjectives, 73, 110, 119, 127
adverbs, 62, 66, 73, 119, 127
after reading survey, 169, 171–72
alphabetics, 77
annotated copy, 133, 179
annotating, xii, 28, 150–51, 156, 159, 175–76, 179
annotations, 150–51, 156, 173, 175–76, 179
assessing, xiii, 25, 28, 139, 146–51, 156, 169, 171
automaticity, 15, 19, 24, 67
auxiliary paragraph structures, 85, 90, 102–3
auxiliary verb, 64–65

backtracking, 19
Barrett's taxonomy of reading comprehension, 6
base words, 20–21, 72–74, 167
basic knowledge, 48–49
Bloom's taxonomy of educational objectives, 5–6, 178
branched ideas, 25, 28, 117

branching, 28
building coherence, xiii, 110, 113, 117–18, 120, 128–36, 143, 147, 175, 179
bulleted list structure, 93

causal explanation structure, 99–100
chapter titles, 88
chapter topics, 88–89
chapter webbing, 157
charts, 8, 44
cinematic images. *See* dynamic images.
clarifying, after reading, xiii, 10, 25, 28–29, 85, 139, 146, 154–56, 167, 169, 171, 174–76, 179; clarifying options, 151–56
clarifying, before reading, xii, 15–17, 33, 36–37, 49, 85, 147, 161, 179; reading goal, 34–35; reading purpose, 35
classified nouns, 51–53, 56, 59–60, 62, 126
classified things, 52, 59–60
clustered ideas, 28
college reading events, 5
comparison structure, 97–98
complex nouns, 51, 56, 59, 62, 66
complex sentences, 59, 67–68, 75
compound nouns, 59, 61–63
compound sentences, 67–68
compound-complex sentences, 67–68
concept of definition maps, 167–69
concepts, 22, 28, 32, 56, 92, 110

conceptual knowledge, 91–92, 105
conjunctions, 22, 99
consequential explanation structure, 100
considerate texts, 23
consonant digraphs, 70
consonants, 20, 69–71, 74
consonant blends, 20, 70, 74
content weighting, 135–36
coordination, xi, xiii, 4, 6–7, 9, 11, 13, 35, 54, 118

definitional knowledge, 90–91
dependent clauses, 67–68
depersonalized actions, 52–53, 57
derivational suffixes, 21–22
described nouns, 56, 59–60, 62
developing knowledge, xii, 18, 48–49
developing topic knowledge, 147–48
diphthongs, 71
dynamic images, 55–56

effectiveness, 10, 15, 146–48, 156, 169, 173, 180
embedded glossary structure, 103
enhanced annotating, 151–53, 155, 157
enhanced annotations, 155–56, 175
entry-level knowledge. *See* basic knowledge
essential reading skills, xii, 6
essential topics, 133–34
evaluative structure, 98–99
example structure, 102–3
exemplars, 140–43, 149, 157–58

fact stream structure, 101–2
factorial explanation structure, 101
fixed images. *See* static images
flows of meaning, 85–87, 142
formal linguistics, 77
formulating, xiii, 18, 24, 54, 111, 118–31, 136, 175, 179
formulations, 24, 120
forward motion, 19–21, 59, 62, 67, 75, 77

generated expectations, 17, 46, 148, 171
generating expectations, xii, 10, 15–17, 31, 33, 37–45, 49, 147, 157, 159–61, 163, 165, 173–75, 179

goal-oriented reading, 85, 90, 103–4
grade band, 19
grammatical test, 62
grammatics, 77
Greek and Latin roots, 11, 20–21, 69, 72–73, 76
guided questioning, 157

history journals, 138, 147

idea development, 113, 134
idea identification, 6
image previewing, xiii, 157, 159–60, 174; questions, 160
images, 2, 17–19, 23, 29, 31–33, 37, 44–46, 53–58, 114, 159–60, 174, 176, 179
independent clauses, 67–69
inferencing, xiii, 3, 5, 15, 18, 22–23, 25, 54, 77, 84, 89, 104–10, 118, 136, 147, 155, 175; main idea inferencing, 107–10; paragraph topic inferencing, 104–7
informational texts, ix, 3, 15, 22, 45, 57, 77, 85–87, 90, 92, 102–5, 110, 128, 178, 182
informational writing structures, 22, 85, 90, 92; type 1, 93–95; type 2, 95–100; type 3, 100–102
italicized words, 42

jigsaw groups, 10
journaling, 157–58

key terms, 41–42, 102, 114, 162, 165
knowledge activation. *See* activating knowledge
knowledge activation guide, 47, 158

learning event, xii, 13
learning framework, 13
learning cycle, 16,
learning goals and objectives, 37
learning outcomes, xii, 17, 27, 84
leveled texts, 19
levels of schooling, 4–5
line drawings, 44
linear representations, 120–21, 125, 129, 131

main ideas, xiii, 2, 4–5, 10, 17, 22–24, 25–26, 34–36, 54, 76, 82–84, 87, 89–90, 93, 95, 101–10, 114–15, 131, 139, 149, 155, 174
mediational practices, xi–xiii, 3, 156–82
mediated reading experiences, 2, 7
mediated reading instruction, ix
mental actions, 7, 15–17, 29, 33, 54, 84, 110, 118, 140
mental picture, 54–55
mental representations, 6, 25–26, 28
middle grade reading events, 5, 113; delimitations, xi
middle grades, ix, xi–xiii, 1, 3–5, 15, 44, 59; defined, xi
morphemic elements, 72, 74
morphemic resources, 76

nonhierarchical reading guides, 178–81
note-making table, 11–12
numbered inset list structure, 94–95
numbered offset list structure, 93–94
numbered statements, 141–42

optimal positioning, 104, 136
optimal preparedness, 41, 44
optimal productivity, 29
optimal rate, 2
optimal readability, 176
optimal reading experience, xii, 15
optimal speed, 19, 21, 59, 67, 75, 77, 176
optimal student learning, xii–xiii

paragraph key words, 89, 140
paragraph topic identification, 89
paragraph topics, 3, 10–11, 13, 22–24, 26, 81–84, 86–87, 89, 92–93, 95–97, 99, 101–2, 104–6, 108–9, 115, 128, 130–31, 155–56, 175
passive verbs, 64–65, 108–9
personalized actions, 52
personalized accounts, 56
personalized doings. *See* personalized actions
perspectives, 9, 13, 98, 114, 177
phonic elements, 20, 69, 74, 75

phonic resources, 76
phonic segmentation, 74
phonics knowledge, 20, 59, 69, 72
photographic images, 19, 159
phrasal verbs, 21, 65–66
prefigured outline, 145–46
prefixes, 20, 69, 72–73, 76
prepositional phrases, 21, 67
presentational structures, 85
previewing, 17
problem and solution structure, 96–97
processes, types of, 15
program materials, 9
proper nouns, 41–42, 56, 59, 61–62, 102, 105
punctuation marks, 21–22, 59, 68, 75
purposeful reading, 103–4

qualifying structures: clauses, 67; phrases, 67
question and answer structure, 95–96

reading actions: consolidating actions, 14–15; orienting actions, 14–15; sustaining actions, 14–15
reading comprehension, 5–6, 13, 15, 28, 145–47, 150, 156, 178
reading cycle, ix, xii–xiii, 9–29
school reading events, ix, xii–xiii, 5–6, 13, 34, 50, 104, 182
reading event, defined, xi, 4
reading, for understanding, xiii,15, 18, 22, 36, 54, 77, 84–87, 90, 92, 102–3, 110, 118, 128, 143, 171, 175, 179
reading fluently, xiii, 15, 18–22, 24, 50, 53–54, 58–76, 110, 118, 173, 175, 179
reading goal, 10, 13–17, 22, 24, 28, 33–37, 48, 54, 76–77, 85, 103–4, 114, 138–39, 140, 147, 151, 159, 174
reading guides, 173, 175–81
reading objectives, 11, 17, 34–37, 114, 158, 173
reading outcomes, 13–14, 16
reading pedagogy, ix
reading phase actions: after reading phase actions, xii, 25–29, 137–56; before

reading phase actions, xii, 16–18, 31–50; during reading phase actions, xii, 18–25, 51–136
reading phases, xii: during reading phase, 13, 15, 18–19, 20, 22, 53–54, 75, 87, 104, 113, 118, 136; after reading phase, 13, 15, 24–26, 28, 54, 139; before reading phase, 13, 15–17, 24, 29, 33, 135, 139
reading processes, 13–14, 16, 118, 156
reading purpose, 5, 11, 33–35, 37, 46, 103–4, 113, 147
rearticulated meanings, 28
reconfigured outline, 145–46
reconfigured texts, 28, 143
reconfigured webs, 143–45
reconfiguring, xiii, 6, 16, 25–28, 139, 143–46, 169, 171
reconstituted topics, 28
repeated words, 109–10, 133
representations, 25–28, 30, 115–16, 120, 122, 125, 126–29, 143
rereading, xii, 11, 115, 132, 150–54

school reading events, 5–8, 12, 14, 34, 51, 104
section headings, 17, 25, 82–83, 88–89, 97, 101, 117, 119, 127–28, 148, 176, 179
section topics, 25–26, 38–39, 82, 86–89, 92–93, 100–101, 133–34, 146, 179
selective reading guides, xiii, 175–78
sentence-building knowledge, 59
Shippensburg University, ix
simple noun, 56, 59
simple sentences, 67–68
simple verbs, 59, 63
social sciences, xii, 3–4, 99; fields, 3
starred ideas, 134
static images, 55
stylistics, ix
suffixes, 11, 20–21, 52, 69, 72–74, 76
summaries, 10, 26, 44, 49, 139–42, 161, 163, 169

summarizing, xiii, 15, 25–26, 139–42, 146, 156, 163, 169, 171
supporting ideas, 22, 87, 127
syllabication, 11
syllables, 20, 74; unaccented, 20
systemic functional analysis, 15
systemic functional linguistics, vii, 15, 77

teacher-directed closed word sorts, 161–63
templates, 135, 166–69, 171, 176, 179
terminology cubing, xiii, 159, 165–67
text-building knowledge, 92–93, 102
text-building structures, 110
text comprehension, 113
text linguistics, ix
think-alouds, 172–75
transitional words, 22

underlined words, 21, 42
unifying elements, 134

verb groups, 63–68, 110
viewing, 17–18, 45, 48–49, 91
visualized content, 18–19
visualized images, 54–57
visualizing, xii, 18–19, 51, 53–58
visuals, 54–55
vocabulary processes, 77
vowel digraphs, 70–71
vowels, 20, 69–71, 74

web representations, 128–34
WH-type questions, 95, 178
word identification, 6, 21, 69–74
word-building knowledge, 11, 19–21, 59, 69, 72–76
wording, 143
word-segmenting knowledge, 20, 59, 69, 74, 76
written previews, 1–3, 157–59, 161–63

YES/NO-type questions, 95, 178, 182

About the Author

Don K. Philpot is a teacher, teacher educator, and writer. He is the author of *Character Focalization in Children's Novels* and numerous works of fiction for children and adults including *Assignments, The Moons of Goose Island, Numbering, The Victorian House, Formations & Lines*, and more. He received his doctoral degree in language and literacy education from the University of British Columbia in Vancouver and specializes in the areas of reading pedagogy, children's literature, children's literature stylistics, and disciplinary literacy. He has been actively involved in K–8 education for four decades and joined the Reading Faculty at Shippensburg University where he teaches courses on reading comprehension, content area literacy, children's literature, reading instruction for English-language learners, and most recently American Sign Language.

CPSIA information can be obtained
at www.ICGtesting.com
Printed in the USA
LVHW091904140920
665972LV00011B/111

9 781475 843989